PRICKLY PEARS
OF PALESTINE

Prickly Pears of Palestine
1st Edition
August 2006

Published by Eye Books Ltd
8 Peacock Yard
London
SE17 3LH
Tel: +44 (0) 845 450 8870
website: www.eye-books.com

Set in Garamond and Frutiger
ISBN 10 1 9030705 2X
ISBN 13 9781903070529

British Library Cataloguing in Publication Data
A catalogue record for this book is available from the British Library

Printed and bound in Denmark by Nørhaven Paperback A/S

Front cover photograph is used with kind permission of Abed Omar Qusini

PRICKLY PEARS OF PALESTINE

Hilda Reilly

Published by Eye Books

Also by Hilda Reilly

SEEKING SANCTUARY
- JOURNEYS TO SUDAN

Reviews for Hilda Reilly

"Reilly's writing is a powerful example of sympathy combined with dispassion."
Amazon.co.uk

"A memorable account based on weeks of extensive journeys throughout the Occupied Palestinian Territories and contacts with its people."
Ibrahim Darwish
Al-Quds Al-Arabi

"At last a book that acknowledges that there are two sides to every story. Hilda manages to present a fair and accurate picture of an oppressed nation that has been so often demonised in Western Media.

At the end of the day, her story shows that behind the headlines, the Palestinians are no different from any other nation. Hilda does not patronise nor pass judgement, she simply observes. The power of the story lies in the ordinariness of Palestinian life; they are ordinary people trying to lead an ordinary life under extraordinary conditions. It is a timely piece that goes a long way to explaining how the world has arrived at what is euphemistically called "clash of civilisations". A must read for anyone wanting to understand the extraordinary juncture of history at which we find ourselves."

Waseem Mahmood OBE, program director of International Media Support. Author of "Good Morning Afghanistan"

ACKNOWLEDGEMENTS

I would like to thank the staff and students of An-Najah University in Nablus for their help and hospitality during the writing of this book, and most especially Dr Rasmiya Hanoun and her family in Nabi Elias for their boundless generosity.

CONTENTS

CONTENTS

PROLOGUE

It was the summer of 2004 and I had just finished writing a book about Sudan. I started casting around for another project and as my mind roamed over those parts of the world that attract me – Africa and the Arab countries – I realised that in my mental landscape of the Middle East there was a void which corresponded to Palestine. For all that the word *Palestinian* is constantly in the news there were few images that came to mind in association with it other than those connected with conflict: the angry chanting from *keffiya*-clad heads crowded together in funeral processions, the wailing of black-veiled women standing on the rubble of demolished homes, the earnest pleading of moustached politicians as they beg for a halt to the bloodshed. As for Palestine itself, did it still exist or had it long since disappeared into the great geo-political mill that swallowed up places like Yugoslavia and Czechoslovakia and regurgitated them, fragmented and rebaptised? One heard of the Occupied Palestinian Territories but, come to think of it, rarely of Palestine.

Around the same time I came across a report[1] produced by a group of Glasgow academics who had carried out a study on the public's understanding of the Middle East conflict. The results were startling. They revealed a widespread ignorance about what must be one of the most widely reported and most longstanding struggles in the world today – the dispute between Israelis and Palestinians.

Misunderstanding was rife about the most basic issues. Many people thought that the Occupied Territories were 'occupied' by the Palestinians. Others thought that the term referred to a border dispute between two countries which were both laying claim to a piece of land that separated them. Many had no idea that the occupation was a military one and assumed that the occupiers were simply the people living there. Some thought that the settlers were Palestinians. The majority of the interviewees had no idea where the Palestinian refugees were from, some suggesting Afghanistan, Iraq or Kosovo.

When questioned as to who was at fault, most thought that the Palestinians were the aggressors, that the Palestinians were trying to grab Israeli land, and that Israeli military action was invariably in response to Palestinian attack.

Digging deeper to find what lay at the root of these misconceptions, the researchers found that they were consistent with an uneven news coverage of Middle East events.

Israelis were twice as likely to be interviewed as Palestinians. US politicians – who tend to support Israel – were quoted twice as often as the more neutral British politicians. Israeli deaths and injuries were reported far more frequently than Palestinian ones, giving the impression that the Israelis suffered many more casualties than the Palestinians.

Analysis of the language used revealed that words with negative connotations were often used in talking of the Palestinians but much less so of the Israelis. Israeli deaths at the hands of Palestinians were described by words such as 'murder', 'atrocity', 'savage'. Israelis killing Palestinians were merely 'angry' or 'wielding a big stick'.

Added to this bias in reporting were the difficulties inherent in trying to cover a conflict with such a long and complex history. With an audience attention span of about twenty seconds per news item, presenters are unable to go into the detail which would explain what led up to any one event. They may say that the Israelis invaded a refugee camp in retaliation for a suicide bombing but have no time to say what the suicide bombing was in retaliation for, and even less to go back through the whole chain of preceding cause and effect.

The chain leads back some 4,000 years to the time of Abraham, the patriarch revered by Jews, Muslims and Christians alike, whose story is told in the Bible. In the Book of Genesis

God called on Abraham to leave his home in Ur, in present-day Iraq, and to travel to the land of Canaan where he promised him that his seed would inherit the land and that they would become a great nation. Although seventy-five at the time and childless, Abraham later had a son by Hagar, his maidservant, called Ishmael, and later still another child by Sarah, his wife, called Isaac. The Arabs are believed to be descended from Abraham through Ishmael, the Jews through Isaac.

According to the Jewish and Christian religions, when Isaac was a young man God ordered Abraham to sacrifice him as a test of his obedience. Abraham prepared the fire to make a burnt offering of his son but God stayed his hand at the last minute, telling him to slay a ram instead. The same story is found in Islam, the only difference being that Ishmael, not Isaac, is to be sacrificed. This event is pivotal to all three religions.

Over a period of centuries the descendants of Isaac conquered the land of Canaan. Under the leadership of David (who killed Goliath) they captured the city of Jerusalem and made it their capital. Solomon, the son of David, built a vast temple there on Mount Moriah (where Abraham had prepared to sacrifice his son). This temple, known as the First Temple, was destroyed by King Nebuchadnezzar who conquered the Israelites and took them into captivity in Babylon. After their return from exile they built another temple on the same site. The Second Temple became the focus of Israelite religious and national life and was the scene of a number of events in the life of Christ. It was destroyed in 70 AD along with most of the city when the Romans, who by this time controlled the region, suppressed a Jewish revolt. All that remained of the temple was a stretch of wall. Known as the Western Wall, or Wailing Wall, it still stands today and is the main focal point for Jewish prayer and pilgrimage.

The events of 70 AD, followed by further conflict between Jews and Romans some sixty years later, resulted in the Jews being driven from their land and scattered far and wide, an event known as the Diaspora. Roman rule came to an end in the fourth century AD when Jerusalem was incorporated into the Byzantine empire by its founder, Emperor Constantine.

The first Muslim contact with Jerusalem came about 500 years later. The Prophet Muhammad is believed to have travelled overnight from Mecca to Jerusalem on the back of a supernatural animal which took him to Mount Moriah, or Temple Mount. From there he ascended in a visit to heaven. Shortly after Muhammad's death Jerusalem was captured from the Byzantines by the Muslims and declared a Holy City of Islam. Since then Temple Mount has been occupied by a vast Islamic complex, including the Dome of the Rock and Al Aqsa Mosque. It is regarded as Islam's third holiest shrine and, bounded as it is by the Western Wall, is a potential flashpoint for confrontation between Muslims and Jews.

After being fought over by Muslims and Christians for a couple of hundred years during the Crusades of the twelfth and thirteenth centuries, the Holy Land, as Palestine was then called, remained under Muslim rule – first of the Egyptian Mamluks, then the Ottoman Turks – until the end of the First World War.

Although the population had remained predominantly Arab, the Jews were never entirely absent from the region. Their numbers in Palestine increased as the Jews of the Diaspora were driven further afield by a mounting anti-semitism, with some of them choosing to return to the land that their ancestors had left.

By the mid-nineteenth century support was gathering among both Jews and Christians for the idea of establishing a Jewish state. In 1897 the World Zionist Organisation was set up, its aim being the creation of a Jewish homeland in Palestine. In the late nineteenth and early twentieth centuries more Jews moved to Palestine, buying land and forming communities. In 1917 Lord Balfour, the British Foreign Secretary, stated in a letter, which became known as the Balfour Declaration, that the British Government 'view with favour the establishment in Palestine of a national home for the Jewish people'. The Balfour Declaration was to ring down through the following decades as a clarion call of betrayal and duplicity in the ears of succeeding generations of Palestinians.

After the First World War, the area now covered by Israel, the Occupied Palestinian Territories and Jordan was mandated by the League of Nations to the British. Under the terms of the mandate, Britain was to implement the Balfour Declaration and facilitate Jewish immigration. During the 1920s and 1930s the seeds of conflict were sown with the rapid expansion of the Jewish population, Arab rioting, and the formation of the Haganah and the Irgun, both Jewish militant groups. Towards the end of the Second World War Irgun declared war on the British rulers of Palestine and embarked on a guerrilla war of independence.

After the Second World War Britain granted independence to the region lying to the east of the Jordan River, now known as Jordan, but retained their mandate in the region west of the river, still called Palestine. Following the Nazi genocide European Jews were now flooding into the area. The Jewish fight for independence grew more vicious with bombings and killings which prefigure much of the Palestinian militant activity of later years.

In 1947 the United Nations voted to divide Palestine into two parts, one Jewish and the other Arab. Israel was set up as an independent Jewish state, but the Arabs rejected the UN plan. Britain, whose mandate had now been brought to end, withdrew, leaving its former charges to their fate. War broke out between the Jews and the Palestinian Arabs who were supported by Arabs from neighbouring countries. During the course of this war hundreds of thousands of Palestinian Arabs were forced to flee their homes in what was now Israel – an event known as the *Nakba* (catastrophe). By 1949, the Israelis had defeated the Arabs and had taken even more land than that allocated to them by the UN. The bulk of the land remaining to the Palestinians (the West Bank) fell under the control of Jordan, while a further sliver of land in the south-west (the Gaza Strip) came under Egyptian control. Jerusalem was divided, with West Jerusalem belonging to the Israelis,

East Jerusalem to the Palestinians.

In 1967 the Israelis, threatened by Arab armies gathering on its borders, launched an attack in which they captured the West Bank, the Gaza Strip and East Jerusalem. Since then Israel has continued to occupy these conquered territories in defiance of a UN resolution ordering them to withdraw. In addition to the military occupation, Israel started a programme of settlement construction, installing communities of Israeli-Jews throughout the West Bank and Gaza.

This downturn in the Palestinian situation generated support for the burgeoning Palestine Liberation Organisation, headed by Yassir Arafat, and the 1970s was a period bloody with battles, assassinations and hijackings.

Over the next two decades the Palestinian fortunes see-sawed. A Palestinian uprising (*intifada*) in 1987 was followed in 1993 by the controversial Oslo Accords which gave the Palestinians limited self-rule under the newly-formed Palestinian National Authority (PNA) but fell far short of their expectations. Shortly afterwards Israel began to be subjected to a rash of suicide bombings, a second *intifada* broke out in 2000, and in 2002 Israel started to build the controversial Wall, or Separation Barrier, between itself and the Palestinians. In April 2003, the Quartet (the United Nations, United States, European Union and Russia) published the Road Map Peace Plan which aimed at the achievement of a two-state solution by 2005. By the summer of 2004 this solution was still nowhere in sight.

Despite the endless media discussions about the rights and wrongs of all this – perhaps because of them – I felt that most people generally perceived Palestinians one-dimensionally, as either victims or terrorists, depending on their own political perspective. I decided to go and spend some time there to see for myself. I wanted to put some human flesh on these bare stereotypical bones. I wanted also to try to tease out the tangled currents of the conflict in a way which would make it comprehensible for the bewildered news consumer.

As regards the political situation, my own feelings were that although I thought the Palestinians had been gravely wronged by the events of 1948, it was unrealistic to expect any turning back of the clock. The state of Israel was not going to be dismantled. But I strongly believed that the occupation should come to an end, that the Palestinians should be given every help to establish their own state and that amends should be made for the injustices they had suffered.

[1] Bad News From Israel: television news and public understanding of the Israeli-Palestinian conflict, by Greg Philo and the Glasgow University Media Group

CHAPTER 1

Having decided to spend some time living in Palestine, my first step was to find something to do there to give some structure to my stay. An internet search took me to An Najah University in Nablus, a city in the West Bank, where they wanted help in editing texts for a website. I emailed the university and got a reply from someone in the Public Relations department called Ala Yousuf saying they would be very pleased to have me. 'You can go ahead in order to join us,' he wrote, ending rather curiously with the words: 'Welcome home.'

The next step was to find out a bit more about practical and political issues. I contacted the London branch of the International Solidarity Movement, an organization which provides non-violent support for Palestinians in their struggle against the occupation, and arranged to attend one of their orientation weekends.

The orientation was held in a squat in Stoke Newington and was run by a Jewish man called Raph. This was the first surprise. In my naivety it hadn't occurred to me that any Jewish person would be an active supporter of Palestine. There were seven other participants: Emily, fresh out of university; Simon, a middle-aged business type; Sarah, an Islington Christian; Thomas, a French boy in his gap year; Samwa, a forceful Pakistani woman; Gilly, a New Zealander with dreadlocks who was a professional activist and had just spent two months living up a tree in Wales to stop a road being built; and Samia, a Pakistani woman who, like me, was going to work on a project not connected with ISM. We did a crash course on the history of Palestine, explored cultural issues, motivation and the concept of non-violence, did role plays of situations we would be likely to encounter, and discussed practicalities.

One of the role plays involved arrival at the airport. Raph impressed on us the importance of not giving any hint to the Israeli authorities that we were involved with ISM or any other volunteer project in Palestine. Although in theory foreign visitors are free to travel around the West Bank, in practice the Israelis try to prevent it, especially in the case of people who are there to support the Palestinians, even in the most neutral capacity. To hinder this, people arriving at Ben Gurion airport are subjected to extensive grilling and even searches. Anyone suspected of being on their way to work in the West Bank runs the risk of being refused entry. We each ran through our various cover stories: doing archaeological work, going on a pilgrimage, visiting friends, or just wanting to see the tourist sights of Israel. Raph warned us not to carry anything that indicated any connection with Arabs or Arab countries. For me that meant getting a new passport, leaving behind my diary and address book which were full of Arab names, changing my mobile phone because it had an Arabic keypad, and checking my handbag to get rid of the Sudanese coins still lurking at the bottom.

By the time I was ready to go it was early September 2004. I mentioned to a friend, Helen, what I was about to do.

'Hilda, you do realize, don't you, that I'm Jewish?' she said.

I hadn't known. She told me that she had many family members in Israel and had been visiting the country regularly for about ten years. Her cousins were in the army and were robustly anti-Palestinian. One of them, a girl doing national service, had talked to her about seeing soldiers firing their rifles at the feet of a Palestinian prisoner at a checkpoint and laughing about it.

I was concerned that Helen might feel antagonistic about my plans but I was wrong. She was open to talking about it and willing to help in practical ways. 'This is the worst time of the year for anyone wanting to travel to Israel,' she told me. 'This month there are three Jewish festivals. The planes are all full and the prices shoot up. But I know a travel agent

9

who specializes in flights to Tel Aviv. I'll give her a call right away.'

She phoned the agent who had one seat left on a charter flight in a few days' time, at a price even lower than I had been expecting to pay. I started to dither while Helen sat with the phone in her hand. 'You haven't got time to mess about, Hilda. You take this flight or you might not get another chance for weeks.'

I took out my credit card and booked the flight.

I hadn't had any more news from Ala Yousuf after our first exchange of emails. Two later emails I sent remained unanswered and I couldn't get through on his mobile. But I had decided to go ahead anyway. I was confident that if things didn't work out with An Najah University there would be plenty of other things to do.

I arrived in Jerusalem early one morning and checked into the Jaffa Gate Hostel in the Old City. A taxi driver I spoke with was pessimistic about my chances of being able to travel to Nablus, which lay about forty miles to the north. 'It's surrounded by the Israeli army,' he told me. 'They don't let foreigners through the checkpoints there, not for Nablus.'

I called in at the Faisal Hostel in East Jerusalem, the gathering point for ISMers, and heard much the same story. Nablus, I learned, was currently the most sensitive spot in the West Bank. Both the Old City in the centre of the town and the outlying refugee camps were believed to be hotbeds of militant activity, and movement in and out was rigidly controlled by the army. 'Even getting in by the back roads is difficult now,' said one ISMer who had been based there recently. He was referring to the routes taken by those who wanted to circumvent the checkpoints.

I tried again to call Ala. This time I got through.

'Hello, welcome,' he said when I introduced myself and told him where I was. 'Welcome home.'

He seemed unperturbed at my news about the transport problems. 'Someone will come and pick you up tomorrow,' he said. 'Phone this number.'

I called the number. The man I spoke to noted the address of the hostel I was staying in and said he would come for me at seven the next morning.

I spent the rest of the day in Jerusalem's Old City, visiting the Church of the Holy Sepulchre which occupies the probable site of Jesus Christ's crucifixion and burial, and wandering along the cobbled alleyways of the souk, past shops bursting indiscriminately with souvenirs and knick-knacks connected with Islam, Judaism and Christianity. Stars of David and *shofars* shared shelf space with Koranic scrolls, pictures of Mecca, rosary beads and crucifixes. Vendors pestered passers-by to come in and look. 'Only look, no need to buy,' they begged. I stopped to look at some T-shirts. The vendor put his arm round my waist, squeezing me. 'Just buy something small. Look at this cross. Only fifty shekels. OK, you don't want to buy so I give you something free. What do you want?'

'Nothing, thank you.'

'What's wrong with you? I offer you a present and you don't want it!'

He wheeled away in disgust and with the same spiel grabbed a couple of middle-aged European women. I tried on a pair of blue sandals in the shop next door before deciding that I didn't need them. The vendor followed me down the lane knocking ten shekels of his price with every step that he took. 'Business is very bad, no tourists. Just eighty shekels. OK, seventy shekels. Sixty then. Come back, please.' The voice trailed off in defeat.

I turned into the Via Dolorosa, the route which Christ took on his way to Calvary and which is marked out with the Stations of the Cross. Just past the fifth station, where Simon of Cyrene was co-opted to help carry the cross, I stopped short at a sign outside a perfume stall.

> *Happy September 11*
>> *Is the immune system anti-semitic for resisting disease?*

> *USA dollars not honoured in this store*
> *Jewish occupation is terrorism with a larger*
> *budget*
> *Israel is America's only friend in the Middle*
> *East, however, before the 'state of Israel' America*
> *had no enemies in the Middle East.*

The owner, a man with a bushy beard and an American accent, was talking angrily with a fat Russian man.

'I have two wives,' said the bearded man. 'Yes, we have multiple wives so that we can have multiple children so that we can drive the Jews into the sea.' He pointed to a photo on the counter. 'This is my family.'

'Your daughter looks sad,' said the Russian man.

'Yes, she is sad because of what is happening here.'

At seven the next morning a middle-aged Palestinian man called Yassir picked me up in a van. He offered me half of his breakfast, a sandwich of plump, moist falafel in pitta bread.

'Thank you. How long will it take to get to Nablus?' I asked

'One hour and ten minutes.'

This seemed amazingly precise considering the stories about road blocks and delays. I asked Yassir what I should say if the soldiers asked where I was going.

'Say you're going to the Samaritan mountains. Say you've heard there are some interesting ruins there. You have the right to go. Don't worry.'

I did worry. 'You have a typical East European paranoia complex,' a Hungarian friend had once told me, remarking on my tendency to feel automatically in the wrong if I'm suspected of being so. It was kicking in now.

I'd never heard of the Samaritan mountains. I started flicking through my guide book for information but found nothing. My fears were fuelled by a news item broadcast a couple of weeks after the ISM session. Samia, along with two other Pakistani women, had already travelled to Israel and, despite their strict

Islamic dress, had made it through the airport. A day or two later a twenty-strong squad of armed soldiers burst into their bedroom in a Jerusalem hotel in the middle of the night and arrested them. They had subsequently been deported, even though the judge at their hastily arranged hearing could find no reason to complain about them.

At the first checkpoint Yassir drove round a line of waiting cars. He explained that he was an Arab-Israeli, one of some one million Palestinians living in Israel. As such, he had an Israeli number plate and didn't have to queue up or be questioned. We made the same detour at the second checkpoint and then took a road up into the mountains. We stopped in a village where Yassir said he could take me no further because Nablus lay in Zone A. Seeing my mystified look, he told me that the Occupied Palestinian Territories were divided into three zones: A, where the Palestinian National Authority had full civilian and security jurisdiction, B, where the PNA controlled only civilian matters, and C, (about seventy-three per cent of the total) which was under full Israeli control. Israeli citizens (including Arab-Israelis) were only allowed to enter Zones B and C.

'Don't worry,' Yassir said. 'Another car is waiting for you further ahead, down the mountain.' He showed me where I should go and told me to leave my bag with him. It would be delivered to me in Nablus in about an hour, he said. How, I knew not, but nevertheless I handed it over. Right then, being separated from my toothbrush and a change of clothing was the least of my anxieties. I clambered over a wall, jumped over some clumps of barbed wire, ran down through some fields, all the time tensed for the sound of soldiers' shouts or, even worse, the whizzing of bullets past my ears, and found the waiting car.

We zigzagged down the slopes of Mount Gerizim and into the outskirts of Nablus. I was entering one of the oldest cities in the world, and one with an intimate historical link to the present conflict. Genesis chapter 12 reports that it was in Shechem – the former name of the city – that God made the first of his promises to Abraham that the land would be gifted to his descendants. The Jewish Talmud speaks of it more darkly as 'a place where bad things happen'.

We drove on past tier upon tier of apartment blocks, bone-white in the blazing sun and stacked up on the mountainsides like a wedding cake conjured out of Lego cubes. The driver took me to the university, a stylish modern campus high above the downtown area. A security guard showed me up to the PR department and introduced me to Ala, a man in his mid-thirties, lean, taut and springy.

'You are welcome,' he said. 'Welcome home.'

The project I was to work on was Ala's brainchild, born of an incident involving a refugee. In 1937 the man in question had given a family photograph to a friend. In 1969 he asked the friend to give it back to him as he had lost everything he possessed in the *Nakba*. But the friend too had lost everything, including the photo. The day after hearing about this Ala started work on a website for the documentation of all aspects of Palestinian life. His aim was to ensure that the stories of his people would be recorded for posterity and made freely available through the internet. He worked with an urgency and single-mindedness fired not only by his sense of Palestinian identity but also by his personal experiences of the Israeli occupation, and by a fear of people dying or things being lost before they could be documented.

Ala lived with his extended family in a house in the Old City area of Nablus. In 2002, during an Israeli invasion, the house was taken over by the army and turned into a military headquarters. All seventeen family members were herded into two rooms and held there for a week. The soldiers brought in weapons, rockets and bombs and fired them from the house, which was in turn shot at by the Palestinian militants returning fire. Arrested Palestinians were taken to Ala's house where they were interrogated and beaten. They lay piled up on the stairs, tied and blindfolded. One of the prisoners who refused to was shot in the stomach. Ala and his brothers were forced to carry him out to a tank, the soldiers being unwilling to expose themselves to enemy fire. Ala's younger brother was taken by the Israelis and used as a human shield. Pushing him ahead, the soldiers shot from behind him, resting their guns on his shoulders. They propelled him into a house to protect their own entry, dropping him in from the roof. When he shouted out to warn the occupants, the soldiers beat him. They returned him to the house the next day, unconscious.

I was to learn these and many other stories later. In the meantime we talked about security issues.

'You've come to the hottest place in Palestine,' Ala told me and warned me to be careful about going to the Old City where the Israeli army made regular incursions to root out suspected militants. He warned me particularly against looking at anyone I saw with a gun. 'If you do and he's assassinated by the Israelis the next day, you'll be blamed.'

The university, I learned, had a reputation as a hotbed of terrorism. Of the many Palestinian militants killed and arrested, a fair number, as well as several suicide bombers, had been students at An Najah which was reviled in the international media as a training camp for this sort of thing.

'This is the university of terror, the university of death, the university of Hamas,' Ala said. He was quoting opinions expressed in some of the anti-Palestinian internet sources. 'We would sue the people who say these things but we're up against publications like *The New York Times* and *The Jerusalem Post*. What can we do?'

In answer to his own question he was doing what he could with his website, providing an information service to counterbalance the negative images projected about both Palestine and An Najah University. This was what I was to work on and I would start the next morning.

Ala called over Falastine, one of the students who helped with the website, and asked her to go with me to the flat I'd be living in. Falastine was a tall, stout girl with a pleasant round face. She was studying English and spoke it remarkably well although she was only eighteen. It was thanks to Celine Dion, she told me as a university car took us back up the hillside. 'I love her songs. I learned a lot of my English from them.'

Falastine's four brothers had all been sent abroad to study for safety reasons. She too had wanted to study abroad but, as her brothers were already away from home, she didn't think it would be right to leave her parents.

I asked her how she felt about studying at An Najah University.

'I think it's beautiful. Everything is nice.'

'What about the reputation that An Najah has outside Palestine?'

'I think it's wrong. It's all lies. They're very normal students. The students come here to study, to live their lives normally in the right way. You are here and you will see the situation. It's very peaceful. If there's any problem it's from the Israeli military.'

The car stopped at a block of flats set well off the road. My flat was on the ground floor, tucked away at the back. It had a small kitchen/living room, a bedroom and bathroom. Falastine took me to a nearby grocery store to stock up on a few essentials and went back to the university.

The door bell rang. I opened it and found a small, dumpy woman, her face encased in a floral wimple which reached down to mid-thigh.

'*Salaam alaykum*. Welcome. I am Umm Ahmed. Your neighbour.'

Umm Ahmed (meaning mother of Ahmed; Arab women are often addressed as Umm plus the name of the oldest son) was not only my neighbour, she was also my landlady. She and her family lived in a bigger flat next door. She took me round there to meet them: her husband Suleiman, a lecturer at An Najah, her two daughters, Muna and Manal, who were students, and her son Amjad, a shy boy of twelve. Ahmed, the older son, lived in Ramallah where he worked for a mobile phone company. We drank mint tea in a sitting room furnished with massive brocade armchairs and a monumental mahogany sideboard. Suleiman had studied in the United States and spoke good English.

I was beginning to worry about the fate of my bag. Seven hours had passed since Yassir had said it would be delivered in an hour. 'Don't worry,' said Umm Ahmed. 'I will lend you clothes.' This did little to reassure me as Umm Ahmed was neither my size nor my style; nor were the girls, who wore ankle-length coats with *hijabs* outside the house and track-suits inside. She pressed on me a jacket several sizes too big for me, saying it might be cold in the evening.

Later I went back to the grocery store to buy bread. Sultan, a young man I'd met in the morning, was still there. He was a student and his family owned the store. A couple of other young men were lounging around the counter with him, watching a programme of video clips on one of the satellite channels. Mohannad and Osama, also students, were from villages outside Nablus. They shared a flat nearby with other students and went home only at weekends. Most students in their position rented accommodation in Nablus, they said, because of the difficulty in getting through the checkpoints every day. Young men in particular were subjected to lengthy questioning and often detained or turned back for no good reason.

On the way back I found Suleiman sitting outside with a neighbour, Abu Mahir. They were sitting round an upturned kerosene tin which they were using as a coffee table. Suleiman introduced me to Abu Mahir (father of Mahir) and called on Amjad to bring another coffee out.

Abu Mahir was mid-thirtyish, scrawny and a chain-smoker. He had spent nine years in prison. Suleiman translated for me a complicated story involving an attempt to kill an Israeli, an escape to Jordan and exposure by an informer. Despite all this, plus having no job, he seemed, apart from his constant smoking, to be a very laid-back sort of character.

Back in my flat I turned on the television just in time to see a news item about Israel. There had been a suicide bombing that day in Jerusalem. The bomber was a young woman from Askar refugee camp in Nablus.

At nine o'clock the doorbell rang. A taxi driver handed over my bag.

My flat was about half a mile from An Najah. I walked there the next morning, down through a mountainside suburb which had the look of a not-quite-finished construction project. The roads were strewn with rubble and rubbish, and straggly yellow gorse, withering thistles and weeds sprawled over areas of wasteland. The pavement, where it existed, had a line of olive trees planted along the middle, forcing pedestrians either into the road or perilously close to the steep bank which fell away at the other side. Above it all the balconies of the apartment blocks were bright with pots of flowers, climbing plants and bird cages.

When I arrived at the university I found posters of the suicide bomber from the previous evening's news stuck up all over the campus.

'We don't agree with this,' Ala said when I asked about it. 'It is not the right way. But they are young. They are teenagers. It is a teen thing. There will be an incursion today. The Israeli army will go to Askar and destroy the house of her family.' This was the invariable Israeli response to a suicide bombing – demolition of the family home. 'She was a friend of Mohammed's sister,' Ala added, referring to a man I had met the previous day. (A few days later I asked Ala if there would be any chance of me being able to talk to the family of the suicide bomber, of Mohammed introducing me to them. It was out of the question, he said, because of the fear of Israeli retribution. Even Mohammed, who had said at first that the girl was a friend of his sister's, subsequently denied it. 'This kind of acquaintance is dangerous,' Ala explained. 'They attack the friends of the suicide bomber and then the friends of the friends.')

I commented on how easily I had travelled from Jerusalem to Nablus without passing through any checkpoints. Surely it was just as easy for Palestinians if they put their minds to it.

'Of course. The checkpoints are just there to humiliate us. It doesn't stop people who are determined to get through.'

To put me more fully in the picture Ala gave me a collection of reports written by some of the students for the PR department. I read through a catalogue of stories of atrocities at check points and prisons, with students being arrested for no apparent reason, subjected to gratuitous harassment and torture. But as I read I was struck by the tone of passivity, the lack of any sense of outrage. There was more a sense of weariness, as if they were saying only, 'Please stop all this.' This tone was in strong contrast to the ideas projected by the media of a widespread virulent violence infecting the entire Palestinian population. Even when the writers admitted to supporting a militant ideology, it was in a half-hearted sort of way, as if they did so only because they could see no alternative.

During the morning I edited some academic abstracts. Ala had accumulated about two hundred summaries of scientific dissertations written by research students which he wanted to put on the website. The English on the whole was competent but in the cases where it wasn't the meaning was unclear so there was little I could do to improve it. I struggled with the technicalities of 'Finite element analysis of reinforced concrete cross-vault shells' and 'Effect of altitude on the blood chemistry of soccer players in the West Bank', already wondering how their authors had been able to concentrate on such subjects in the midst of the daily mayhem of occupation.

Later on Falastine dropped by and we went out to a nearby restaurant. The Oriental House was clean, comfortable and subtly exotic. The clientele was mostly trendy young people, many of the women in jeans or dungarees. A young woman at the next table smoked a *narguila*, tossing a head of blonde-streaked hair and haughtily exhaling clouds of smoke.

We ordered falafel and salad. Falastine recommended a herbal tea made from local wild plants. She was interested in alternative medicine and had experimented with macrobiotics which she had learned about by watching the programmes of Mariam Nour, a Lebanese health food guru. 'You know, it's not just about eating,' she said. 'It's about a philosophy of life. She said free your mind, look at the essence of things. I started to read about this, about spirituality which is the science of the soul. It helps you to understand yourself and to understand the world around you.'

I asked her if this kind of approach helped her to see any kind of solution to the conflict.

'Well, the solution of fighting, I think we can put it aside because if you want to fight and make war there has to be two sides and here there is only one side, that's the Israeli side. We have no arms. We have nothing to fight with but our bodies and of course to go and stand in front of the tanks, but faith and hope cannot destroy the tanks.'

The suicide bombing of the day before and the posters at the university were still looming large in my mind. 'Why do some people become suicide bombers?' I asked Falastine. 'Do you understand what's going on in their heads?'

'Well, yes, I think so. The situation drives them to do it. I hear their stories. Many of them, the Israeli soldiers shot their father in front of their eyes or their brother or one of their family, so of course they are so mad and so angry. If somebody comes and just shoots one of your family, the person you adore most, with no reason, wouldn't you go mad? You know, we shouldn't judge the people who do these extreme things, we have to put ourselves in their place and see how they think and how they feel. I know I would go mad and I would hate them endlessly – but I don't know if I would be a suicide bomber.' She laughed gently. It didn't seem very likely.

Whether it was the result of the New Age teachings of Mariam Nour or an inherently sanguine disposition, Falastine had a truly relaxed attitude. She talked calmly about incidents which I was soon to realise were typical examples of daily Palestinian fare – seeing her cousin shot dead in front of her eyes when she was aged only six, being arrested at gunpoint by Israeli soldiers who had confused her with a suspected suicide bomber of the same name. 'Well, yes, I guess I'm lucky,' she said when I commented on her positive attitude. 'I'm able to cope with things like that. It's my nature.'

In the afternoon Asem, another of the students who helped Ala, took me into the centre of town to do some shopping. We took one of the shared taxis which queued up outside the university.

Downtown Nablus occupied the base of a bowl formed by the mountains of Gerizim and Ebal. On first sight it seemed to have an old-fashioned air about it. The goods in the small shops were displayed any old how as if the principles of window dressing were unknown here, the coffee shops – barren and utilitarian – had the uncongenial atmosphere of a Salvation Army hostel, with men sitting around puffing desultorily on *narguilas*, and the office buildings were drab and dreary. It could have been the backdrop to a black-and-white B movie. But when we turned off the main streets and into the souk we plunged into animated technicolor.

I stocked up with vegetables at stalls stacked high with an unexpectedly wide range of produce. The aubergines alone came in multiple varieties, from pale pink and smaller than a thumb to grotesque dark purple, the size and shape of a donkey's testicles. A cheese vendor offered me a curious object that looked like a dirty snowball. 'Milk and yoghurt and rice,' he said. 'Try it.' I did. It tasted like rancid parmesan. I bought a block of soft white feta instead. We stopped at a *knafe* shop where a man was pouring a yellowish mixture onto a metal plate the size of a cartwheel set on top of a brazier. '*Knafe* is a Nablus speciality,' Asem said, ordering two servings. It was a syrup-drenched dough cooked on a layer of white cheese and sickeningly delicious.

The souk formed part of the Old City, a warren of centuries-old buildings networked with arched alleyways. 'I used to live here,' Asem told me as we came out of the *knafe* shop. 'In this street I saw my friend killed, shot by Israeli soldiers. I saw it from my house. It was during the invasion of 2002, when

Nablus was put under curfew for ninety days. No one was allowed to go out. My friend, he went out and he was killed.'

All around us the walls of every building in sight were plastered with posters bearing names, faces and dates. 'These are the martyrs,' Asem said, 'the people who have been killed by the Israelis, the people who have died in military operations.'

The Palestinians used the word martyr to refer to all those killed by the Israelis, whether actively involved in armed resistance or unwittingly caught up in conflict, and to all suicide bombers. They usually described suicide bombings as military operations. I asked Asem what he thought of the latest suicide bombing in Jerusalem. 'It is not right,' he said.

The next day was Friday, the Muslim holy day. When I went out in the morning Suleiman and Abu Mahir were busying themselves around an oil drum buried deep in the ground, coaxing flames from a layer of burning coals at the bottom of it. Once they had got the coals glowing nicely they filled the drum with several chickens spiked onto a metal pole and covered it with a layer of clay. The cooking would take about three hours, Suleiman said. In the meantime, he and Abu Mahir were going to pick figs. 'Come with us,' he said.

We got into Abu Mahir's car – an ancient little Ford that looked as if it had been rescued from a scrapheap – along with Abu Mahir's two young sons, Mahir and Hani. We drove through the outskirts of Nablus and into an area of olive groves. A mound of earth and rock piled up across the road brought us to a halt. Behind us a taxi disgorged a group of men who set off on foot towards a village up the hill.

Mounds like this blocked many of the minor roads between the towns and villages, Suleiman told me. They were put up by the Israeli army to restrict the movement of the Palestinians. We got out of the car and walked the remaining distance to the fig trees.

The plot of land the trees stood on belonged to Abu Mahir's wife's sister's husband's family. They lived in a village at the other side of Nablus, about ten miles away; normally a short enough distance but the travelling difficulties imposed by the army made it impossible for them to harvest the fruit.

We filled several buckets and basins and headed back home. Abu Mahir put on a cassette and we bounced along the unsurfaced track to the sounds of a music that could have been French but wasn't. 'That's Hebrew music,' Suleiman said. 'Abu Mahir got to like Hebrew music when he was in jail.' This surprised me. I would have thought that the situation in which he was exposed to it would have conditioned him against it. Even more surprising, Abu Mahir had also learned Hebrew in jail and spoke it well. 'Why did you do this?' I asked. 'It's the language of the oppressor surely?' Abu Mahir shrugged off this suggestion. It was something to occupy his time, he said. I later found that many Palestinians were reasonably fluent in Hebrew, particularly those who had worked in Israel before the *intifada*, and had no qualms about it.

Suleiman had invited me to eat with them, so after the clay cover had been hacked off the subterranean barbecue, I followed the trays of steaming chickens into the flat where the table was already laid with platters of rice cooked with peas, carrots mixed with sliced nuts, and tomato and cucumber salad.

After the meal Umm Ahmed asked if I could help them set up an internet connection. They had just bought a new computer and so far had been unable to get online. The stumbling block seemed to be the options available for indicating the country they were in. There was no mention of Palestine or West Bank or any other related name anywhere on the list. I asked them what they thought their country would be called in this sort of situation. Nobody knew. I selected Israel. Umm Ahmed said this couldn't be right. But it worked.

At Sultan's shop in the evening I met up again with the two students, Mohannad and Osama, and a couple of other neighbours. Abu Jaffer was about fifty, leaned heavily on a stick, and looked like a mercenary fresh from battle in some war-torn banana republic. He had studied in Glasgow, worked as an engineer in the Gulf, set up a solar heating factory in Jordan, made a fortune from it, lost it all, become manager of a casino in Jericho, and was now running a second-hand furniture shop in Nablus. The other man, Abu Fayad, seemed to be the focus of a heated discussion. He ran in and out of the shop, backwards and forwards, shouting angrily. Sultan introduced me to him but he paid no attention. Out he ran again, leaned into his car, came back with a couple of photos and thrust them into my hand. I looked at the first one. It showed a good-looking young man. I looked at the second and saw what seemed to be a huge chunk of barbecued meat, a side of beef perhaps, lying on a bed. The remains of a hand and foot attached to it were all that showed that it had once been human. Abu Fayad snatched the photos back and left the shop.

'That was his younger brother,' Sultan said. 'Killed in an Israeli rocket attack.'

I came away from Sultan's with two invitations – lunch with Mohannad and Osama the next day and pot luck at Abu Jaffer's house whenever I fancied.

The meal with Mohannad and Osama was served in a bedroom, or at least, in a room furnished with two single metal beds and a couple of stools which we used as tables. They shared the flat with four other students and paid the equivalent of about £25 a month each.

The conversation focused on financial matters while we ate (lentil soup, charred chips, sliced tomatoes and bread). Since I'd been in Palestine I'd noticed that everyone seemed to complain about having no money and about the impact of the occupation on the economy so I wanted to know how they could afford things like rent, university fees and the mobile phones that they all had.

'My father gives me money,' said Mohannad.

'But where does he get his money from?'

'He is a trader. He works in Israel. He goes there but not

through the checkpoints. It is very dangerous.'

Before the *intifada*, many Palestinians worked in Israel, travelling there every day. That was no longer allowed but many, like Mohannad's father, carried on illegally.

Osama, who had done the cooking, ladled out more of the lentil soup for us. He seemed always to be the object of banter from the others but said little himself, only smiling mysteriously. He was slim and boyish-looking, as if not fully grown, both physically and in personality.

Osama bin Laden's name came up.

'Do you like Osama bin Laden?' I asked.

'Oh yes, we love Osama bin Laden!' Mohannad leapt up, full of enthusiasm. The strip lighting behind him fell off the wall with a crash.

'Why?' I asked, as Mohannad sorted out the tangle of cables and fixed it back up again.

'In Palestine everybody loves Osama bin Laden,' said Osama, with his usual enigmatic look.

'Why?'

'Because he war to America,' shouted Mohannad, sitting down again.

'Why is that good?'

'Because Bush war to Islam, he kills Islamic in Iraq, in Afghanistan, in Sudan, in all Islam. Bush is bad. Osama bin Laden is good.'

Abu Jaffer lived on the ground floor of a block of flats further up the road. When I called round he and his wife Muna were sitting outside on the terrace with his brother Irfan and his sister-in-law Huda.

Huda was in her mid-thirties and had an alluring, gypsy-like manner. She was smoking a *narguila* and chattering into a mobile, dark eyes darting from one to the other of us as she spoke.

'She's talking to her son,' Abu Jaffer told me. 'He's in prison in the Negev.'

Fahdi, the son, had been arrested by the Israelis two years

previously because of some involvement he had had with the Al Aqsa Brigades, the militant wing of Fatah. He was now halfway through a four-year sentence.

'We are proud of him,' Irfan said. 'He's not a thief, he's not a criminal. We feel proud because he defends our country. Even the children three years old don't want the occupation. When the first *intifada* started Fahdi was only five years old and he was throwing stones at the soldiers. When he gets out of prison he will get married and have a son and in twenty years' time the son will be in prison. However long the Israelis stay here there will be war.'

Abu Jaffer reeled off a list of all the other family members who had been in prison, including his father, his uncle, his brothers, his cousins, and even Huda who had spent a day in jail under suspicion of smuggling letters out for her jailed brother-in-law.

'They came and took me away while I was preparing *molokhia*,' said Huda who had by now finished her call. She puffed on the *narguila* and passed it over to Irfan.

Irfan was in a lugubrious mood. 'The future is dark here in Palestine. I am afraid of the future. It's not just me thinking this, it's everybody here.'

I asked them what they thought of Yassir Arafat who seemed to be a controversial figure, not only internationally but among the Palestinians themselves. Many non-Palestinians still regarded him as a terrorist, while many Palestinians felt that he had betrayed them by yielding too much in the Oslo Agreement. At another level, both at home and abroad, he was widely considered responsible for endemic corruption and nepotism in the Palestinian Authority.

Irfan defended him staunchly. 'I like Arafat because there are no leaders here except Arafat. For fifty years he's been here with us, with the rebels. For us he's like Fidel Castro, it's like Cuba.'

Abu Jaffer disagreed. 'Most people in Nablus hate him. Most Palestinians hate him. I hate him.'

Throughout this conversation Fatima, one of Abu Jaffer's

daughters, had been hovering at my side, homework in hand, bursting in each time there was a break in the exchange. 'What's the past participle of come?', 'What's an infinitive?', 'Why is this the past tense?' I answered as best I could. The youngest daughter, Lolo, wanting her fair share of attention, insisted on reading to me the story of *The Paper Bag Princess* in Arabic before I left.

CHAPTER 2

A number of students helped regularly in the PR department so I got to know them. One of them, Islah, invited me to her *tai kwan do* class to see them doing their end-of-course test. I went over to the gym. Seven girls dressed in white trousers and belted tunics with black trim were sitting on a bench like magpies perched on a branch. The instructor put them through a programme of individual exercises – kicking, turning, thrusting their arms out, as the magpies transformed themselves one by one into souped-up marionettes. Islah achieved the highest score and moved straight to green belt status, the others to yellow.

Afterwards we walked over to the canteen.

Islah had poise, self-confidence and charm. Her small, trim figure was always neatly dressed in trousers or jeans with an Islamic coat and a *hijab* tucked into the collar. She spoke English with an American accent and her speech was peppered with young generation colloquialisms.

She talked to me about her brother who was currently in jail, accused of being an accomplice of a suicide bomber. 'He was arrested on the basis of evidence given by a Palestinian witness, so they said. He was told that he would get five years if he agreed to go on trial without the witness but that he'd get seven years if he insisted on the witness being cross-examined. He insisted on the witness. The witness didn't appear. The Israelis said he was ill. But he still got seven years.'

I asked her how the spectrum of opinion about the conflict fanned out among Palestinians generally.

'Well, nobody would ever admit that they'd be prepared to be a suicide bomber. The nearest would be admitting to sympathising with them, sharing their ideology. I suppose I tend towards that end of the spectrum. The opposite extreme would be people who would accept all of the Occupied Territories being part of Israel as long as there was peace. But very few people are like this. The only one I know of is my uncle.'

In the canteen we joined a few of the other students. They started a discussion about occupation and colonialism, drawing parallels between their own situation and those of the American-Indians and Latin-Americans. Islah thought that the Israeli occupation was made doubly reprehensible by the fact that the occupying forces were heterogeneous. She grabbed a sugar bowl and set it on top of her coffee cup. 'This is occupation by just one entity,' she said. 'The sugar is occupying the cup.' She removed the sugar bowl and picked up the menu, brandishing it so that its pages flapped open. 'Now look, this is made up of different pieces of paper.' She rolled it up and put in the cup. 'This is like the Israeli occupation because the Israelis come from many different sources, from different parts of the world. They're not homogeneous. This type of occupation is worse.'

Meanwhile Falastine, who had joined us, had embarked on a story about her brother who was studying in Greece. 'He was transiting once through Cyprus and when he showed his travel document at passport control the woman shouted over a colleague, "Hey, do you know what Palestine is?" The man said, "I don't know. I guess maybe it's the capital of Gaza." They roared with laughter.'

Although the male students whose homes were outside Nablus generally rented accommodation in the city, many of the female students travelled every day as they were less likely to be harassed at the checkpoints. Camelia and Fida, two students in the English department who lived in Tulkarim, a town about twenty miles away, invited me to go home with them for the weekend. The first question which came to mind was the risk of my being hassled on the way out of the city. As a foreigner I wasn't supposed to be in Nablus in the first place.

No problem, said Ala. The soldiers would let me through on the way out and to get back in again I could walk round by the mountain route.

The three of us took a taxi to Beitiba checkpoint, just outside Nablus. We would have to go through the checkpoint on foot and get another taxi at the other side.

The checkpoint was near a quarry. Great slabs of rock lay alongside the road and the olive trees and cactus plants were covered with a grey patina of quarry dust. A long line of people queued at the turnstiles. 'There were 500 people in the queue when we arrived yesterday,' Camelia said. 'You can imagine how long it took and how hot and tired we get waiting.'

As each person passed through, their papers were examined by a soldier. Other soldiers looked on, rifles at the ready. 'I'll go first and explain to the soldiers that you're coming to visit us,' Fida said. 'Then all you have to do is show them your passport.'

Fida went ahead and spoke with the soldier on checking duty. Three other soldiers gathered round, listening to her story and glancing over at me. She seemed to be getting the third degree. Eventually she called me over. The soldier riffled through my passport.

'Where are you going?'

'To Tulkarim, to visit friends.'

'How did you get into Nablus?'

'From Jerusalem.'

'Did you pass a checkpoint?'

'I don't know.'

My reply could hardly have been more inane.

'How do you think you could pass a checkpoint without knowing about it?' The soldier waved his rifle in the direction of the corrugated iron shelters for the queues of travellers, the checking desks and the military look-out points. 'You are in Nablus illegally. You didn't go through a checkpoint. I can't let you pass. You have to go back to Nablus now or we'll call for the military police.'

I pointed out that if I could just pass through the checkpoint

I would no longer be in an illegal situation.

'Wait a minute.' He went over to speak with a colleague.

While he was away a couple of women who had been standing around – clearly not Palestinian from their Western style of dress – came up and introduced themselves. They were from Machsom Watch, an Israeli human rights organisation whose members monitored the checkpoints in an attempt to curb the abuse of Palestinians by the Israeli army. I told them what had happened. They advised me not to try arguing any further. 'If the police come they'll take you straight to Ben Gurion airport and deport you,' one of them said.

The soldier came back again. 'You can't go through. Go back to Nablus. The only way you can leave is through Huwara checkpoint. Maybe they will let you through.'

I was struck by the illogicality of accusing me of being in Nablus illegally and then sending me back there. If it was illegal, why didn't they call the police? I supposed it was because they didn't want to go to the bother of getting the police involved in a situation which presented no conceivable threat but at the same time they felt they had to pay some minimal lip service to the rules.

Camelia and Fida were by this time at the other side of the barrier. I waved goodbye to them and turned back. I had at least got off more lightly than the British MP Ian Gibson who, the week previously, had been held at a checkpoint for more than an hour in a Palestinian ambulance after suffering a stroke in Ramallah.

Saed, a lecturer at An Najah, invited me to visit the cemetery with him. He wanted to show me the grave of his mother who had been shot by Israeli soldiers two years previously.

As we walked across the university car park a volley of gunfire rang out.

'Would that be the army?' I asked. 'Down in the Old City?'

'No,' Saed said. 'It's much closer. This is dangerous.'

The shots continued, very near now, as if the bullets were whizzing about our ears. We bent double and scuttled like cockroaches for the car.

'I've no idea what's going on,' Saed said, turning the key in the ignition, 'but we'd better get out of here.'

I started to fasten the safety belt.

'No, we don't use these here,' Saed said.

'In the UK you have to, it's the law.'

'Well, here it's better not to. You never know when you might have to get out of the car quickly.'

Saed drove cautiously down towards the gate and stopped to ask one of the guards what was going on. All he could tell us that was that the shooting was further up at the main entrance to the university. Saed turned left and we sped down An Najah Street where the cemetery lay at the lower end of the hill.

We went to Saed's mother's grave. The stone slab was surrounded on three sides by stone benches and sheltered by a corrugated iron roof covered in climbing plants. Behind it lay the grave of her cousin who had been shot before her eyes thirty years before her own murder.

Saed had brought a broom with him. He started to tidy up the grave as he spoke, sweeping the rubbish lying around it. 'It was really shocking. We were sitting peacefully in front of the house, in the garden. My mum was sitting embroidering, and my dad was picking thyme and I was next to them. Two army jeeps stopped in front of the house, so maybe like maximum thirty metres away from us, in plain view. It was Friday so it was very calm, there was nobody in the street. Then the jeeps stood, you know, for a few seconds longer than I thought was normal. Just as I was thinking that, they started shooting at us, shooting directly at us. At that time I didn't know that my mum was hit because I was standing behind the glass door of the balcony and the glass debris hit me in the neck. I thought that I was hit with a bullet and I fell on the ground and started screaming. I thought the bullet had penetrated my neck, the left side of my neck. So I started screaming to my dad to come and help me. I didn't know that my mum had got hit. I was bleeding heavily from the neck and I thought I was going to die and then I noticed my mum had fallen. So I ran to her and she was pale and her eyes were wide open, and I started talking to her, mum, mum, you know. She didn't respond. I wanted to lift her and when I put out my hands to carry her, my hands were filled with blood.'

Saed had stopped sweeping and was leaning on his broom.

'So I started screaming at the top of my lungs to the neighbours, screaming, screaming, and then the neighbour who lives in front of us came running, then another neighbour rushed in. They came and carried my mum away and I knew that she was, you know, she was martyred.'

The neighbours put Saed's mother into a car and took her to hospital. In the meantime, the jeep, which had driven to the end of the road, came back again.

'I was afraid that they were going to kill me and my neighbour so I started waving my hands and shouting don't shoot, don't shoot, and I came and stood in front of the jeep. I started screaming and saying, you killed my mother, why did you kill my mother? I was screaming and screaming. And then the guy next to the driver he aimed at me.'

Saed, who lived for a long time in the United States, sounds American. He believed it was his accent which saved him.

'The guy hesitated, then he shot in the air a few times and the driver said to my neighbours, 'Take him to hospital.'

Saed's injuries turned out to be fairly superficial. After being treated he went to the hospital where his mother had been taken.

'When I entered people were shaking hands with me and kissing me so I knew that my mum, you know… And I went in and my dad was shaking and he was crying… terrible. And then they brought her. I saw her and I kissed her and… terrible.'

Saed sat down on the bench opposite me.

The family had lodged a complaint, he said. 'We had an Arab lawyer from Israel and they were to bring them to trial. So far it has been two years and the Israeli army have not given the results of the investigation to our lawyer. They wanted to basically make the whole thing die. We made a huge campaign against them in the media, interviews with *The Los Angeles Times*, in *The New York Times*. We made a feature with *The Philadelphia Enquirer*, with the Canadian newspapers, all over. And you know, we say this very clearly, we're doing this not only for the sake of our mother but in order to save other innocent civilians, in order to make the next Israeli soldier hesitate a little bit before killing a Palestinian civilian in such outrageous cold blood. Like you saw in Gaza the other day, this soldier shot twenty bullets, twenty bullets at this kid, thirteen years old, and the chief of staff is accepting his story. What kind of soldier is it that shoots a kid? The problem is with their system. The Israeli military system encourages all soldiers to be trigger happy because there are no questions asked.

'It seems like the Israelis, they think they're above the law, they're above any morality or international legality. I don't know how they can get away with it. I know that part of it is because they get so much political support from stupid morons like George Bush, who calls Sharon a peace man. Sharon, who by any standard is a vampire, to say the least, who doesn't drink milk in the morning, he drinks blood every morning because he cannot survive without blood. This guy, if you look at his CV it's basically one massacre after another, and he's the prime minister of Israel. How can they ask us to respect Israel or the Israeli society when they elect a person like this and keep him in power? We are not against Jews as Jews. The problem is with Zionism as an ideology. It has done more harm to the Jewish people by creating this big ghetto, the so-called Israeli state.'

Saed started sweeping again. I asked him if he would consider it acceptable for Israel to stay the way it is now and for the West Bank and Gaza to become a Palestinian state, in other words, the two-state solution. He said that he would, but only as a first step towards one secular democratic state encompassing both Israel and Palestine. He pointed out that there were already one million Palestinians living inside Israel

– the Arab-Israelis – and about four million refugees scattered throughout other countries who should have the right to go back to the homes they or their families lost in Israel. One of the problems with this solution from the Israeli point of view is that the Arabs would increasingly outnumber the Jews as they have a higher birth rate.

Saed agreed. 'That's the problem for Israel. You cannot have a Jewish state and call yourself a democracy. You can have a Jewish democracy. But don't say you're a Jewish state and a democracy for all your citizens because the Palestinians who live inside Israel are second-class citizens. And you know, democracy doesn't mean anything when you deny the indigenous people the right to go back to their homeland. We start a two-state solution and then the refugees come back and we create a society with equality for everybody.'

Saed finished his sweeping and suggested we take a walk to look at the other graves, many of which were adorned with posters of martyrs.

As we walked around we met a number of other visitors. Saed knew them all. They shook hands and embraced. Sometimes they stood at a grave with hands cupped, murmuring words of prayer.

A family – mother, father and brother - sat at the grave of a twenty-three-year-old martyr. 'We want peace,' the father said to me as the mother wept. 'You are welcome,' he added. 'We like you but not your government.'

We moved on. 'This boy was deaf and mute.' Saed pointed to a stone slab decked with photos and flowers. 'He was playing with a toy gun. An Israeli soldier saw him. They shot him in the neck, so he became paraplegic. He couldn't speak, he couldn't hear and he was paraplegic, and he lived like this for one year. Then after that he died. Twelve years old.'

Grave after grave had a story of conflict associated with it: the graves of six people gassed by soldiers during an invasion of the Old City, the grave of the man who took Saed's mother to hospital who was himself shot a year later, the grave of a twelve-year-old girl shot the week before I arrived in Nablus, and many more.

'This grave is for a family of eight killed when their house in the Old City was bulldozed. They brought a D9, one of the biggest Caterpillars. They bulldozed their way in without giving any warning to the residents of this area. And this family couldn't get out. They killed three generations.' Saed read out the names and the relationships on the tombstone. 'One of the women was pregnant and there were three children. And what really hurts is that no questions were asked, no trial for the soldiers who did this. Nothing. No condemnation. Nothing. Just... *hallas*, just accept the fact that we bulldoze.'

The next day I discovered the source of the gunfire at the university gate. It had started as an argument between some drivers of the taxis which lined up at the gate to ferry students into town. One driver had tried to jump the queue and another tried to stop him. The argument got more heated. One of them pulled out a gun and started firing it in the air, then some other men got out their guns and they were all firing in the air in a sabre-rattling sort of way. 'It's very regrettable,' Ala said. 'There are a lot of problems in Nablus caused by people getting guns and going around in armed gangs. They get the guns from Israelis who are only too happy to contribute to a destabilising of Palestinian society, and it's difficult for the Palestinian police to deal with it as they're not armed themselves.'

CHAPTER 3

As in any other university, the country's political parties were represented at student level at An Najah. Hamas representatives currently held the majority of seats on the Students Council, the remainder being in the hands of Fatah, Islamic Jihad and several smaller factions. The various political presences were in strong evidence on the campus, partly because of the ongoing conflict situation and also because the university was shortly to hold its first Students Council election since 2001. Normally they were held annually but they had been cancelled during the *intifada* because of their inflammatory potential.

I noticed that some banners had appeared outside the exhibition hall and that people were streaming in and out.

'It's the PFLP,' Fida said. 'They're putting on an exhibition. Let's go and see it.'

The PFLP (Popular Front for the Liberation of Palestine) was established in 1967 in an amalgamation of three Palestinian fighter groups. Vigorously anti-western, it was responsible for many guerilla actions against Israel, including the hijacking of Israeli planes in the 60s and 70s. Camelia, whose father belonged to it, told me that it had toned itself down since then and now pursued a more moderate socialist agenda.

Fida and I entered the exhibition hall through curtains of soft black material and passed into a corridor lined with the same black. The strident percussive strains of a funereal music blared from loudspeakers. I felt as if I was going into the ghost train at a fair.

A young man introduced himself to us. He was Hafiz, a fine arts student, who had designed the exhibition and was only too pleased to show us round.

The fairground effect overlaid with macabre overtones continued, with stands in black cut-out. Various exhibits were devoted to the memory of individual martyrs, with photos of their funerals and of key events in their lives. Hafiz pointed to a blood-stained tee-shirt with bullet holes in the front which was pinned to the wall. 'This martyr, before his death he said that if he was ever shot in the back his body was to be left where it fell as a sign of his disgrace. We are showing this blood-stained tee-shirt as proof that he was shot from the front.' Another stall displayed a raggedly torn shirt and trousers. They had belonged to a militant shot in the street. The family had not been allowed to collect the body and it had been attacked by dogs. Next to it a series of exhibits illustrated prison life: scarecrow figures suspended from the ceiling by a rope (prisoners were kept like this with no food for days, said Hafiz), an assortment of model ships and other ornamental items made by prisoners, a box of sand with black polystyrene hands and candles sticking up out of it.

The exhibition lightened up a bit towards the end with a mock-up of a typical room in a shared student flat, designed to draw attention to the difficult conditions imposed by the occupation, most students having to rent accommodation in Nablus rather than travelling from home daily. A series of innocuous-looking photos of the campus followed. These, said Hafiz sternly, were supposed to show that conditions in the university were not good enough, citing inadequate provision of rubbish bins as an example. We thanked him for the guided tour and Fida dashed off to a lecture.

A few days later the PFLP stands had been cleared away and the Hamas women were putting others up in their place.

'Shall we go?' suggested Camelia.

The Hamas exhibition was an odd mixture of market and propaganda, and much jollier than the PFLP one. Students crowded gaily round stalls where *hijabs* and *jilbabs* were arrayed alongside glamorous evening dresses. They poked around among the jewellery and the makeup, sampling perfumes from dagger-shaped bottles, testing palettes of eye shadow and blusher, trying on rings and necklaces. They jostled each other at toy stalls and bookstalls, and rummaged in the bric-a-brac of worry beads, olive wood key rings and embroidered goods. Two booths side by side were devoted to the Koran and the founder of the Muslim Brotherhood. Next to them was an immense polystyrene model of Al Aqsa mosque with a padlocked chain round it. The chain was there, Camelia said, because extremist Jewish elements threatened to destroy the mosque and build something of their own in its place. A cartoon beside it mocked the other Arab countries for standing by and ignoring the plight of the Palestinians. A model pen hung poised over a broken star of David lying in a pool of blood. 'It's meant to show that education is the most effective way of making progress,' said Camelia.

A wall covered in photos of slaughter and atrocity commemorated events from the *intifada*. In one of them a dead Palestinian lay with his live baby daughter posing beside his head. Another showed a badly injured baby in hospital. Camelia was scathing: 'The baby was a suicide bomber, of course,' referring to the tendency for Israeli aggression to be justified as a reaction to a perceived threat, even in the most unlikely circumstances.

A big black bin stood crammed with the usual sort of campus rubbish – paper cups, plastic bags, empty drink cans, scrunched up sheets of paper; sticking out of it were pieces of card marked Oslo, Geneva, Road Map, a graphic statement that all these agreements, accords and proposals could be consigned to the garbage bin of bad ideas.

We came to a herbal remedy stall with bowls of seeds, leaves, roots and dates, and bottles of water and oil. 'These are the things that the Prophet advised us to do,' Camelia said. She pointed to a poster with sayings in Arabic rendered into rather quaint English. 'He who eats seven ajwa dates in the morning of each day shall not be influenced by poison or witchcraft on that day,' I read. 'Cover the pot and close the drinking vessel because there is one night in a year's time whereby a certain epidemic will come down and pass through every exposed pot and unveiled drinking vessel and it integrates therewith. Verily do acquire the black seed for it is a cure for any disease except death. Eat olive oil and anoint your body with it for it comes from a blessed tree.'

One of the Prophet's pieces of advice was to clean your teeth with a siwack, a stick taken from the arack tree. 'The siwack is a disinfectant for the mouth and is pleasurable to God. It has a very delightful smell and taste resembling mint plant.' I bought one for five shekels, about 70p sterling, which seemed rather a lot for a piece of twig. It turned out to have more of a potato flavour and was definitely less effective than a toothbrush.

'Zamzam water is a drink for whatever intention; when you drink zamzam water with an intention for healing it will be so as per God's whim,' the poster promised. 'Zamzam water is from the sacred well in Mecca,' Camelia explained. 'It is very good for our health.'

The last exhibit was a set of steps covered in a white satiny material, strewn with artificial flowers and birds, bedecked with flashing fairy lights, and with photos of martyrs and bunches of grapes hanging over it.

'What on earth is this?' I asked Camelia.

'It's the stairway to paradise by which the martyrs ascend into heaven.'

A crowd was gathering round it, generating the same warm, natural, happy atmosphere as at the clothes stalls and the herbal pharmacy.

After that it was back to the macabre with an Islamic Jihad exhibition. A mural round the entrance depicted the head and shoulders of Fathi Shikaki, the founder, with globules of blood dripping from underneath it. Inside the decor was black, blood red and gloomy, like a filmset for Dracula's lair. Aggressive music pounded out with frequent mention of Allah.

With Camelia I walked round what was now becoming a familiar parade of images: *dishdasha*-clad Arabs in other countries leading the good life contrasted with Palestinians in military fatigues carrying rifles and the Koran; Palestinians cold and hungry in desert prison camps; Palestinians grieving for dead militants, queuing at checkpoints, being tortured.

Suddenly, as we stood in the claustrophobic dimness watching a martyr's funeral on a computer screen, two masked men in military dress and carrying rifles burst in. For a couple of seconds I was rigid with fright, firstly, because the very image was fear generating, secondly, because I thought some kind of attack was afoot, and thirdly, because I feared that no matter what their agenda might have been, seeing a foreigner in their midst they would immediately lay into me as a suspected spy, or take me hostage, Baghdad style. In those few seconds a whole lot of terrifying scenarios flashed through my mind in the same way as your life supposedly flashes in front of your eyes as you drown. The face masks – woollen, with holes for eyes and mouth – were chilling, triggering memories of terrorist groups in the seventies, hijackings, ruthless treatment of victims. Then one of the men started helping the other to fix his rifle (which I now saw was a toy one) with sticky tape. Camelia asked what was going on and they explained that they were there to role play Israeli soldiers at a checkpoint.

We moved on to inspect the art exhibits, red paintings on black cloth done by prisoners in Megiddo prison camp. 'Suffering produces creativity, of course,' said Camelia in her dry fashion. 'The purpose of this work is to show that Palestinians still have art in their heart. We are not just terrorists as we are represented. We practise art just as American and British and other people do.'

A terrific din was coming from a table covered with model houses and neat gardens. In the middle of it a tank was blasting off rounds at a militant who lay bleeding on the ground. 'A resistance operation in a settlement,' said Camelia. 'Maybe this land is his own land, or his father's land. It has been taken. It is occupied.'

On the way out we passed another table. On it was a rectangular pool lined with polystyrene bricks, the water dyed blood red, with a yellow sailing boat in the middle. 'The boat is carrying the souls of the martyrs to heaven,' said Camelia.

'I found all that quite disturbing,' I said to her as we left.

'Well... how do you think we live?' she asked.

Ramadan started in mid-October. The evening meal at which the fast was broken, *iftar*, became the social focus of the day.

Abu Jaffer's family had invited me to eat with them. We sat round the kitchen table waiting for the *muazzen* to signal the setting of the sun. As the Koranic reading was broadcast from the mosque, Fatima, the second daughter, prayed, turning towards Mecca with her hands cupped in front of her and lips moving silently. The others bustled about putting the food on the table. When the *muazzen* finally called *Allahu akbar* they all broke their fast in the traditional way with a date.

While we helped ourselves to turkey and *molokhia* (a green vegetable stew with a grassy flavour), Abu Jaffer predicted that the Al Aqsa mosque would soon collapse. 'It's foretold in the Koran and the Torah. The Israelis have been digging under it, trying to find the remains of Solomon's Temple and that's undermined it.' The family all agreed that this would sound the death knell for any peace negotiations.

After the meal we watched BBC Prime on satellite television. Fatima went into her bedroom and reappeared robed from head to foot in her white praying clothes. Again turning towards Mecca, she bowed and knelt through the prescribed ritual of devotion while the rest of us watched Sean Connery on the Parkinson show.

The next day I dropped in at Abu Jaffer's second-hand furniture shop in the souk. As we walked over to a bakery to get some bread we heard the short, sharp serial explosions of gunfire. Nobody turned a hair or even stopped what they were doing to look around or ask questions. Abu Jaffer said it was probably people shooting in the air as a preliminary to a party to celebrate the life of one of the martyrs that was being held in the evening. As we watched the rounds of dough being tossed into the cavernous log-fired oven a boy came in and said he'd just seen an informer being shot. Abu Jaffer shrugged.

Abu Jaffer had asked a friend of his, Ali, a big beefy man who had fought with the Al Aqsa Brigades, to take me to visit a soap factory. The production of soap made from olive oil had once been one of the mainstays of Nablus's economy. Over recent years the industry had been decimated, a victim of both the conflict and competition with products from EU countries.

The factory, which was in a cellar-like building, was open but had not been operational since it had been bombed by the Israelis. It was guarded by a small, excitable man called Mahfooz. Both he and Ali had been shot during the course of the fighting that had taken place there.

Mahfooz showed me around, describing volubly and with extravagant gesticulation the soap-making process, the bombing and the fighting, all at the same time.

Sacks of soap and drums of oil lay haphazardly on the floor, untouched since the day of the fighting. I climbed up onto a platform and looked into a vast vat where the caustic soda and olive oil were cooked. It looked like a scene from Poe's *The Pit and the Pendulum*. As I looked down I remembered Samah, a young woman from one of the old aristocratic families of Palestine who worked at the university, telling me that some of the older family members had talked to her of how they used to punish people who couldn't pay their debts by taking them to the soap factories and throwing them into the vats of boiling soda and oil to die, even as late as the 1930s.

That evening I had *iftar* with Irfan and Huda's family. They lived a few hundred metres down the hillside in a flat adjoining a barber's shop where Ashraf, the twin brother of Fahdi, worked. 'Ashraf used to be a car mechanic,' Irfan said as he introduced me, 'but when Fahdi was arrested he took over the shop for him.'

Ashraf had been arrested along with Fahdi but was

subsequently released. 'He had no connection with any militant group,' Irfan said, explaining that at least one son in a Palestinian family will always remain free of any suspicion so that they will be able to look after the rest of the family.

Huda and her thirteen-year-old daughter Ataa covered the table with sheets of newspaper and laid out a steaming bowl of *maqlooba* (a rice and vegetable dish), stuffed cabbage, salad and yoghurt.

As we sat down a frail old man wearing a dressing gown and holding a catheter bag in his hand tottered in from another room. Irfan introduced him. 'This is my father. He's 105.' Irfan settled him in at the head of the table and piled food on his plate. Throughout the meal the old man, who had been a stonemason – the best stonemason in Nablus, said Irfan proudly – reminisced about the time of the Turks and his memories of the First World War. So Irfan said anyway, but to me his words were barely distinguishable.

Ashraf had recently got married and he and his wife Samer lived in the family flat. When we had finished eating they put on a video of their wedding. A series of stills focused on their faces as Celine Dion belted out *The Power of Love*. Samer wore a voluminous white dress covered with a Red Riding Hood-style of cape. Ashraf draped her with some gold bracelets and necklaces – the dowry – and they danced together, with Ashraf brandishing a sword which he then used to cut the cake.

Huda and Samer shared a *narguila* while Irfan busied himself in the kitchen making *knafe*. Ataa had pulled out a keyboard and was playing the Palestinian national anthem. She opened her English text book and pointed to the opening lines of *My Love is Like a Red, Red Rose*. 'Do you know this song?' she asked. 'We can't sing it at school because we don't know the tune.' I picked it out on the keyboard and wrote the notation in her music book. We sang it together while Huda chattered on the phone to Fahdi.

When I got back, Suleiman and Abu Mahir were outside drinking coffee and the air was snapping with the fire crackers that Abu Mahir's children were playing with. Since the beginning of Ramadan, these firecrackers had been going off all over the place every evening. At first I had thought it was gunfire. Surely, I asked the two men, the pistol-like report of firecrackers must be unsettling for Palestinians. Suleiman agreed. 'This is a very bad thing. It upsets people who have lost friends and family to Israeli guns, or who have been involved in any shooting.'

One of the children put a cracker into my hand and showed me how to set it off by throwing it onto a stone. I looked at the wrapping. 'Fun trick noise makers', it said in English, followed by some words in Hebrew.

'They're manufactured by settlers who sell them to the Palestinians,' Suleiman explained. 'Some of the militias try to prevent retailers selling them by threatening them and others demand protection money so that they can continue to sell them. It's all a big racket.'

'Can't the police do anything?'

'The police are useless. They're not armed so they're impotent against the militias. The Israelis have empowered the militias by not allowing the Palestinian police to be armed.'

He finished his coffee. 'Come in and see Umm Ahmed.'

Umm Ahmed was just serving up more Ramadan delicacies – two plates of pastries like Cornish pasties, some filled with cream cheese and some with a walnut mixture, deep-fried and drenched with honey. Already feeling bloated after a cheese one, on top of Irfan's *knafe*, I wanted no more, but no sooner had I swallowed the last mouthful than Umm Ahmed was lifting a walnut one onto my plate. I washed it down with *tamarhind*, a dark, sugary Ramadan drink, as we watched a Syrian serial in which a man was beating a screaming woman in a sleeveless black cat suit. I'd been surprised at the kind of programmes popular with Palestinians, many of which seemed to be at odds with an Islamic lifestyle. Yet every house I'd been in had satellite television. It was one of the few sources of entertainment available to Palestinians. Suleiman had dishes for two satellite companies, plus a third one for digital. 'Digital is for the wrong things,' he told me.

'What kind of wrong things?'

'Sexy. Many people have digital here because Nablus is very conservative.'

'Well, why would they want sexy programmes then?'

'Because they have double standards.'

'*Ahlan*,' said the stallholder, a trimly-built man in his fifties with close-cropped, curly, greying hair. 'You are welcome.'

'*Shukran.*'

I was standing in front of a herbal medicine stall. Bottles of liquids and dried leaves jostled for space on the shelves. The walls were lined with posters of martyrs.

The man introduced himself as Waddeh, asked me where I came from and assured me again that I was welcome.

I asked him about his products.

He took a bottle off the shelf, opened it and put it under my nose. It smelled like cider. He began to explain in an idiosyncratic English, delivered slowly and deliberately like lilting poetry.

'This is for people who are fat and who want to be thin. With this you can lose ten kilograms in forty days. It is from apple. And this' – he pointed to a plastic bag filled with stalks – 'is for people who are crazy. This is very old medicine. It is the medicine of Mohammed. Whose blood is bad, when he visits us he needs just two weeks and he is well. We smile when we see who is ill in this world and the modern doctors can't do anything for him. In our business it is simple, from the herbal and the natural.'

He opened a jar of greyish powder. 'This is for kidney stones. No need for operation.' He opened another jar. 'This is from eighty-six herbs. Who has his stomach wrong, that is very easy. He takes this and in just one week his stomach is very, very nice.'

I pointed to a bottle containing a colourless liquid and a male doll, like a toy Action Man. 'What's this?' I asked.

'This is for girls who want big breasts,' said Waddeh. The

doll, which was too big to have passed through the neck of the bottle, had presumably increased in size after being put into it to demonstrate the properties of the liquid. 'Not drink, touching,' Waddeh added, making a circular rubbing motion on his chest. 'I am sorry, I cannot speak English well. I forget the words. My mind... It is since ...' He pointed to a boy in one of the posters. 'This is my son.' He pointed to the date, April 2002. 'They killed him.'

Waddeh's son Rami had been shot in the course of fighting in the streets of the Old City. I asked him if he had other children.

'Yes, this is my son.' He pointed to a young man in a shop across the way. 'All the time he is sad, weeping for his brother's death. He too says he is ready for death. And I have a twelve-year-old, Ahmed.'

The boy had been caught up in a recent army incursion.

'At ten o'clock at night the shooting started. Everyone in the town was running to give help to others. Ahmed was running to see what happened. He found hands on the ground, ears, noses, fingers.' Waddeh picked up a paper bag from his stall and mimed dropping things into it. 'He was picking up bits of bodies and putting them into a bag like this.'

A man with a black and white *keffiya* wrapped round his nose and mouth gangster-style appeared in the alley, darting in and out of the stalls, distributing photocopied sheets. He thrust one into my hands.

'What's this?' I asked Waddeh.

'This man is from the Al Aqsa Brigades[2]. The paper is about Arafat. They are criticizing him.'

I asked Waddeh what he thought of Arafat.

'In the past Arafat is a very good man but when he began to give Sharon and the Israeli government everything, believe me, his way is very wrong. He always say hello to Sharon. He does what Sharon want. But he must say bye bye to this kind of talking. He must stay and listen to the Palestinian people.'

'Everyone who is walking in the Old City here is a fighter. We want the peace, we say hello to any friend. But tell me, in which way can we love the Zionist? In your country, if any enemy coming to your town, you will feel you want to face the enemy. In every family in Nablus now you can find that the soldiers killed their father or their mother or their son, or they have someone put in prison. Every woman, every wife, every mother, is very black. That man,' he nodded to a stall stacked with bales of furnishing material, 'he is my brother. His son is in prison. He is eighteen years old and he is sentenced for twenty years. Why? Because he had many friends who were wanted by the Israeli army.'

A young man from a neighbouring stall joined us. His right hand was missing, lost in the same fighting as Rami.

'Sharon, he is the new Dracula,' Waddeh continued. 'But I want to say to Sharon one word – thank you. Why? Because the foolish Sharon wake up all the Palestinians to face the Israeli people.'

Waddeh lit a cigarette. 'It is bad for my health, I know, but I want to go away from this life because I have nothing to live for. I am waiting. I want to go the same road as my son's road. My heart is stone, the tear in my eyes is like the snow.'

A Koranic reading blaring from a radio in a stall nearby was drowning out Waddeh's words. I said goodbye and left. The stalls were closing and the atmosphere was febrile as people hurried to get home in time for *iftar*. I walked out of the souk and into heavy traffic and hooting horns.

I started to cross the street, heading for the cash dispenser at the bank on the other side. As I did so, I heard the familiar sound of Ramadan firecrackers. Then I saw people rushing over to where the sounds were coming from, to a man lying on the ground. This time, it seemed, the sounds were not fireworks; they were gunshots. The car horns rose to a crescendo. A group of Palestinian policemen stood still in the midst of it all, as impervious to what was going on as waxworks in Madame Tussaud's. I withdrew to the pavement and the shelter of a stall where a man in a red fez was selling Ramadan drinks, saffron yellow and plummy brown, in plastic bags like the ones goldfish are sold in.

'*Esh hasal?*' I asked him. What's happened?
'One man shoots a gun,' he replied in English. 'No problem. Welcome to our country, number one Palestine.'
Another informer had just been gunned down.

[2] Military wing of the Fatah party

CHAPTER 4

I climbed up six flights of dingy, dirty stairs and emerged into a clean, comfortable office. I was in the campaign headquarters of Hussam Khader, an imprisoned member of the Palestinian Legislative Council.

The campaign, which aimed at defending the rights of Palestinian prisoners, was being managed by Hussam's brother Ghassan, a vigorous, Italianate-looking man who spoke urgently, the words tumbling out as if he was afraid that he wouldn't have enough time to say everything he needed to say.

Hussam Khader had fallen foul not only of the Israelis but also of Yassir Arafat for being openly critical of corrupt practices in the Palestinian Authority. 'Say to Arafat the name of Hussam Khader and he will get like this' – Ghassan stretched his arms and flapped his fingers. 'He will get nervous. Hussam was always fighting corruption and the PA is against him because of this. The PA doesn't do a good job to support the Palestinian people. They don't have a good strategy. Hussam aimed to make Palestine like Singapore but now it is like Singapore for five per cent of the people and like Somalia for the other ninety-five per cent. Arafat for me is like Saddam Hussein. He is a dictator. He told Hussam to leave the Legislative Council. Hussam said to him, I am not in your company, I am elected by the people, and Arafat said, I am the people.'

Ghassan complained also about the way in which Arafat and the PA reportedly looked after their own with the money coming to Palestine in international aid. 'Just last week I heard that Arafat paid for a friend of his to get his teeth fixed. I saw the paperwork myself. And meanwhile people in the refugee camps are living on less than two dollars a day.'

Ghassan lived in Balata, one of the refugee camps in Nablus, which was subject to almost nightly harassment by the Israeli army.

'One night they came to my door at three in the morning. They were looking for one of my neighbours. They told me to knock on his door to get him to open up. I refused. The soldiers put a gun to my head. They said, fuck you, we can kill you. So I did it. I went to the door and there were ten guns aimed at me, ten spots of light shining on my chest from the telescopic sights. The neighbour was arrested.'

It seemed to me like the kiss of Judas. 'Didn't you feel embarrassed about having to betray him like this?'

'No, they understand.'

Hussam Khader had set up a cultural organisation, the Jaffa Centre, in Balata refugee camp. Ghassan introduced me to Walid, one of the people who ran it. He invited me to visit the Centre.

We met in Ghassan's office and walked down past the vegetable market to the taxi ranks. Walid pointed to one of the ranks.

'All the taxis there are cars stolen from Israel and painted.'

'Don't the police take any action?'

'There is no effective police force. Crime is dealt with between families. But there is very little crime. Here you are safe. If we didn't have the occupation, our life would be perfect.'

We drove out from the centre of town, past the stumps of some old Roman columns, then past a bombed building whose crumpled storeys lay collapsed in on each other like the layers of a half-eaten mille-feuilles. 'It used to be a prison,' said Walid. 'The Israelis hit it with an F16. They wanted to kill one of the prisoners. He wasn't killed but twelve policemen were.'

We got out of the taxi at the entrance to the camp, just opposite a church built over what is believed to be Jacob's well where Christ met the Samaritan woman and spoke to her of the water of life, as told in the gospel of John.

The word camp implies an impermanence which was belied by the buildings themselves. Although generally poorer and with fewer facilities and comforts than most other parts of Nablus, the inhabitants live in houses much like any others.

Walid showed me round the Jaffa Centre where educational and social activities were run. The building was new. The previous one had been destroyed when the Israeli army shelled the camp's electricity generator.

Four years after the start of the second *intifada* the Israeli army was still maintaining a presence around the camp with frequent invasions, shootings and arrests.

I sat in the office with Walid and another Walid and two Mohammeds. They described how life in the camp was affected by the ongoing siege situation, the damage to property, the curtailment of activities, and worst of all, the deaths and injuries.

'Here in Balata they killed seven children in one week,' one of the Mohammeds said. 'They came to the south of the camp in jeeps and started taunting children through their loudspeakers. "Where are the men? Where are the brave people?" they shouted. So the children threw stones. The soldiers waited for any child to get closer to the jeeps. They shot a child in the knee. He fell down. A soldier opened the door of the jeep and shot him five or six times. This kind of thing happened seven times in one week. The people who saw the act they said it was just a hunting party for the soldiers. Just target training.'

I asked what Amnesty and the other human rights people were doing.

'Nothing. I met a woman from Amnesty six months ago. She came to the camp for one hour on her way from Jenin to Jerusalem. You will see them sitting in their offices in Ramallah, but nothing happens in Ramallah.'

'What did she do here?'

'She just listened to our stories. That's all. Palestinians don't count as witnesses. Even an international[3] will not count if he speaks against Israel. Once they killed a child four years old.

They shot him in the head. They said he was armed – a child four years old!'

The penalty imposed on an Israeli soldier for killing a Palestinian without justification, they said, was 100 shekels, about £14 sterling.

'They shot these children in the head, the chest, the neck, the leg,' said Walid. 'The soldiers, they know the result. They will have to pay 100 shekels, that's all. Yet if a Palestinian kills an Israeli soldier he will be jailed for life. And what is the international community doing about our situation? Nothing. They don't even know about it. I met a woman in an internet chat room who didn't know anything about Palestine. She didn't even know where it was. So I told her, and I told her about the conflict here. Then she referred to 9/11. This was just three months after it happened. So I said to her: "What was that?" I asked her when it happened, who was responsible for it and so on. She was amazed. She said: "How come you don't know anything about it?" I said: "That was three months ago and it lasted just a few hours. The Palestinian conflict has been going on for fifty-four years. How come you don't know anything about that?"'

Walid thumped his fist down on the table and stood up. 'Come and have a look round,' he said.

We went down to the basement where a drama class was going on. A teacher with a cadaverous face was directing a group of teenagers in some kind of musical. The girls wore traditional black dresses with red and yellow embroidery, the boys baggy black trousers and waistcoats. They acted out some rural scenes, interspersed with *dabka*, a style of Palestinian dancing rather like Irish dancing. The participants formed a line, holding hands and jumping up and down with the body rigid, then broke up into little circles, pirouetting with one hand held high above the head.

Upstairs again, I went into an English class where Annalisa, an Italian woman who was spending a couple of months in the camp, was teaching English to about a dozen schoolgirls. We talked for a bit about the careers they wanted, mostly as doctors and secretaries.

Annalisa lived in a flat opposite the Centre and her nights were often disturbed by army activity.

'Last night it was very noisy,' she told me. 'About eleven o'clock my neighbour came and asked me to go up to the roof to see what was happening. The camp was surrounded by soldiers and there were lots of explosions. I didn't stay long. I was very nervous. On the roof you're a target for the soldiers.'

I wanted to have a look round the camp. Walid asked Ahmed, a student from An Najah, to take me.

The buildings were fairly rough and ready, the walls either bare breeze blocks or covered with a coat of cement. The alleyways between them were often barely more than the width of our shoulders. Children played in the cemetery; there was no other open space for them. Many of the children had lockets containing photos of martyrs hanging on strings round their necks.

Ahmed took me to see a house which had been demolished recently by the Israeli army. He pointed out all the features, much as an agent would take a prospective purchaser round a show house in a new estate. The front wall was missing. Inside the remains of the stair and upper storey had collapsed to the ground. The man they wanted had escaped.

Back at the Jaffa Centre the English classroom had been turned into a circus, with kids walking on stilts, riding unicycles and juggling. The kids were excited and, unusually for Muslims, boys and girls were engaged in physical horseplay, throwing each other around, hitting and pulling each other. Some of the girls were hanging on to me and stroking my hair.

I left them to go and visit Jacob's well.

The church above the well is no longer used for services, the last priest having been killed by settlers in 1979. In the absence of tourists it is rarely visited, but a caretaker is on hand for those who do turn up. He took me inside and down into a crypt to see the well. Talking very quickly, he raced through the story of Christ and the Samaritan woman at such a rate that

I could barely catch his words. He clearly knew it by heart and had rattled it off hundreds of times before. A bucket of water lay on the brick rim of the well. The caretaker poured a dash of it into the well to show how long it took to hear the splash when it hit the bottom forty metres below. Then he poured some into a glass for me to drink. His performance over, he ushered me over to a stall where he had some religious knick-knacks for sale. He kept repeating that his guided tour was free so I took the hint and bought some little earthenware pots of well water and a few ageing postcards.

I went out to Balata camp again a few days later to meet up with Annalisa. I walked up from the main road in the dark of early evening, surrounded by children trying to snatch at my hands, putting their arms round my legs, shrieking, high on post-*iftar* excitement. Fire crackers were going off like artillery shot. A boy was running around with a bag of *tamarhind* with a hole in it, using it like a water pistol to squirt the drink at people.

Annalisa had just finished her English class. A few minutes after I arrived Claus, a chef from London who had been staying in the camp, burst in with bagfuls of presents he had been buying to take home. He started to unload them. A bundle of Hamas tee-shirts, several *keffiyas*, a sheaf of Hamas wristbands, a handful of Yassir Arafat keyrings, and gold earrings for his sister. The last item was a white tunic and trousers with a wide black belt and a full-length coat with a hood.

'A Jedi outfit,' said Claus, wriggling into it. 'Made by a tailor in Nablus. Four hundred shekels. I'm going to wear it for going to football matches back home.' He strutted around while Annalisa and I admired it. The cape wasn't quite right, looking more like a monk's cowl than a Jedi hood but not bad at all for a tailor working only from a picture in a comic strip.

Before leaving Claus was going to visit Jayyous, a village near the Green Line which separates the West Bank from Israel, where he had spent a few weeks the year before. Annalisa was going with him and they invited me to join them. I decided not to after my previous experience of trying to get through the checkpoint to go to Tulkarim.

'You'll be OK,' said Claus. 'You don't look like a hippy.'

I wasn't reassured. Claus did look like a hippy so being with him would be a liability. As well as that, it was the olive season when many ISMers came to help the Palestinians with the harvest. The three of us – an eager young Italian idealist, an eccentric hippy type and a woman around early-retirement age – were probably pretty representative of ISM's demographic make up and would be likely to attract attention. I stuck to my refusal.

Ahmed, the boy who had given me the guided tour of Balata, came in with three of his friends, Ibrahim, Hamid and Rami. Rami was complaining about the travel restrictions. The only way he could get out of Nablus through a checkpoint was to pretend that he was going to Jordan. As a student in Ramallah he had to apply for a permit to travel to Jordan – a process which took time and money – every time he wanted to go there.

At least he felt much safer in Ramallah. 'There you aren't surrounded by soldiers all the time,' he said. 'Since the beginning of the *intifada* about 5,000 people have been shot here in Balata.'

That worked out at about one in four of the population.

The one in four of this group who had been shot was Ibrahim, a nineteen-year-old with thick black Buddy Holly glasses, a snub nose and a rueful grin. He pulled up his shirt to show a torso stitched together like a patchwork quilt with long scars running just under the heart, down across the stomach and into the abdomen. He had been gunned down by soldiers while walking along a road in the camp. His brother and another boy carried him to a bus in the main road outside the camp. The bus took him and three others who had been injured at the same time to hospital. Ibrahim spent two weeks in intensive care.

Ibrahim's story triggered an avalanche of similar accounts from the others.

Hamid's house had been blown up. 'Soldiers came and told my mother to leave, they told her you can't take anything. My sister, they wouldn't even let her put her shoes on. They took them 500 metres away and then they blew up the house. We lost everything, all our belongings. They destroyed it along with the house of our neighbour. They did it because our neighbour was a leader of the Al Aqsa Brigades. But he had been killed eight days previously! Then they went to the cemetery and shot his tomb. My brother saw them doing that, my mother and sisters also.'

'This kind of collective punishment isn't working,' said Ahmed. 'The more they punish the Palestinians, the more the Palestinians hate the Israelis.'

Hamid described how a friend of theirs, Ahmed el Katib, had become a suicide bomber after one of his neighbours, another leader of the Al Aqsa Brigades, had been killed by the Israeli army.

'Ahmed was very sad about this. Then he saw the Al Aqsa leader's cousin go to Jerusalem to make an operation. We saw that it was a normal thing, *yanni*, because someone from his family was killed. After one year Ahmed decided to make an operation. The last time we saw him was in the market. He shook hands with us, we had no idea what he was going to do. When he did it, we were doing our *tawjihi* exams. When they told us it was no problem. When my brother told me we ran to his house to see his family. They were sad and crying. But as well as sad they were very proud.'

'It is the best way to get freedom,' Rami said.

Hamid agreed. 'If the Jews attack us with rockets or planes, there is a rocket from Palestine to make an operation in Israel.'

'And this rocket is much smarter because it knows where it is going,' added Ahmed. 'The worst thing for an Arab is not humiliation for himself but for his family, his parents, brothers, sisters. They're defending their families. Ahmed did the operation in the village his family came from, in Kfar Saba.'

I'd arranged with Ahmed to go and visit the local *masaharati* – a person who goes round in the middle of the night during Ramadan to wake people in time to eat the pre-dawn meal. On the way there Ibrahim invited us to call in at his house. He took us to an upstairs room to meet his grandfather who was disabled. He lay in a bed with a pulley arrangement for pulling himself up, a scarf wrapped tightly round his head.

Ibrahim's mother brought us tea and we talked about the village near Haifa on the Mediterranean coast where the family had originally come from.

'The British are to blame for everything,' said the old man in the bed. 'Not the people, but their government.'

'You mean the government sixty or seventy years ago?' I asked.

'Then and now, it's all the same.'

I asked the family if they wanted to go and live in Haifa.

'Yes,' shouted Ibrahim's twelve-year-old brother before the others could open their mouths. But when they did they all agreed with him.

I left with Ahmed and Ibrahim to go to the *masaharati*'s house, picking our way through the dark alleys using the screens of our mobiles phones as torches. The street lights had all been knocked out by the army.

The house of the *masaharati*, whose name was Ali Hassan, was big and cavernous. His wife showed us into a room on the ground floor. With its white plastic chairs ranged against the walls and a bouquet of artificial flowers covered in cellophane lying on a low table, it felt like an undertaker's waiting room.

Ali Hassan strode in, wearing a thick winter *jellabiya* and a woollen bonnet. He shook our hands vigorously and sat down beside me, poised eagerly for conversation.

The job of *masaharati* is a traditional one in Muslim culture and something similar to a town crier. Ali Hassan described how he goes out at 2 a.m. and walks through the streets, banging his drum and reading verses from the Koran. Although we were talking through an interpreter he engaged me directly, looking straight into my eyes, addressing his words and gesticulations to me alone.

With the Israeli occupation the job is a dangerous one. One of the *masaharatis* in Askar camp had been shot dead while doing his work.

Ali Hassan goes to the authorities before Ramadan to register the fact that he will be out in the streets during the night but he is not immune.

'Last year I was beaten up by soldiers, then they handcuffed me.' He stood up and demonstrated, holding his hands behind his back. 'They took me to a house where a wanted man was hiding and used me as a human shield. They wouldn't allow me to take my medicine. I have high blood pressure and diabetes.' He pulled out some packets of pills to show me what he took. 'By the time they let me go it was after sunrise and I couldn't take it.'

The soldiers left the house without releasing him or even telling him they were going. The mother of the family had to free him by cutting through the plastic handcuffs and ruined three knives in doing so. The soldiers had also broken his drum. He showed me where the big silver drum was patched. Then he put it on and beat it with great resounding thuds. He was a wonderfully theatrical character, the flow of his words as he told his stories sonorous and reverberating like the roll of his drum.

I asked him what he did as a day job. He took out a card and handed it to me. Under his name I read:

Municipality of Nablus – Funeral Services – Health Department.

'I wash the bodies of the dead.'

For this he earned 1,350 shekels (about £200 sterling) a month. His wife did the same job for female bodies.

I asked him if he had to deal with people he knew in the camp, the ones who were killed in the course of hostilities. He explained that the bodies of martyrs don't get washed. 'They are like the people killed in battle and it is to honour them in the eyes of God that they go to the grave unwashed.'

Ali Hassan was fifty-one and had been born in Nablus. His parents came from Jaffa. I asked him what kind of peace he would like to see.

'I want a peace based on fairness and love between people, that brings to all sides their rights. We have our rights and our lands that were owned by our parents and our grandparents and we want them back. We want a peace that brings freedom and respect for our religious sites and our religion.'

For non-Muslims the Ramadan month alternated days of scheming how to eat and drink without being seen with evenings of trying to avoid being force fed beyond satiety.

I bumped into Annalisa in the souk. She had just bought some fruit and she was hurrying home to eat it before her class. 'I can't keep food in my flat because it brings out the cockroaches and I can't eat in the Centre because they think I'm fasting with them!' she explained.

Since I had last seen her she had attempted to travel to Jayyous with Claus. At Beitiba checkpoint they had had to separate as there were separate queues for men and women. Annalisa got through without too much difficulty but Claus didn't. She had had no way of knowing what was happening to him as the men's queue was much longer and slower than the women's and Claus didn't have a mobile. She waited for two hours before deciding to give up. At this point she was stuck. She couldn't go to Jayyous without Claus because she didn't know anyone there but she couldn't get back in through the checkpoint, firstly because she was a foreigner and secondly because she had told the soldiers she was leaving the country.

Fortunately she remembered having met an Italian woman in Jerusalem who worked in Ramallah. They had exchanged phone numbers. She called her and arranged to go and stay with her for a couple of days. Her description of Ramallah, her friend's lifestyle there, her beautifully furnished flat, the kitchen stocked with wine and beer, the absence of the army, made it sound like a cosmopolitan paradise compared with Nablus.

An email had already arrived from Claus. He had been turned back at Beitiba for the same reasons as I was. An attempt to get through the other checkpoint at Huwara met with the same response at first but he stood his ground, insisting that he was on his way out of the country and finally they let him through. Annalisa had tried to get back into Nablus through Huwara. The soldiers turned her away, saying it was dangerous and it was their job to protect her by keeping her out. After a series of phone calls to contacts in Nablus and taxi drivers outside Nablus, she managed to get herself ferried back in illegally through the usual kind of relay arrangement. The whole business of travelling around the West Bank was like some crazy board game.

One of Ala's projects involved interviewing older refugees to compile an oral history of the *Nakba* of 1948. He introduced me to one of them, Abu Raed, who lived in the Al Ain refugee camp in the centre of Nablus.

Al Ain had the same kind of rough and ready unfinished look as Balata. Abu Raed lived with his wife and an unmarried daughter called Reem on the top floor of a house, with other family members living below. He was a trim man, nattily dressed in a short-sleeved blue shirt and navy trousers, and with a full head of greying hair brushed back from his forehead, almost a Dirk Bogarde lookalike.

Until 1948 Abu Raed had lived in the village of Yazoor, near Jaffa. His family had owned large tracts of land where they cultivated oranges for export. At the time of the *Nakba* Abu Raed was fourteen.

'I remember my land and what happened with the Jews,' he said. They attacked Yazoor every night with bombs.'

Like so many others I spoke to, he complained bitterly about the British. 'The British gave the Jews everything they wanted – planes, tanks, guns to fight the Palestinian people. But if they came to our houses and found a single bullet they demolished the house.'

When the trouble broke out Abu Raed was sent away with

his three sisters and three younger brothers. The three older brothers stayed in the village with their father to defend it. 'But defend it with what?' he asked rhetorically. 'The Jews had tanks, planes, automatic weapons while we had only guns.'

The defensive action was doomed to failure and eventually the whole family ended up living in tents in a Red Cross camp in Nablus. Later on, when the refugee camps were set up by the United Nations Relief and Works Agency for Palestine Refugees (UNRWA) in 1950, they moved into Al Ain. Now, almost sixty years on, they are still there, in camps populated not only by the original refugees, but by their children, grandchildren, and even later generations.

And still they hang on to the hope that they will return.

'If now you ask me do you want to go back, my answer is yes. Believe me, I will go back if I have to live in a tent,' Abu Ra'ed insisted.

Reem, who had spent all her life in Nablus, also wanted to return to Yazoor.

'It is our country. The name is changed now and there are many factories but it is still our land.'

'Do you think you'll go back?'

'I hope.'

'But do you think you will?'

'I think no.'

And sixty years on they were still subject to military aggression. Reem described how they had just recently had their house invaded by the Israeli army.

'Soldiers came and everyone was put into one room and forced to stay there for five hours while they searched the whole house. There were fourteen of us, including several babies. One of them was only three days old. My niece who is five needed to go to the bathroom. I said, I'll go with you. She said, no, I'm afraid they'll kill me, I don't want to go to the bathroom. When the soldiers left they set off a smoke bomb and when we opened the door we couldn't see anything, I couldn't even see my fingers in front of my face.'

Abu Raed followed with a more disturbing story. His nine-year-old grandson had been shot in the head by Israeli soldiers.

'He was coming home from school and he went into a shop to buy candy and when he came out he was shot. His brain was outside his body.' He pointed to his temple to show me the entry point and then to the back of the head where it had exited. 'Two other boys were shot at the same time. One of them managed to drag the other two back into the shop. When I heard the news I was mad. My wife, I thought she had lost her mind.'

Abu Raed got up and searched through a drawer. He pulled out a document and handed it to me. It was a medical report. *Bullet injury 20.2.03. The patient was injured by a bullet and sustained severe head injury with brain hemorrhage and brain tissue out. Underwent urgent surgery, s/p cranioectomy, L+ occipital bone, removal of the multiple bone fragments.*

Despite the severity of his injuries the child had survived and made a complete recovery.

We turned to the television as the news presenter had started to talk about Yasser Arafat. For some days there had been increasing speculation about his health, with rumours about a mysterious illness which the Palestinian authorities had been quick to deny. Arafat himself now appeared in the *maqata'a*, his Ramallah compound, looking like a pixie in a jumpsuit and a woollen bonnet. To Reem's relief it was announced that he was suffering from gallstones. 'I was afraid it was something more serious,' she said. We switched over to CNN where the newscaster was claiming that the cause of his illness wasn't yet known as the diagnosis couldn't be made in Ramallah.

I asked Abu Ra'ed what he felt about Arafat.

'He is our leader,' he said, and refused to be drawn on the subject.

I met more of the original refugees in the camp of Askar Jadid, east of Nablus. I'd gone to meet Amjad, director of a community development centre there.

Amjad had been sentenced to five years in prison at the age of fifteen for throwing stones at settler buses.

'When we were in jail we learned all about Palestine and about our land. Jail for me was like the baccalauriat in Fatah, in Abu Ammar. We made the jail a university for Palestinian studies. I have children now. I teach them that their land is not here, it is in Jaffa.'

Abu Ammar was the name Arafat had chosen as his *nom de guerre* and was widely used by Palestinians as an affectionate nickname for him. It was fairly common in the Arab culture to choose such names, particularly ones of historical significance. In Arafat's case, the allusion was to Yasser ibn Ammar, a companion of the Prophet Mohammed.

Amjad had just returned from Norway where he had taken a group of the camp children on an awareness-raising tour. He showed me a video of their trip. A group of young *dabka* dancers came spinning onto the screen. Amjad pointed to one of the boys. 'This is Malik, the leader of the group. You see that all the boys wear a *keffiya* when they're dancing. Now Malik no longer wears one. He gave his *keffiya* to his friend Bashar. The *keffiya* was used as his shroud, it has gone to the tomb and now Malik won't put a *keffiya* on when he dances.' Amjad was referring to twelve-year-old Bashar Zabara who had been shot in the neck by Israeli troops during an incursion after a suicide bomber from Askar had carried out a mission in Tel Aviv.

We got into Amjad's ancient car and drove off to visit Khamis, a refugee from Jaffa. The camp buildings, many of which had bullet and shell holes, were covered with posters of the latest martyrs, including one of Bashar Zabara. As we stopped to look at it a small boy came up to us.

'I was with Bashar when he was shot,' he said.

'What were you doing?' I asked.

'Throwing stones.'

He mimed firing a rifle.

'Soldiers!' he shouted, and ran away.

'You know,' said Amjad, starting the car again, 'I don't like to kill anyone but we have the right to our state, the right of our refugees to go back. The suicide bombers don't go from nothing, they go from a bad situation. Osama, one of the suicide bombers from this camp, he saw many of his friends killed in this *intifada*. He spoke with himself, he said, I must kill people in Israel because they kill us. I remember when he saw the Israelis firing rockets and he saw his friends in the mosque without medical help, without anything, and another five killed. He saw that. I saw him crying. For that he went to Israel.'

We drew up outside a house in a dilapidated alley. The front door opened directly onto a small room furnished with three beds, a couple of small tables, a wardrobe and a television. On the bed nearest the door a man of about seventy-five sat cross-legged under a blanket.

Khamis Abdel Hamid was used to telling his story to foreign visitors and was a bit of a star turn. Sitting bolt upright and without any preamble, he launched into a diatribe against the British with the theatricality of a Shakespearean tragedian.

'The British are responsible for everything,' he declaimed, 'for the *Nakba*, for the establishment of Israel, for the suffering of our people. Before the British there was no discrimination between Arabs and Jews. We lived in harmony. The British are the main reason for the conflict between us now.'

He bore out Abu Raed's accusation of British partisanship. 'If an Arab had a knife, the British put him in prison, if a Jew had a gun, the British gave him another one.'

Khamis had been living in Lydd until forced to flee at the age of eighteen.

'They attacked us at 2.30. I was on my way to the coffee shop. Then I heard the dumdums. It was Ramadan, it was July, we were thirsty, we were rushing to the mountains. There was Hagana, there was Stern. Eighty per cent of the people sheltering in the mosque were slaughtered. I remember it as I see you now. I will never forget that time. It's in my mind, like a film recorded for television. I can't describe the terror of that time. You were escaping from that place and they were shooting at you. It was exactly like the judgement day.'

Khamis had visited his old house twenty years later. 'There

was a Jewish person living there. I said to him, this is my house. No, he said, it's mine. Go away or I will shoot you. It is something that encourages you to drop your tears. I cried till I had no more tears left. I went to the cemetery where my brother was buried and I read the Koran. And now they think they can compensate us by giving us some bread. I am not in need of their bread. This is not the home of Sharon. He can find his father's grave in Russia, but not here. They are slaughtering people every day here and nobody in the international community cares.'

I asked Khamis to tell us about his life as a child.

'My life as a child? It was not better, it was *better* than better. It was an excellent life. That land is our holy land.' Khamis took the opportunity to renew his attack against the British. 'The Jews took it with the help of the British, they didn't do it alone.'

We dropped in next on the family of Abdel Mohsen, a refugee from Haifa. Abdel Mohsen was a stern and Scrooge-like man, white-bearded and tightly buttoned into a tweed coat. He held up his hand, palm outward, in a kind of stop signal when I went to greet him, nodding curtly when I was introduced.

Abdel Mohsen lived on the ground floor of a three-storey house, the rest of which was divided into flats for some of his sons. Although it looked relatively comfortable, with several sofas, a vase filled with peacock feathers, and a big wooden sailing ship, it still managed to retain, like so many refugee houses, a bare and unlived-in atmosphere which seemed to declare that the residents didn't expect to be there for long.

For many years Abdel Mohsen had done construction work in Israel, leaving home at four in the morning and returning at four in the afternoon. Until the *intifada* many Palestinians had worked in Israel, now there were very few – those who crossed into Israel illegally or those who had special permission. Abdel Mohsen complained about the detrimental effect this had on the Palestinian economy.

I asked him if he had resented having to go to Israel for work.

'I had to do it to feed my family. Everybody had to do it because there was no work here.'

'Would you like to go back to live in Haifa?'

Abdel Mohsen's wife butted in before he could answer. 'No, no.' Noura, his daughter, contradicted her. 'She's only saying that because the Israelis forbid it. All the people dream about going back. Me, I dream of this.' She added that the people living in the camps were discriminated against by the local residents.

Several girls came clattering in from school, Abdel Mohsen's grandchildren. They were excited to find we were talking about Haifa, a place which had always been presented to them as a kind of El Dorado and their natural birthright.

'Yes, yes, we want to go back,' they cried.

'Why?'

'To live in a good place by the sea,' said Samar aged thirteen.

'To see the sea, here it's not good,' said Sabreen, twelve.

'To see the sea and to go back to my family's country,' said Hiba

'To be near the sea and to have a nice house' said Duha.

Arafat's health was soon the focus of attention for the international media. Amidst worries about the kind of care he could be given in Ramallah, the French government stepped in and offered to provide treatment for him. Christiane Amanpour of CNN, commentating as Arafat was airlifted to Paris on 29 October, expressed surprise at the small number of supporters present at the *maqata'a*, illustrating what I was beginning to see as a deep divide between the international perception of Arafat and the views of many Palestinians. Abroad he was regarded as the main stumbling block to peace whereas at home he was often criticized for yielding too much to Sharon and Bush.

Down at one of the local grocery shops I asked if people were worried about Arafat.

'Some sections are, some sections think it's time we got rid of him,' said Ismail, the owner. It was clear from the way he spoke that he was one of the latter.

Ismail, a retired engineer, was something of a politician. He had stood for the previous legislative council elections and more recently had drafted a blueprint for a binational state which he was emailing to people all over the world as a solution to the conflict. He believed that if Arafat died there would be anarchy, with all the militias fighting each other for power.

In the souk I spoke with Waddeh who said he thought that Arafat was already dead and that they were covering it up to give themselves time to sort themselves out and work out a strategy. In any case he didn't think it would be a loss. 'For us he's been dead for ten years.'

After *iftar* at Umm Ahmed's house we sat around watching the latest events on television. I asked Ahmed, who worked in Ramallah, if people there were concerned about Arafat's ill health.

'Very few.'

'What'll happen if Arafat dies?'

He clapped his hands, snapped his fingers, swayed and whooped, and grinned at me.

Then he took a photo out of his wallet. It was of himself with Arafat, taken when he visited him in his compound four years previously.

'What did you talk about?' I asked, curious.

'Nothing,' he said, in a tone which suggested that there couldn't be anything that he would have to say to Arafat. But he still seemed pleased to have the photo.

One of the sisters switched channels and we watched the histrionics and melodramatic posturing of a Syrian soap for a bit. I asked Suleiman why the French were being so helpful to Arafat.

'Because they are nice people. They're not like the British.' He gave me a sideways roguish look to reassure me that no offence was meant.

However he didn't hold out any hopes for the French doctors

being able to save Arafat as he believed that he had been poisoned, either by the Israelis or by people in the Palestinian Authority.

I went down to Sultan's shop later to get help with a jar of jam I couldn't open. The boys there said they were sad. As well as the ones I already knew were two more students, Hussam and Ahmed. 'We all love Arafat,' said Hussam. The others agreed and they all kissed their fingers. Despite the avowed sadness Mohannad was in a frisky mood. He started singing a Palestinian song and doing a few steps of *dabka*. Then he broke off to ask me how babies were fed in Britain, cupping his hands round his chest to ask if it was breast or bottle. Intoxicated with the admiration he seemed to be getting from the others he moved on to talk about nappies and to describe in scatological detail, with mime and noises, an intestinal problem that Osama had. They all roared with laughter. Osama, as usual, looked enigmatic.

At the university the next day the students were putting up banners about Arafat. A large crowd had started gathering in the courtyard, wearing Fatah headbands, some with *keffiyas*, holding banners on poles and chanting in the usual demonstration sort of way, with the leaders shouting a question and the others replying.

I asked Sami, who worked in the PR department, about the measure of support for Arafat. He was non-committal. 'Some people support him, some not. We have a democracy here. It's not like other countries in the area where 99.999, an infinity of nines, support the leader.'

I walked across to the canteen with Asem. By this time the procession was marching round the university, upstairs and downstairs, gathering followers as it went. 'Abu Ammar, our soul and our blood we give you,' they sang. Round the courtyards faces filled all the windows.

I asked Asem what he thought of Arafat.

'Listen, he has done many wrong things in the past but he

is our leader and he is sick.'

I put the same question to Saed, saying that nearly everyone I spoke to before his illness didn't seem to like him.

'You've been talking to the politically educated people. He has a lot of popular support. I don't agree with him but now he is sick.'

Saed talked about the tremendous facility Arafat had for establishing personal contact. 'He was always kissing people. Everybody. Everywhere. In hospitals he was always kissing patients, kissing their limbs, their wounds. Arafat was the ultimate kissing machine.'

I had in fact just seen footage of Arafat kissing his doctor's hand which CNN ran repeatedly. I had thought it showed Arafat in a bad light because the doctor was pulling his hand away, rejecting Arafat's gesture as if it was embarrassingly over-sentimental. 'Not at all,' said Saed when I mentioned it. 'It was a very significant incident. It showed his humility. You imagine, Arafat, president of Palestine, kissing his doctor's hand in gratitude. The doctor was pulling his hand away out of respect, to show he wasn't worthy of this.'

On 3 November there was an announcement on the tannoy. The students started cheering and whistling.

'What's it saying?' I asked.

'There's been a military operation in Tel Aviv,' said Ala. 'A suicide bombing.'

Later in the day it was announced that the suicide bomber had been a man from Askar camp in Nablus.

Six or seven young men were in Sultan's shop that evening. They were all being very laddish. One of them was making up stories about Hussam drinking alcohol and going into a room with his girlfriend to kiss her. Mohannad pestered me to take him to London. Hussam said he wanted to marry me because of the money he thought I must have. Sultan said something about Ahmed and a friend. 'What do you call it in Britain when a man marries a man?' he asked me.

'Gay.'

'Yes, that's it, Ahmed's gay.'

They all yelled with laughter and slapped each other's hands.

The Al Jezeera news came on. The first item was about the suicide bombing in Tel Aviv. I asked them what they thought about it. One of them started to say that it made him very happy. The others shut him up, the atmosphere shifting suddenly from laddishness to embarrassment.

Mohannad changed the subject to the upcoming American election. Everyone agreed that Bush was terrible, that Kerry wasn't much better and that Blair was wrong to support Bush. They shouted out the various names, turning their thumbs down after each one. I left them watching a woman on a Lebanese chat show talking about how much she loved her boyfriend.

About ten o'clock a terrific shouting noise started. I went out into the courtyard. The shouting continued, resounding over the whole city. After a while the voice became quieter and more melodious, chanting *Allahu akbar*. I thought it must be something at the mosque, some event associated with Ramadan, and went back inside.

When I arrived at the university in morning it was deserted and the gates were closed. '*Arbaa shuhada imbaarih*,' said the guard who let me in. Four people had been killed by the Israelis the day before. The shouting I'd heard in the evening had been the announcement of the deaths.

Alaa was in the office. 'This is a preventive security measure,' he said, explaining why the university was closed. 'The funerals are taking place today, there may be Israeli tanks in the city, the students might start throwing things at them. It's a question of bad or worse. Bad is to close the university, worse is to lose some of our students. They can catch up with their work later.'

This kind of tit-for-tat action was often taken following a suicide bombing. There had also been the usual destruction of the suicide bomber's family house in Askar. His parents, six brothers and four sisters had been rendered homeless. The explosives also damaged four of the surrounding houses.

I dropped in to see Irfan's family on the way home. Irfan lay curled up on the sofa in a kind of foetal position, wailing about Arafat's condition and claiming that he had been poisoned. 'Even the French doctors say so,' he insisted. Salt had been rubbed into the wound by CNN showing footage of Israelis dancing for joy in Jerusalem to celebrate Arafat's condition. The ancient father was in bed in an alcove, asleep and sitting upright. Ataa switched channels to a pop song quiz show from Dubai. Irfan got up and bustled about with buckets, changing the water in the goldfish tank, still complaining about the schadenfreude of the Israelis.

When I passed Ismail's shop later he was sitting on the veranda beside a big tray covered by a cloth. The shop itself was closed. A group of armed Al Aqsa Brigades shabaab had forced him to close in mourning for the martyrs.

'Would they shoot you if you didn't close?' I asked.

'Of course.' He stretched out his hands in a gesture of impotence. 'Who would punish them?'

We talked for a bit about the latest Arafat news. Ismail had heard the rumour about the poisoning but he pooh-poohed it.

'Why would the Israelis do that? There is no one who could suit them better than Arafat. He is too conciliatory with the Israelis. Why does he always condemn suicide bombers but never the Israelis when they kill our children? Why does he try to please the Americans?'

He began to complain about American hegemony and interference, speaking in slow, measured tones and with grandiose gesticulations.

'The gangs in Iraq who kidnap people like the French journalists and the Italian women are pro-American groups. They do it to blacken the reputations of the Iraqi resistance groups by giving the impression that they are attacking people who are doing good in Iraq The Americans, they have no right to be there. Saddam was a dictator but it was up to the Iraqis themselves to get rid of him.' He flicked his fingers contemptuously. 'Go home, Yankee.'

I left him surreptitiously selling a loaf of bread from under the cloth and keeping a sharp lookout for marauding *shabaab*.

On 6 November, with Arafat gravely ill in a Paris clinic, the Israeli Justice Minister was talking about his funeral, scotching rumours that he would be buried in Jerusalem. 'Jerusalem is a place where Jewish kings are buried, not Arab terrorists,' he declared.

Security was already being tightened in anticipation of his death. It was announced that from now on students would only be allowed through the Nablus checkpoints at the beginning and end of the week. Those (mainly girls) who had been travelling from home daily were now having to find rental accommodation in town.

At the university Hamas and Islamic Jihad were putting on a joint festival in the piazza. Fida, who was rushing off with Camelia to look for a flat, grabbed a couple of first-year science students and asked them to explain to me what was happening. But it was self-explanatory.

Against a backdrop of military motifs a line of ten men in the black and yellow livery of Islamic Jihad marched onto the stage with faces blackened and carrying the Koran. The presenter made a long hectoring speech, followed by two men calling out the names of martyrs. '*Allahu Akbar*,' roared the crowd. 'Death to Israel! Death to America!' A girl in *hijab* and jeans read a poem about the martyrs, her delivery so loud and shrill she would surely have a sore throat for days. Four men in khaki outfits, a kind of Islamic barber's shop quartet, sang a couple of numbers. A comedian came on and did a Rory Bremner act, mimicking the liquid and fruity voice of Yitzhak Rabin, the high-pitched squeak of Ahmed Yassin, followed by Arafat, Bin Laden, Sharon and then Gaddhafi gabbling 'Palestine? Where is Palestine?' The audience loved it. At intervals throughout men in the audience jumped up, shouting slogans. The audience chanted a response each time. Eight young boys wearing red satin trousers and waistcoats, heads encircled with the black and yellow bandana of Islamic Jihad, danced on for a *dabka* performance, standing out as joyous compared with the rest of the programme although the music was still quite military-sounding. The noise rose to a crescendo, with men in the audience dancing in circles, standing on chairs, raising others to sit on their shoulders, clapping hands high above their heads, and then died away. The boys left the stage. The barber's shop four still stood singing in a sober khaki line.

---

[3] Term generally used for foreign peace activists present in the OPT

CHAPTER 5

Ramadan was coming to an end and the university would be closed for a week for the *Eid* holiday. Rasmiya, a lecturer in the psychology department, invited me to spend the holiday at her house in Nabi Elias, a village about twenty miles from Nablus.

This time I had a story prepared for the checkpoint. 'Yes, I've been visiting Nablus,' I told the soldier. 'Now I'm heading for Ben Gurion airport to fly back to Britain.' I tried to give the impression that I was only too glad to be shaking the dust of the place from my feet. He let me through.

Nabi Elias lay about a kilometre from the Green Line separating the West Bank from Israel. It was an unattractive village, with clumps of drab grey concrete-covered houses clustered on a slope rising up from the main road. Rasmiya's was one of the few houses on the other side of the road. The family lived on the upper floor of a new compound which they had recently had built. At ground level there were several shops. One of them was a pharmacy owned by Rasmiya's daughter Shatha, another was an outlet for building materials belonging to her husband Abu Shaddi.

Rasmiya had four children, two of whom – Shatha and Hadi – lived at home. The oldest son, Shaddi, worked in Ramallah and came home at weekends and another, Fadi, was studying in Cairo.

Rasmiya and Abu Shaddi had both been born in the area and their families had once owned large tracts of land there. Rasmiya's parents were originally from Jaffa. During the *Nakba* they walked from there to Azzoun, a small town not far from Nabi Elias. They took with them a herd of twelve cows and her mother carried a box of gold on her head. With these assets they were able to buy land and some houses.

Rasmiya took me up to the roof to show me the surrounding layout. She pointed to an area of housing on the crown of a hill jutting out above the village houses. Had it not been for the very different style of construction, it would have seemed like one urban unit. 'That,' she said, 'is a Jewish settlement. And the hill that it's built on belonged to Abu Shaddi's family.' The land had simply been expropriated for the building of the settlement, with no compensation. When accompanying the Israelis to be shown the land that was to be taken from him, Abu Shaddi had suffered a heart attack. Rasmiya turned to the back of house and pointed to a fenced barrier that snaked over the landscape. This was part of the Wall that was currently being built, theoretically to separate Israel and the West Bank but in fact often cutting deep into Palestinian territory, carving it up into a checkerboard of go and no-go areas, isolating villages and making it difficult or impossible for cultivators to reach their land.

Rasmiya pointed west to where she had an olive grove. To reach it she would have to go through a checkpoint which was only open for a short time in the morning and again in the evening. As a result it had not been possible to do the harvesting or get the insecticide treatment carried out. The trees were now deteriorating.

Shortly after the barrier was built a sheep had got its horns entangled in it, setting off the alarms, Rasmiya told me gleefully. She and Shatha had watched from the roof of their house as soldiers rushed up with jeeps and guns and sirens blaring and then held back, afraid to approach the sheep because they thought it might have explosives attached to it, hidden under its wool. 'They thought it was a suicide sheep,' she said with her great throaty laugh.

While Rasmiya started preparing the food for *iftar*, I went for a walk round the village. The name of the village, Nabi Elias, meant Prophet Elias who was believed to have died there. A tomb, a square stone building topped with a dome in the middle of a field, marked the spot of his supposed burial. A greengrocer invited me into his shop. He peeled an orange for me and insisted that I eat it although it was before *iftar* time. When he discovered that I was living in Nablus he was keen to find out what I thought about the lifestyle there. Being used to the conservative life of a small village, he had the impression that such a big city must surely be a den of iniquity. He mimed a tight body fit to indicate the kind of clothes he thought they wore and asked me if the women left their hair uncovered. I said that some did and some didn't. He looked suitably shocked.

After *iftar* Rasmiya and I went to visit an old aunt of hers. Ala had asked me to go and see her as she was aged about a hundred and was still very alert. He wanted me to record some of her memories for his project.

We walked for a couple of miles, first by the side of the main road which was busy with cars flashing past, most of them with the yellow number plates of Israel. Then we turned off up the hillside. There was no track. I clutched Rasmiya's arm as I stumbled forward over the uneven rock-strewn terrain.

Rasmiya was used to this kind of journey. She had often had to circumvent the Israeli road blocks by using mountain routes to get to Nablus. She strode forward confidently, telling me tales of encounters with soldiers and tear gas, of donkey rides and friendly farmers.

We came to a single-storey house, fronted by a veranda where a shrivelled, bird-boned woman lay on a thin mattress, propped up on pillows. A swarm of relatives were gathered round, the women in traditional black embroidered dresses with light cotton scarves draped over their heads. The men sat stiff-backed in wooden chairs, the women sat on the floor.

The aunt had been in a local hospital and was waiting to be transferred to one in Jerusalem for treatment. The Israeli authorities had said she would have to wait twenty days for permission to go there.

While some of the women passed round tea Rasmiya

encouraged her aunt to talk about her childhood, translating for me the gist of what was said. She spoke disjointedly about the First and Second World Wars, about Turkish soldiers, fleeing Germans desperate for water, dead bodies covering the ground and buried German guns which were recovered and given to Haganah in 1948. She dozed off. The daughters and grand-daughters crouching round her bed stroked her head and her hands. When she awoke she was back further in time, telling a story of having fallen into a well when she was five. A man pulled her out in a bucket. He later married her, when she was eighteen and he was eighty. I was beginning to feel uncomfortable about bothering her but Rasmiya assured me she was happy to talk. I managed to record short snatches, while a girl, one of the great-grand-daughters, scribbled her words. Every time she stopped somebody would say *hallas* and I would switch off the recorder. Then she would launch into her reminiscences again and the girl would wave at me to switch on. But by then I'd missed the beginning. As we got up to leave she started to vomit blood into a bucket, supported in the arms of her family.

After Nablus, Nabi Elias seemed almost like a different country. Nablus, being in Zone A and therefore out of bounds to Israelis (other than soldiers) was 100 per cent Palestinian. Nabi Elias not only straddled Zones B and C, it was also divided by the main road leading from Israel to the Jewish settlements in that part of the West Bank. Most of the shops in the village lined this road and many Israelis, both from Israel and the settlements, did their shopping there. It was strange to see Jewish people parking their cars outside Palestinian shops, being served by Palestinians.

Shatha had opened her pharmacy only a few months previously. Many of her customers were Jewish. I asked her how she felt about her Israeli clientele. 'We have to live with each other. And I am new here. I have to develop good working relationships.'

'But the settlers, they're living on land that was grabbed

from your family!'

'Yes, I know. But we have to get on with each other. People like you are amazed at this but…' She shrugged. 'Some of the settlers are aggressive to Palestinians. Sometimes they attack cars that are left out at night, sometimes they break windows. But some of them are nice.'

It was my second day in Nabi Elias and I was in the pharmacy waiting for Rasmiya. We were going to go to Qalqilya, a big town a few miles away in Zone A.

Rasmiya's car was parked in front of the shop. As we got into it a settler drew up behind us, waving to Rasmiya to move out to let him have the space before she had even put the key in the ignition. Seeing that she didn't move instantly, the settler moved forward, completely blocking our exit. The driver jumped out, raised his hand in an aggressive gesture and went into the supermarket. We were stuck there till he came out again. When he did so he shouted angrily at Rasmiya. 'This kind of thing happens all the time,' she said. She was clearly upset but I felt that I was much angrier than she was. It was reminiscent of apartheid South Africa. Perhaps Rasmiya had become inured to it.

We drove through a checkpoint at the edge of Qalqilya and into the town along an avenue lined with palm trees. Rasmiya, who was a sharp-eyed shopper, stocked up on food for the forthcoming holiday, picking through the fruit and vegetables and going from stall to stall to get the freshest, the juiciest and the best value for each item.

On the way back to the car we met a friend of hers.

'Hilda, this is Mahub,'she said. 'He can tell you all about life here in Qalqilya. I've asked him to take you to see the Wall and then he'll bring you back to the house.'

Mahub, a slim dapper man with rectangular face and chiselled features, had his own glazing business. Until the *intifada* most of his clients had been in Israel which was only a few minutes away by car. At that time most Palestinians were working in Israel because there were more employment opportunities there than in the West Bank. 'Now I cannot get a permit to work in Israel,' he explained. 'But I can work in the settlements. I had to go to work there. I had no choice. If I'm all the time thinking about it I don't know what to do, so I put it in some corner of my mind and go on. Many Palestinians make good money working in the settlements.'

We arrived at the Wall where it curved round the edge of Qalqilya. At first I had a feeling of anti-climax. There was nothing in the wasteland between us and it to give it perspective and it was difficult to believe that the massive stone slabs rose ten metres high. Only when Mahub stood beside it could I see that they did. He also added the psychological perspective.

'Just to see it people feel they are being strangled,' he said. 'It's difficult, so difficult, but what can we do? They are so powerful.'

On the road to Nabi Elias Mahub pointed to the village of Jayyous in the distance and to land that had been taken from it for settlements.

'We thought after the Oslo Agreement there would be no more settlements. But we see no change. Now there are 250,000 settlers in the West Bank, about 215 settlements. They are planning to stay here for ever and they think that maybe after ten, fifteen, maybe even fifty years we will go away. They expect it.'

Talk of Oslo led to thoughts of Arafat. Mahub believed that he was moribund if not already dead.

'They want to announce his death to the people step by step. He has all the people of Palestine in his hand. He is a good leader. There are many things good with this guy. Maybe some people know things we didn't know, but with any leader there are good things and bad things. No leader makes no mistakes.'

Mahub had at one time been involved with a group of Palestinians and Israelis engaged in dialogue about the conflict. He felt that many Israelis had no idea of the conditions which Palestinians were living in.

'When we began to explain that many people when they open their fridge there is nothing to eat, nothing to drink, one of the Jews said: "I don't understand. If I opened my fridge and there was nothing for my children to eat or drink, I would want to take action against the people responsible." Many Israeli people think everything is OK here. They don't understand that there are checkpoints, problems with soldiers, no work, economic difficulties.'

On Thursday 9 November I got up at about eight o'clock. Abu Shaddi was already downstairs in his shop, Rasmiya had gone to a well up on the hillside to get fresh spring water for the tea. Shatha and Hadi were still in bed. I turned on the radio in the kitchen. Traffic roared from the road below and from the loudspeaker of the mosque resounded Koranic verses, but the message of the few broadcast words I could make out and of the lugubrious tone, was clear. Arafat was dead. I switched to the BBC World Service just in time to hear the Israeli Justice Minister saying in an interview that the world was well rid of him. I looked out of the window. A crowd was gathering outside the mosque. A man was propping a pole with a black flag on the end against a lamp-post. The shops, which were already open and packed with provisions for *Eid*, were starting to close again as a mark of respect. At the greengrocers a couple of men were carrying crates of fruit and vegetables back inside. A trio of sheep that had been standing tethered outside the butcher's shop awaiting their fate were led back into a truck for a temporary reprieve.

The reactions in the house were muted. So much had already been said in anticipation of Arafat's death there was little more to say.

'This causes many problems for people,' said Rasmiya, waving her hand towards the closed shops. 'People will lose money, they won't be able to prepare for *Eid*.' Abu Shaddi looked sad and subdued.

By mid-morning the butchers and greengrocers were starting to open again discreetly. It had been announced that food shops were authorised to do business because of the impending festival.

In the pharmacy I found Shatha gift wrapping some cosmetics for a customer who was buying *Eid* presents. I asked him how people were reacting to the news of Arafat's death.

'People here have no feeling about Arafat. They're more concerned about the effects of the Wall and the land grabbing.' He complained about the problems suffered by his fiancé's family who had invested heavily in building greenhouses for their market garden and had lost everything when their land was appropriated.

Abu Shaddi came into the pharmacy and the three of us watched television. Old footage covering the highlights of Arafat's career was interspersed with images of the *maqata'a* being cleared by bulldozers and crowds gathering in downtown Ramallah. The cameras showed a group of Palestinian leaders sitting at a table and zoomed in on Arafat's chair, draped with his *keffiya*.

'I feel sad,' said Abu Shaddi abruptly and went out.

'He is crying,' said Shatha. 'He was overwhelmed by the sight of Arafat's empty chair.'

The television presenter announced that the Al Aqsa Brigades, the militant wing of Fatah, had just changed their name to the Abu Ammar Brigades.

A man in his sixties, a settler, came in and slapped a packet of pills on the counter. 'This is not what I wanted,' he complained in English. 'This is Sinagra, I asked for Viagra.'

Shatha explained that the products were the same, that Sinagra was simply another brand. She took out the leaflet and went over the product information with him. The customer still wasn't satisfied and suggested that Shatha's English wasn't good enough for her to make the comparison. 'Well in that case it should be cheaper,' he said when he was finally convinced. Shatha showed him some documentation to prove that the price was fixed by the Palestinian pharmaceutical authority. The man grumpily stuffed the pills back into his pocket and left.

'Israeli men often go to Palestinian pharmacies for Viagra,' Shatha said. 'In Israel they have to have a prescription but here it's available over the counter. It's the same with the pill. There's no proper medical supervision here.'

I asked her about sexual mores. She said that they had been affected by the *intifada*.

'Students have to live away from home. Sometimes girls see other girls with nice clothes, they say: you too can have nice clothes if you have a friend. It starts by, for example, having lunch in a restaurant, then little by little...' she tailed off.

'What about men? What do they do with their sexual urges in this kind of culture?'

'Well, I suppose maybe they have affairs. A lot of married men have affairs. Before the troubles a lot of them would have affairs with Israeli women.'

She picked up a packet from a shelf.

'Tell me, Hilda, what's this? The pharmaceutical rep said I should stock it for Israeli women.'

She handed me a packet of Tampax.

'You mean to say you don't know what this is?'

'I know it's for periods but I don't know how it works.'

'You didn't come across this kind of thing in your pharmacy course?'

'No.'

I drew a diagram and explained, to Shatha's amazement, the principle of tampons.

Another settler came in, wearing the black suit and white shirt of the more orthodox.

He bought a fruit-flavoured lip salve. As Shatha reached out for a bag to put it in he snatched up the salve from the counter.

'Did you see that?' she said when he had gone. 'He wouldn't let me put it in a bag because he didn't want a bag with Arabic writing on it.'

We watched the scenes in Paris where Arafat's body was being taken on board a helicopter. Another customer, Jalal, was complaining to me about Tony Blair.

'All the people here, they don't feel good about Blair now, since Iraq.' He nodded towards the television where the helicopter was preparing to take off. 'Look what Chirac has done for the Palestinians. From the beginning Chirac supported Arafat and he has agreed to support the next Palestinian leader. Any person who supports us like this, we will feel good about him.'

'What about Arafat? Did you feel good about him?'

'Arafat was like a wall who supported us. Whatever he did, he was our leader.'

I had noticed that since Arafat's illness and death there had been a shift in people's opinions about him. Criticism was more muted, greater acknowledgement was being made of his role as father of the Palestinian people.

Jalal was a tailor. Like the earlier customer he complained about the impact of the Wall. He had previously supplemented his income with the produce of land he owned, land which was now trapped behind the Separation Barrier. He could see it from the roof of his house. 'I see my land and I can't reach it. But a new problem will be when I go to my roof and I see the bulldozers tearing up my trees to build a settlement.'

Jalal asked me what I thought of Tony Blair. I said that I had supported him before the war with Iraq but not since.

'Me too,' said Jalal. 'Four years ago I liked him. Now I don't.' He went on to compare Blair unfavourably with Chirac and waved his hand at the television screen. 'Look what Chirac has done for the Palestinians. Any person who supports us like this I will feel good about him.'

A Jewish woman with sunglasses pushed up into long blonde hair was trying to buy make-up. Shatha spoke no Hebrew. Jalal translated for her.

On television cameras were tracking Arafat's helicopter as it flew from the hospital to the airport for the flight to Cairo. When it landed, the coffin draped in the Palestinian flag was carried to the plane by French army personnel, stepping slowly to the sound of the *Dead March*. Abu Shaddi, who had rejoined us, sat wiping his eyes.

The funeral took place the next day. Shatha's older brother

Shaddi, also a pharmacist, had come home from Ramallah for *Eid*. Together they rearranged products and dusted shelves as we watched the ceremony in Cairo and later the scenes in Ramallah where the burial was to take place. Shatha was horrified at the chaos in the *maqata'a* as a roiling mass of humanity surged and seethed round the coffin, seeming to engulf it, to prevent it from ever reaching its resting place. 'You imagine if Arafat was here!' she exclaimed. 'He would stop this behaviour. Now there is no one in control.'

'Why then, if Arafat had such influence, did he not stop the suicide bombing?' I asked.

'Come on!' said Shatha. 'Israel has all the strong security with army checkpoints and so on. If they can't control it how could Arafat control it?'

We started to talk about the politics of militant action and the definition of terrorism. I felt that a major difference between the Palestinian militants and Osama bin Laden was that it was clear what the Palestinians grievances were but that bin Laden seemed to attack without indicating why he was doing so.

'I don't agree,' said Shaddi. 'Bin Laden wants America to stop interfering in our affairs. The Americans behave as if they are masters of the world. They interfere in Iraq, in Afghanistan, in Palestine, everywhere. All Arab people like bin Laden, not for himself, but because he hits America. And they like North Korea because it is making problems for America. Ten years ago we didn't know anything about North Korea but now we like it. My enemy's enemy is my friend. This is the rule. We know that North Korea is bad and Saddam too. But we like the fact that they stand up to America. In fact, to us America is worse than Israel because it is clear what Israel wants but we don't know what America's position is. There is a reason for the struggle between the Jews and the Palestinians. But the Americans, there is no struggle between us. They are not even our neighbours. So why do they treat us in the way they do?'

Palestinians generally felt that America's interference in the Middle East was motivated by greed whereas bin Laden was acting out of principle. 'Why else would bin Laden, with all his money and his business empire, leave it to go and live in a cave in Afghanistan with nothing?' Shaddi asked me. 'He must have a belief that what he is doing is right.'

Shaddi felt no personal animosity towards the Israelis. In Nabi Elias he often came into contact with them.

'I think we can live together,' he said. 'I have no problem with Jewish people if they want to come and talk. Force between the two nations will not solve the problem. I have a lot of friends who are Jewish. Sometimes we start talking when they come into the pharmacy. We exchange opinions about the situation. "Do you agree with such and such?" "No, I don't agree, this is not good." That sort of thing. But it doesn't go beyond meeting like that. I can't visit them because they're in Israel and here there are no facilities. There are no restaurants, for example. But if I could I would be glad to.'

I'd noticed that none of the Israelis who had come into the pharmacy in the past two days had expressed condolences or made any reference to Arafat's death. I commented on this. 'Yes, I too thought that,' said Shatha, reflectively, as if it had been on her mind but she hadn't liked to mention it.

Shortly afterwards a young Jewish man, one of Shatha's regular customers, came in. Shatha introduced me.

'Hilda, this is Johan.'

Johan lived in Kfar Saba, just at the other side of the Green Line. We talked about the latest developments.

'The ordinary people don't want this conflict,' Johan said. 'Neither the Jews nor the Palestinians. It's all the fault of the politicians. The trouble is, there are too many political parties in Israel, more than twenty, so there is too much scope for disagreement. Just leave it to Shatha and me and we can sort it out easily.'

As an Israeli citizen Johan had to do military service once a year. He talked about the stress of manning checkpoints, the constant worry of not knowing whether or not any individual they are dealing with poses a threat. He described the case of a woman, mother of seven children, who had been a suicide bomber. There was no characteristic profile.

He and Shatha exchanged some friendly banter as she wrapped up his purchases. As he left he said to me, 'This is no life for her. We have to find a solution.'

That evening we went to Qalqilya for Rasmiya and Shatha to get their hair done.

The salon was in the hairdresser's house. It was packed with women wanting to do themselves up for *Eid*. While the hairdresser flitted between two cut-and-blow-dry clients her assistants were busy in corners plucking eyebrows and chins, applying henna and face masks, buffing nails. We had a long wait in the hot, chemical-laden atmosphere.

'The hairdresser isn't married,' Shatha whispered to me. 'Her mother's first husband was a spy for the Israelis and he was killed. Now nobody will marry her because she is tainted.'

She explained how people were often trapped into collaborating, first by inducement and then by blackmail. 'There was a boy in Tulkarim who wanted to go to Canada. He was refused permission, then he was approached by an Arab who said we can help you if you help us. Just tell us what time your neighbour goes to his car. The boy told them and the car was hit by a missile fired from a plane. Then they told him that he must continue giving information. If he didn't, the fact that he had spied would be made public.'

Although it was late when we left the hairdresser's, about ten o'clock, the shops were still open and busy, particularly the clothes shops. Everyone buys new clothes for *Eid*. We went to a shop called Bretty Lady (Arabic speakers often confuse *p* and *b* because there is no *p* in Arabic) to pick up a suit that Shatha had bought. Among the customers hustling round the racks two women stood out. Their heads were bare, unheard of in such a conservative area. They wore jeans and red tee-shirts with the face of Che Guevara across the chest. Their body language and their way of speaking were markedly different from the Palestinian norm. No one in the West would have looked twice at them but in that environment they were as jarring as punks at a Mothers Union meeting.

'They belong to a political group,' Shatha whispered. 'They are the opposite of Hamas. They don't believe in God. People here don't like them.'

The first day of *Eid* is a bit like a Scottish New Year, with everyone embarking on a round of visits to family, neighbours and friends, starting early in the morning. After visits from Abu Shaddi's brother, nephews and cousins, Rasmiya and I set off for her aunt's house. I took the cassette player to let her hear the recording we'd made. When we arrived we found that we were attending a wake. The old woman had died the day before and was already buried. The mourners clustered round us on the veranda, crying anew as I turned on the recorder and we listened to her quavering stories of Turks and Germans and buried arsenals.

In the afternoon a ceremony was held for Arafat in the village community hall. A couple of hundred men sat in rows of plastic chairs in a bare concrete basement area. Two men stood at a table in front, reading prepared speeches into an unnecessary megaphone. As soon as I appeared a man escorted me to the front row and another brought me coffee and dates. A choir of about twenty-five small boys started to sing, fists in the air as they chanted slogans about *al quds*. To finish off they swung into the national anthem with a terrific volume of sound, even the three-year-olds bawling as if fit to burst. Then it was all over. The boys broke rank and charged outside, chanting 'Abu Ammar, our blood and our soul we sacrifice for you.' The man who had welcomed me looked at them, sad and amused. 'Well, he's gone now. He has no need of their blood and their soul.' The boys continued to storm around the village, waving flags and singing: 'Arafat is the nation and the nation will not die.'

By the third day of *Eid* most of the visiting was over and the usual feeling of anti-climactic void that follows any holiday was creeping up. But there was still one more celebration for Rasmiya's family. They were having a surprise birthday party for Mahub who had been asked to drop in for a casual visit.

Both Rasmiya and Shatha were dressed up to the nines. Rasmiya, who took great care about her appearance, was glamorous in a pinstriped trouser suit of deep damson and a grey satin blouse. Shatha, always striking no matter how she was dressed, wore a plum-coloured two-piece with knee-length skirt and knee-high black boots.

After we had eaten the furniture was pushed up against the wall to clear a space for dancing. Hadi put on a CD of pulsating Arab music and the boys took to the floor, pelvises twisting like belly dancers, arms held high and hands clapping above their heads. Hadi took his mother's hand and pulled her out to join him. His cousin Hamoodi, a shy young man but emboldened by the sight of Rasmiya dancing, waved me up to join him. We swayed together. 'Were you can dancing when you young?' he asked, smiling beatifically.

By the time the music came to an end everyone was high with excitement. Rasmiya decided I was letting the sartorial side down in my jeans and jumper. 'You must put some nice clothes on,' she said. 'Come with me.' She took my hand and led me through to Shatha's bedroom where we rummaged through her wardrobe to find something to suit. I went back in, elegant in a long swirling skirt of silvery lurex with a pearly top, to join in more dancing.

The music changed to *dabka* and now even the rather staid Mahub joined in. I rushed out to change again and, to their delight, reappeared in an embroidered black Palestinian dress that Rasmiya had given me. Together we twirled and swooped through the *dabka* routine.

At nine thirty the party came to an end, with Cinderella-like suddenness. The music stopped and Mahub was already half-way to the door before I realized it was all over. The bubbles of gaiety seemed to have been pricked like a balloon and we all went to bed.

As travelling was easier once I had left Nablus, I had decided to visit Israel while I was in Nabi Elias. I wanted to visit the Jaffa area, where many of the Nablus refugees came from, particularly Abu Raed's village, Yazoor. It was only about fifteen miles from Nabi Elias. I had mentioned this to Ala. He reacted with a mixture of rapture and envy. 'If you do this,' he said, 'it will be the most important event of your visit to Palestine.'

To cross the border into Israel I planned to get a lift with an Arab-Israeli who was free to pass through the checkpoint and then get a bus from Koforsaba to Jaffa. But Rasmiya wouldn't hear of me taking a bus in Israel. 'It is dangerous. There have been so many suicide attacks on buses. It is better to pay for a taxi all the way. You don't want to lose an arm or leg. And when you're there, don't sit down in any restaurants. Just buy a sandwich and take it away to eat.'

Rasmiya arranged for someone to drive me to Jaffa in the morning and pick me up again in the evening. In the meantime I phoned Abu Raed's house. Reem answered. I told her that I was going to Yazoor and asked if her father would like me to do anything there for him. 'Just bring back a stone for us,' she said.

My driver, Abu Dya, was an avuncular sort, smartly kitted out in a tweed jacket and tie. We quickly sped across the narrow strip of Israel which lay between the Green Line and the Mediterranean. I told Abu Dya about my plan to visit Yazoor. 'I'll take you there,' he said. 'I know the area and afterwards I'll drop you off in Jaffa.'

We were soon driving through a bleak industrial landscape of factories, workshops, warehouses, used car garages, scrap yards with towering piles of wrecked chassis, and acres of corrugated iron-roofed sheds.

'This is Yazoor,' said Abu Dya.

It was a far cry from the Shangri-la of the refugees' dreams.

A bit further on we came to the residential part, a soulless suburban area of neat villas and apartment blocks. We parked beside a hillock on which stood a few old ruins, all that was left of Abu Raed's Yazoor. I wandered over it, took photos, picked up a few stones and broke off some twigs from the trees and bushes.

Abu Dya pointed to thicket of prickly pears. 'They have been here since before 1948.' He leaned over into the thick thorny leaves and pulled off a pear. 'Take it,' he said. 'For Abu Raed.'

We drove on into Jaffa and Abu Dya left me by the seafront.

Apart from Old Jaffa, an area around the port which had been heavily restored and trendified with art galleries, chic restaurants and boutiques, the town seemed a rather sad and seedy place.

I spent the afternoon in the flea market. Most of the stalls stocked junk: crockery, brass items, old electrical goods, nondescript pictures, fake jewellery, old Bedouin dresses coming apart at the seams, all piled together any old how. Against my better judgement I got drawn into haggling matches with several of the stall holders and ended up with two Iranian chess pieces, a Bedouin necklace and a brass oil lamp in the shape of a camel.

In the evening Abu Dya picked me up and we drove back through the dazzle of downtown Tel Aviv. At the other side of the city we passed through mile after mile of suburbs which seemed to go on for ever, land on which Palestinian villages had once stood and which the families of most of the refugees in the Nablus area had once cultivated. Twenty minutes later we were back in the West Bank.

CHAPTER 6

At the end of the week I went back to Nablus. I had arranged for a mini-van driver to take me to Huwara village. Once there I would take the same route as I had used when I first entered Nablus.

The driver, Hassan, was a speed freak. We streaked across the West Bank to the thumping beat of Hamas music. The lyrics were about the assassinated leader Ahmed Yassin, the tune like a sea shanty. Hassan chattered into his mobile phone with scarcely a glance at the road. I asked him to slow down. He laughed superciliously. 'Do not worry. I am a good driver.'

Halfway to Huwara he rammed on the brakes. A flying checkpoint had popped up in front of us. A soldier approached the van and tossed his head to indicate that Hassan should get out. He backed off, keeping his rifle trained on Hassan as he climbed down. After a lengthy conversation Hassan was allowed to get back into the van. The soldier came round to the other side to talk to me.

'Passport.'

I handed it over. He flicked through it.

'Where are you going?'

I mumbled a story about a cousin in Jerusalem.

'Where have you been?'

'Qalqilya.'

'What were you doing there?'

'Visiting friends.'

'What friends?'

I concocted another story about professional contacts.

'Why are you here?'

'On holiday.'

'Oh yes? In a place like this? That's unlikely.'

'Not if you're a Christian,' I said, squirming at the hypocrisy of my words.

'Good answer,' he sneered. 'OK, it's a strange story, but OK. You can go.'

I met up with my next driver at the petrol station in Huwara. He took me up the mountain, to a checkpoint which was unmanned. 'Go under the gate and walk into the forest,' he said. 'A car is waiting for you further on.' It was dark, cold and spooky. I crawled under the gate and ran into the trees.

Fifteen minutes later I was back in my flat. Loudspeakers in the mosques were hysterically announcing that two boys had just been killed by the Israeli army in the Old City. The words bounced angrily off the mountain slopes in multiple echoes.

Winter had set in during the ten days I had been away. When I left Nablus it had still been hot and radiant. Now, as I left the flat the next morning, Al Makhfia was shrouded in cloud, grey, gloomy and wet. The city below still sparkled faintly in response to the rays of sun penetrating horizontally from the east, creating a curious otherworldly atmosphere.

At the university I discovered that the two boys who had been killed the previous day had been part of a group who were throwing stones at soldiers. One of them was a friend of Asem's. He told me how he had heard the news. 'A friend called and told my mother about it. She didn't want to tell me but I knew there was something wrong. I put the television on and I saw his name on the breaking news, on the newsbar. I couldn't believe it. My friend. I went to the hospital. I carried his body to the cooler.'

'Why do they throw stones when they know the soldiers have no scruples about killing them for it?'

'Their lives are not worth living. Even the young boys. Their parents can't stop them. I too threw stones at the beginning of the *intifada*. When we saw Sharon enter the Al Aqsa mosque we saw there was something bigger than our lives happening.'

I later asked Suleiman the same question.

93

'You can't stop them. It's a peer culture thing and if they don't do it they will be considered cowards.'

'But if Amjad wanted to throw stones, what would you do?'

'Couldn't do anything.'

I looked enquiringly at Umm Ahmed.

She nodded fatalistically, in agreement with Suleiman.

That evening I called round at Abu Raed's house. I showed him the few photos I'd taken of the crumbling buildings on the grassy knoll. He kissed them and pressed the stones and the prickly pear to his heart. Tears flowed.

The buildings were not old Palestinian houses, as I had thought, but Roman ruins. He had played among them as a child. The branches I had brought evoked memories of climbing the very trees I had taken them from. He fingered the twigs. 'Even if they offered me the whole of Nablus in exchange, I would rather go back to Yazoor and live in a tent.'

'Have you been to a Palestinian wedding?' Rasmiya asked me.

'No.'

'Well I have an invitation here. My friend Wael. His son's getting married. I can't go but you can go instead.'

Wael was a colleague of Rasmiya's. She took me round to his office and explained that I would be coming to the wedding.

'*Ahlan*,' said Wael, a jovial man of about sixty. 'And you must come and eat at my house the day after the wedding. I will come and pick you up at your flat.'

'What should I wear?' I asked Rasmiya later, imagining that everyone would be dressed up to the nines. 'I don't think I've got anything suitable.'

'Wear that Palestinian dress I gave you,' she said.

The wedding reception was in a hotel in Al Makhfia. When I arrived streams of men were going through the door, but there was no sign of any women.

'Excuse me, is this Wael's son's wedding,' I asked one of the men.

'Yes, but there's another door for women.' He pointed to a side entrance round the corner.

Inside about 250 women were crammed together, eight to a table. They all wore ordinary everyday clothes, even jeans and jumpers, and I felt ridiculous in the Palestinian dress of an old village woman. I squeezed in at one of the tables, just in time to see the bride and groom, Samar and Yaroub, arriving. Samar was wearing the same kind of white Red Riding Hood cape I had seen in Ashraf and Samar's video. She took it off, revealing a white satin dress, sleeveless and backless, and they sat together on two ornate chairs set on a dais festooned with curtains like a four-poster bed. The guests helped themselves to the jugs of lemon juice and plates of kalawaat set on the table and waitresses came round with big round trays piled high with KitKats. I talked with the woman opposite me but our words were drowned out by the music as Yaroub and Samar started dancing together. A few of the women joined them. A three-tiered wedding cake was brought in, flanked by two torches flaming like oxy-acteylene burners. Yaroub cut it with a sword and he and Samar took it in turns to spoon bits of cake into each other's mouths.

The cake was wheeled away. Back up on the dais Yaroub was festooning Samar with gold jewellery and the guests were leaving their tables to queue up and congratulate them. More trays of KitKat were being ferried in, followed by trays of wedding cake, small squares of cream-covered sponge. People were already starting to leave. The music was getting louder and more women were taking to the dance floor. After another abortive attempt to talk with my neighbours above the din, I too slipped out.

'Your mother-in-law loves you,' exclaimed Umm Ahmed as she opened the door to me. I had called round to ask Suleiman to retune my television which had gone on the blink.

'I don't have a mother-in-law.'

She laughed. 'This is an Arabic expression. We say it when someone arrives just as a meal is being served.'

She sat me down at the table where they were just about to start on chicken, *molokhia* and rice with pine nuts.

Outside the wind gusted and the rain lashed down. Since my return from Nabi Elias the temperature had plummeted. Suleiman was regal in winter clothes – a thick grey pinstriped *jellabiya* covered by a dark blue, ankle-length cloak; Umm Ahmed wore a pink winceyette dressing gown over her clothes, buttoned up to the neck.

After lunch we watched the news on CNN. They were talking about the presidential election to be held following the death of Arafat. Mahmoud Abbas was still being touted as the front runner.

'He will give away East Jerusalem and the right of return,' said Umm Ahmed. 'The people don't want this.'

'They will kill him,' said Suleiman in his usual laconic fashion.

The next item was a story about the Travelodge Inn which was offering one night free at Christmas to any couple called Mary and Joseph.

'What's an inn?' Umm Ahmed asked.

I explained and told them the story about the birth of Jesus in a stable because there was no room at the inn, talking in Arabic for Amjad's benefit. Amjad, who was usually very shy, seemed amused by my recounting of the Christmas story in bad Arabic and loosened up. 'In the Koran Jesus was born under a tree,' he said. He took a copy of the Koran from a shelf and started to look up what it said about Jesus. Muslims revere Jesus as a prophet and they believe, like Christians, that his mother was a virgin. But they differ as to his death. Amjad looked up the relevant surah and Muna translated the gist of it, which was that Jesus was not crucified and that Judas, who resembled him closely, was killed in his place.

About an hour after Umm Ahmed's copious lunch Suleiman knocked at my door. Wael had just arrived at his flat looking for me. This was the day Wael had invited me to eat with his family, but as I hadn't seen him at the wedding because of the segregation of the sexes, and as neither knew the other's address, I assumed he had forgotten about it. I hadn't bargained for Arab hospitality. Knowing only that I lived in Al Makhfia he had checked out all the local grocery shops until he found someone who recognized my description. Having roughly pinpointed the area where I might be found and knowing that Suleiman lived in that area, his flat was the next port of call. Of course there could be no question of protesting that I had already eaten more than enough for one day and I was whisked off to Wael's flat in Rafidia where Yaroub and Samar and their families were seated around a gargantuan spread.

I sat beside Abdulla who had lived in Germany for some time before returning to Nablus to set up a delicatessen. After the start of the *intifada* he had had to close it because he was threatened by the *shabab* who didn't want him to sell imported goods. 'They are uneducated, these people. They couldn't tell the difference between goods from Israel and America and those from other countries.'

I'd been surprised by the amount of Israeli and American products I'd seen in shops. Why didn't the Palestinians boycott them, I asked. According to Abdulla, there was no alternative. The Palestinians couldn't be self-sufficient and Israel was able to prevent them importing from elsewhere as everything had to pass through Israel. I felt that he was painting the picture a little blacker than it actually was, given that the shops overflowed with goods from non-hostile countries such as Turkey, China and Indonesia.

Wael joined us with a slice of *knafe* for me. I begged to be excused, having forced down a bowl of soup and a plateful of prawns, stuffed courgettes and stuffed aubergines on top of Umm Ahmed's chicken. He cut the *knafe* in two. 'You eat half and I'll eat half,' he said, forking it into his mouth and asking me which church I belonged to.

'None.' I chose my words carefully as Muslims generally can't understand how anyone can have no religious affiliation. 'I'm a free thinker.'

I needn't have worried.

'That's what I like,' said Wael. 'Free thinking. I don't think people should be regimented by religion.'

By this time I was caught up in the train of the wedding festivities which were continuing the next day at Abdulla's house. We sat down to another excellent meal which was eaten in the usual hasty Palestinian fashion. Wherever I'd eaten, regardless of the quantity or quality of the food, I'd noticed that Palestinians generally treated meals as a means of putting an end to hunger, to be dispatched as quickly as possible. There is no sense that food is to be savoured, lingered over. As soon as the last mouthful is swallowed, even before some have finished, people get up and the plates are swept off the table. This utilitarian attitude was emphasised by the table covering which was often pages of old newspapers or a sheet of plastic.

We moved through to the sitting room for coffee. A couple of women handed out thimble-sized cups and another woman came round with a long-spouted brass pot. At the same time I could hear whooping noises in the kitchen. I went through. Samar and the younger women were dancing, some of them with scarves tied round their hips, wiggling and swaying. Abdulla's wife, vast in purple velour, came in, yanked my scarf from around my neck and tied it round my hips. She took my hand and we ondulated with the others, between the sink and the fridge, in segregated celebration.

CHAPTER 7

It was 28 November and the campus was buzzing. This was the eve of the election for the Students Council and campaigning was at its height. Every few yards as I crossed from the gate to the PR office students from one or other of the various political groups represented pressed publicity material into my hands.

Each of the seven groups was to put on a show on the open-air stage during the day.

Tasneem, one of the English students who helped in the PR department, dropped by and suggested I go over with her early to get a good place.

Tasneem was the daughter of the Head of the Sharia Department. She had a high cheek-boned face of serene virginal purity and was always immaculately presented. Today she wore a white *hijab* and navy tailored wool coat. Round her neck was the green and white scarf that declared allegiance to Hamas.

We went to the raised area in front of the library where the other female Hamas supporters were gathering. In the lower area below us the Hamas men were lining up in parallel ranks.

Tasneem asked me what I thought about the Muslim attitude to women.

'I don't understand the need to keep women apart from men and covered up,' I told her. 'It suggests that people are so highly sexed they won't be able to stop themselves making sexual advances if they see somebody of the opposite sex.'

'No, not really, it's just to protect us.'

I thought that this merely confirmed what I had just said.

Several of Tasneem's friends – Naima, Samia and Maryam – joined us, jostling around and questioning me about my religious beliefs.

'Have you read the Koran?'

'What do you think of the Koran?'

'What do you think of Islam? It is a very beautiful religion, don't you think?'

The questions were coming thick and fast.

Maryam tried to calm the others down. 'Islam leaves people free to choose their religion,' she said. 'There is no pressure.'

People with bags of accessories were going around distributing scarves, headbands, wristbands and stickers. Naima draped a Hamas scarf round my neck and took a photograph. Samia thrust a Hamas badge into my hand and started reading the words written on it. 'Repeat this after me,' she said. It was the shahada, the text recited when converting to Islam. Maryam, clearly embarrassed, told her to let up.

The Struggle Block, an extreme leftist group with very little support, was gathering on the stage. The PFLP group, in their red and white livery, was behind us shouting slogans. The Islamic Jihad people in yellow and black were to the side of us, giving some preliminary blasts on their trumpets and drums. I looked down and saw that the Hamas men had broken rank and were milling around. Five minutes later they had re-arranged themselves and were standing again in parallel lines, but at right angles to the ones before. A group of them were bringing in on their shoulders a big green cut-out of Palestine covered with white flowers. The whole effect was like a cross between a scout rally and a medieval battle line up.

When I next looked down, the Hamas lines had switched to a diagonal pattern. The men were now facing Mecca and about to pray. The praying seemed to go on for ever. 'Look, he's crying,' said Naima, pointing to one of the Hamas men.

'At the last election Hamas made a model of an Israeli plane and suspended it from the roof and they fired a rocket at it,' Samia told me. 'This year they're not allowed to do that sort of thing. Now they're talking only about improving the university facilities, getting better educational opportunities. Before they were carrying guns and talking about militant action. It's much better now.'

I asked the girls the difference between Hamas and Islamic Jihad and why they preferred Hamas.

'They are similar, like brothers and sisters,' Naima explained. 'That's why you see many students wearing both Hamas and Islamic Jihad scarves. They are both based on Islam, but Islamic Jihad is more narrowly focused on militant activity. Hamas has very good social programmes. They help the students. That's why we support them.'

The DFLP[4] people were now marching onto the stage carrying big pictures of the party's founder, Niaf Hawatmeh. A woman started singing a tuneless song. The Hamas people had finished praying and were involved in a process of complicated manoeuvres, forming groups identified by different uniforms depending on what they were carrying – posters, musical instruments, flags.

A great fanfare of trumpets and drums accompanied Islamic Jihad who were on next. They delivered their manifesto in a series of ear-splitting harangues. 'They shout loudly because they are very religious,' said Naima.

Hamas were already advancing towards the stage as Islamic Jihad moved off, men and women streaming in from several directions, the men carrying big fringed pennants, the women carrying small pennants with no fringes. A man with a voice so loud he didn't need a megaphone led the chanting of slogans which drowned out those of the departing Islamic Jihad. A group of women carried the map of Palestine, a group of men carried a model of Al Aqsa mosque. Some of the women carried babies wearing Hamas headbands and clutching Hamas pennants in their chubby fists. The male rearguard in single file carried posters of Hamas leaders and martyrs. From the giant stage backdrop – which was changed for each of the factions – loomed Ahmed Yassin and Abdel Aziz Rantisi, two of the founders of Hamas, both of them assassinated by the Israelis. They were flanked by a militant with raised fist and biceps like Arnold Schwarznegger.

The girls were lining up in threes to parade onto the stage.

Naima pulled me in between herself and Samia. I wriggled out and let them go ahead without me.

Seeing me on my own, a small pasty-faced girl introduced herself. Israa, an English student, didn't support any group and hadn't decided yet if she would vote. She pulled a photo out of her bag. Round about a beaming Yassir Arafat stood Israa and nine other girls. As achievers of the ten best *tawjihi* results in the country they had been invited to meet him at the *maqata'a*.

'What did you think of him?' I asked.

'A great man. He was so kind with us, joking with us. The minister of education was there.' She pointed to a man in the photo. 'He was saying something about men and women and Arafat interrupted him. He said, "No, not men and women. Women and men."'

'Who would you like to replace him?' I asked

'There is no one like him.'

The Fatah students were gathering behind us in a riotous band. The female dress covered the full gamut, from full face cover and *jilbab* to jeans and tee-shirts. At the front four little uniformed girls with red berets and black neckerchiefs prepared to lead them onstage. A group of men carried a coffin for Arafat and black flags. They wore his trademark black and white keffiyah tied pirate-fashion round their heads. Compared with the Islamic groups they were very disorganized, straggling all over the place. An unco-ordinated shouting of Fatah slogans began as the Hamas performance rose to a finishing crescendo. 'This group will shake the ground! *Shabibi*!' one lot yelled over and over again. 'Abu Ammar is the light of the eye,' bawled others. The Fatah children gave a drum roll and the procession got underway as the Hamas backdrop was hastily removed and another showing Arafat and the Palestinian flag was put up in its place.

The following morning, election day, a full-blown fairground atmosphere prevailed. Music blared from loudspeakers, people holding sheaves of scarves handed them out, and the ground was littered with discarded pamphlets.

In the PR department I commented to Ala on the difference between the behaviour of the Islamic groups and Fatah. He laughed. 'That is your first impression and it is the right impression. You know, there is story about the Prophet Mohammed. During a battle once he told a group of men to stand on a mountain and not to do anything until they were given a new order. So now Muslims are always very orderly, they always do as they're told.'

I asked him if support for Hamas was related to a person's degree of religious devoutness.

'Not at all. Many people vote for Hamas because they have a good social programme, even people who are not religious. Me, for example, I don't pray, I'm secular, but I'm closer to Hamas than to Fatah. Here in Nablus, Christians and Samaritans vote for Hamas because of their political agenda. It's nothing to do with their religious ideology. They support the refugees and the right of return, not like Fatah.'

I logged on to my computer and started editing an article about a doctor who was working as a taxi driver. The reason, he claimed, was the bad economic situation caused by the conflict. This struck me as not entirely fair. Palestine has reportedly one of the highest rates of doctors per capita in the world.

'Isn't this because students are pushed into medicine by their families for reasons of status?' I asked Ala. 'Not everything is the fault of the Israelis.'

Ala agreed. 'But it's true that the economic situation has deteriorated seriously. After 1991 about 360,000 workers were no longer able to cross over into Israel to work because of the suicide bombings. Then there was the loss of income from the 400,000 Palestinians living in Kuwait who became homeless after the first Gulf War. Every Palestinian family in the West Bank had a relative in Kuwait. Another thing is the impact of Chinese imports. My father used to have a plant for making shoes. He had to close it because of the Chinese shoes coming in. In Nablus alone 120 workshops had to close.'

There was a flurry of activity outside, the sound of raised

voices, accusatory tones. 'What's happening?' I asked.

'A fight,' said Ala.

'Involving who? Fatah?'

He laughed. 'Of course.'

I walked round the campus with Camelia, Fida, Iman and Khadija, all keen Hamas supporters. Iman and Khadija shared the flat that Camelia and Fida had moved into before *Eid*.

'Hamas didn't accept the peace process with Israel,' Iman told me. 'The kind of process we've had since 1992, Oslo, etc, isn't a peace process, it's a surrender process.'

Fida chimed in. 'All Palestinians want peace but this is not peace because it is based on exploitation of the weakness of Palestinians. Weak, because we don't have weapons. The process is not between two states but between oppressors and occupied.'

'What kind of peace do you want?' I asked.

'We need justice,' said Fida. 'No interference from the superpower America, no biased interference. Real peace would be applying international laws of the UN. We also need good leadership after Arafat, peace be upon him. He was a great man. He was able to make a balance in the Palestinian parties. For the time being what we want is no interference in our election. We don't want characters imposed by Israel, by other people.'

A crowd of chanting Hamas supporters went by. 'For the sake of God we are doing this. Our loyalty is to God, to Palestine, to Prophet Mohammed.'

Camelia was explaining why she was going to vote for Hamas. 'I think they are the best because they're not materialistic, they're humble people, and they don't try to force their will on others by fighting and guns like the Shabibi. The Shabibi are troublemakers. If they control the university everything will be in chaos. They get money from Fatah, money that Arafat was giving for course fees and books and so on, but it's not distributed to everyone, only to the Shabibi supporters. Hamas looks after all the students.'

The other girls meanwhile were talking about Tony Blair. I asked what they thought of him.

'I like Tony Blair for his face,' said Khadija. She giggled coquettishly. 'But his politics? He is a wicked politician, like his partner Bush. They are two of a kind.'

The factions had their headquarters set up in curtained-off areas throughout the campus. I spoke with Rafik, one of the Hamas candidates. I complimented him on the impressive precision of the previous day's performance.

'All the instructions we follow are from Islam,' he said. 'We follow the orders of the leader and we have only one leader so we are well organized. If there is more than one leader cracks appear in an organization.'

I asked about the differences between Hamas and Islamic Jihad.

'There are small differences only. We have the same ideology, the same objectives and goals. There are just some small differences in the way we reach our goals. But perhaps you can speak with our leader about all this.'

He went behind the curtain and came back with Wajdi Al Aruri, the leader of Hamas in the university. Wajdi was an older man. He had been in prison six times, he told me, so hadn't been able to study when he was younger. Now he was studying fine arts.

I asked him about their manifesto.

'We will continue to help the students and support them. And we will continue fighting the occupation in an Islamic way. I believe that the results of the university elections are an indicator of Palestinian opinion generally.'

'You know, I suppose, what a very negative image people in the West have of Hamas. What would you say in response to that?' I asked him.

'I would ask them to imagine that they are occupied by someone in their countries. What would they do? How would they appear to the whole world? Would they fight for their rights or would they not fight for them? Hamas seeks for the true peace without losing our rights. I hope that there will be a better balance of opinions in the West and that there will be justice in Palestine. We have our heritage, our culture. We are well-educated and civilised people.'

He disappeared again behind the curtain.

The Hamas candidates were obviously busy with their last-minute canvassing but I got talking to Husam, an engineering student, who was going to vote for them. I was still trying to identify their position, particularly as regards militant activity.

'Listen, if you want my opinion, if you are talking about the military operations which happen inside Israel – what they call suicide bombings – they are unacceptable for the majority of the Palestinian people. If you want to fight and you feel yourself strong, you have to fight with army against army. But if they refuse to give us our state, if they refuse to give us at least our daily bread to eat, if they refuse to let us go to our universities, our schools, it is wrong. We can't fight them with stones. We did this in the first *intifada* in 1987, fighting them with stones, but they retaliated with guns and hundreds of stone-throwers were killed so the Palestinians started to change their resistance to the way that you see now. And if we take into consideration that there are no civilian Israelis because all of them come to our land and take it from us, then we have absolutely the right to kick them out of Palestine. I don't accept what's called the suicide bomber but I and the majority of the Palestinian people understand them because when you destroy my house, when you kill my family, my father, my brother, my sister, what do you want me to do? When you see how they freeze every aspect of our life, when you go to Huwara checkpoint and see all the humiliation, what do you ask me to do? They have to change but there will be no change unless the whole world gives it attention. Because... oh Mr Bush, oh Mr Blair, oh Mr... leaders of the free world... but no one can hear us, so after all this conversation I'm telling you that I am with the resistance at least to kick Israel out of our territories. If they give us just ten per cent of normal living, if they start to deal with us as humans, not as animals, we will surely start to change our point of view against the Israelis.'

The results were to be announced in the late afternoon. In the meantime I went home. Going back to the university at about four I heard someone calling my name from the top of one of the apartment blocks. I looked up and saw Camelia leaning over a balcony draped with Hamas flags. 'Come up,' she shouted.

I took the lift up to the ninth floor. Camelia, Fida and Iman were in the kitchen clearing their lunch plates off the table.

'If Fatah wins I will never go to the university again,' said Iman.

'Me too. I will quit,' said Camelia. She dumped the frying pan into the sink. 'Please God, let Hamas win.'

'We *will* win, we *will* win, we *will* win,' sang Fida, wiping the table top.

'I'm not going to wear my Hamas scarf now in case we don't win,' said Iman.

'You're not confident?' I asked

'Yes, I am. We will win. But if we don't I'll feel so ashamed.'

They were running around now, in and out of the bedroom and bathroom, fixing their *hijabs*, shrieking their hopes and fears.

A megaphone boomed in from the university.

Iman screamed. 'They're saying Fatah have won in all the faculties except engineering. Oh no!'

'Not possible,' said Fida. 'They don't know yet. Nobody knows till the results are announced officially.'

They all dismissed the megaphone as premature Fatah bragging.

We hurried down to the university. The campus was packed. The president of the outgoing Students Council was speaking.

'He's very nice, everyone likes him,' Fida said to me as we pressed into the throng. 'He's a gentleman. He's been imprisoned by both the Israelis and the Palestinian Authority.'

'It's not the end of the world if we lose,' the president was saying. 'Even Prophet Mohammed had some hard times.'

'He's preparing us for bad news,' said Camelia.

'Fatah get a lot of financial support, especially from the Palestinian Authority,' said Fida, already preparing excuses for a Hamas defeat.

'They have a lot of sympathy votes because of the death of Arafat,' Iman added.

'If we don't win, it's OK,' the president continued. 'Our belief is in God, not in elections.'

I teetered on the edge of the raised flowerbeds, pressed up against a thorny rose bush. Below me a woman held a baby with a Hamas scarf tied round its white woollen bonnet. Fatah men were beginning to appear on balconies waving *keffiyas* to a rising swell of cheers.

The president started to lead the *maghrib* prayer. Camelia prayed in a fervent whisper, one hand over her face.

The prayers included some verses from the Koran.

'He's chosen verses that suit the situation that we are losing,' Fida muttered to me.

A Hamas girl beside me was already crying. 'It's not official yet but you can tell from the verses he's chosen,' Fida continued.

The results were announced. Fatah were the winners with thirty-nine seats, Hamas were second with thirty-seven. A roar of applause arose from the Fatah supporters.

In the Hamas area I was surrounded by fallen faces. The girls were devastated.

'You know, Hilda,' said Camelia, 'I can't imagine An Najah university with a Fatah council.'

'But there are only two seats difference.'

'I know, but the leader will be Fatah so everything will be Fatah.'

A barrage of gunshots supplemented the cheers of Fatah. A tracery of bullets soared red into the dusk sky.

An old sheikh was now speaking. He told them that three Israeli soldiers had been killed by Hamas that day. There were more cheers.

'We are not against Israeli citizens that we are showing our happiness,' Iman said to me. 'But they oppress us so much.'

The outgoing president was speaking again. 'We are slaves of God. We will do what he wants us to do.'

The gunshots were sounding inside the campus now. All around me people were looking alarmed.

'They're crazy, these Fatah people,' said Camelia. 'This will drive the Israeli soldiers to come here.'

The president of the university, Rami Hamdalla, spoke briefly, struggling to make himself heard above the hubbub, then everyone started to disperse. Many of the Hamas women were crying and hugging each other. The Fatah people were rejoicing.

Circles of *dabka* dancers, arms round each other's shoulders, tossed their feet in the air. A Fatah man handed me a KitKat. Outside, traffic jammed the street, drivers hooted their horns, and students crowded round stalls selling corn on the cob, plastic cups filled with boiled chick peas, and coffee from big Arab urns.

I met Ala on the way out.

'Are you happy or unhappy?'

'I'm happy that the democratic process has been respected.' Clearly there were things that he wasn't happy about but he didn't elaborate.

I put the same question to Sami.

'*Noos noos*. Half and half. I am sad that there were guns inside the campus.'

The celebrations continued the next day. Fatah people were standing at the university gate, handing out a Turkish version of Mars Bars to everyone who entered. Inside more Fatah people were preparing the stage for the festivities.

I dropped in to Rasmiya's office. Shaddi's fiancé Amani was there and we went out together to the veranda to watch the party preparations down in the courtyard. Amani was happy about the two seats that Islamic Jihad had won. 'They have done well because it is the first time they are standing on their own. Before they were with Hamas.'

We got talking with Randa, a Fatah supporter who had butted in when she heard me comparing the Fatah people to a rabble of rowdy football fans. Was I right, I asked her.

'Well, they are a little bit disorganized.'

'More than a little bit surely? What about the guns on the campus?'

She rejected any suggestion of Fatah involvement.

'That must have been people from outside. No student would have a gun, that's for sure.'

She was optimistic that Fatah would act democratically. 'The council orientation is now Fatah because the council president is Fatah, but in our Islam we can't take a decision alone. We must take opinions from all sides. I think all students are happy with the result.'

'What about the political differences between Fatah and Hamas?'

'Well, Hamas, their first ideas are about Islamic ruling.'

'And Islamic Jihad?'

'They are our brother and sisters. There are so many things we agree about as well as the things we don't agree about. We think the Palestinian government should be for all, for Muslims, for Christians, for everybody. I think Islamic Jihad is just for Muslims. Also they want to get into war with Israel. In Fatah we have two choices: peace, we want to try that first, and only after that war. But the right of return and Al Aqsa, we can't let that go. We don't want to say we want just peace, we want a right and fair peace.'

We went down to join the rapidly gathering audience. Men were still fiddling with the sound system. Bursts of music kept blasting out and stopping abruptly. An old woman in traditional dress was sitting beside Randa. With each burst of music she clapped and whooped. 'She's from the Old City,' Randa told me. 'She's from Fatah, so she's very happy for us and to be with us.' A group of Fatah men came tumbling down the steps from the library, chanting at the tops of their voices.

'Eat bananas, eat bananas, let God take whoever doesn't like us winning,' they yelled.

A bunch of Fatah girls were trying to get a procession under way, all shouting at each other about which way to go. They couldn't seem to decide. Randa excused them by saying that a celebration was more enjoyable if it wasn't organized.

A voice announced over the tannoy that classes were cancelled for the rest of the day. A host of balloons and streamers were released from the roof, the music struck up again and a line of men carrying banners and posters started moving towards the stage. Men were being tossed in the air. Girls were acting as cheerleaders, clapping and shouting.

'Yassir Arafat would be very happy today,' I said to Randa. 'By the way, do you think he was poisoned?'

'Yes, by Israel. I am sure of it.'

'Some people say he might have been poisoned by Palestinians.'

'No. Maybe by the hand of a Palestinian, but Israel was behind it.'

A band of children were now coming down the steps, wearing red caps and carrying drums as big as themselves.

A man on the stage was shouting a speech with many references to Abu Ammar.

'Our victory is a gift for Abu Ammar, for the martyrs, for all the people of Palestine. This victory is for the poor people, for the parents of the young men and women killed. We want to thank all Fatah members for this victory…'

Behind him the stage was packed with Fatah men. Some of them were smoking, some were talking into mobile phones. One was reading a newspaper.

An argument broke out between Randa and a woman in front who had jumped up onto her chair to get a better view, waving her flag and blocking those behind. She refused to budge.

The presenter led the audience into a prayer. Like the music it proceeded in fits and starts as somebody fiddled with the microphone.

More women complained to the woman standing on the chair. She yelled back at them and stayed where she was.

'Hi to the other groups and welcome with us.' Randa did a running translation for me as the presenter spoke. 'Our university is for all students. We say to Hamas, there is a day for us and a day for you. We have a message for Marwan Bargouthi: you will remain our symbol, the symbol of the Fatah students.'

Finally responding to the complaints, the woman in front told us all to solve the problem by standing on chairs ourselves.

'Our fighting will not be complete until all prisoners are out of Israeli jails.'

The presenter finished his speech and everyone stood for the national anthem. Only the old lady remained sitting, holding a baby in a white shawl which had been thrust into her hands by its mother who needed her own hands for flag waving.

Next the skirl of Scottish music rent the air as a band of pipers approached the stage. Behind them came the Fatah president carried on the shoulders of other men, like a haggis being piped in to a Burns supper. Someone handed him a baby as he was deposited on the stage.

With the baby under his left arm and waving the Koran in his right hand he started to speak. The baby started to holler. It was passed from one man to another and then down from the stage. The crowd clapped and roared and stamped their feet. *Shabibi, Shabibi, Shabibi*, they shouted.

'We give this victory to Abu Ammar and to Ahmed Yassin and to every martyr. We will follow the road that Abu Ammar showed us,' continued the president. The men on the stage behind him continued to smoke and talk on their mobiles, and Randa continued to translate the speech for me. Much of it was just a repetition of what the previous person had said. The outbursts of rhythmic chanting grew more frequent, the atmosphere more emotionally charged, the speakers more fervent. A list of martyrs' names was read out with a fanfare of music and cheering after each one, then the names of prisoners.

A Hamas man came on to make a congratulatory speech, then a PFLP man. The presenter took over again, wearing the scarves of several factions plaited into one. By this time he was losing his voice.

A video conference between groups of students from An Najah and from a university in Indiana was scheduled for that afternoon. I left the Fatah celebration and went over to the library to join the participants.

The video-link was giving problems. I sat with Islah while the technical people fiddled about with plugs and cables and talked to her about my perceptions of Hamas and Fatah.

'You are so right,' she said. 'It's like, there was this Fatah guy, he bumped into me, and he was laughing and saying, "Oh, sorry, *habibti*." But it was like, he didn't really care, you know, he thought it was funny. Then another time, I bumped against a Hamas guy. He was so solicitous. He said, "I'm sorry, sister. Are you OK?" And once I had a problem with registration. I was just standing around looking puzzled and some Hamas girls approached me. They said, "Are you OK? Can we help you?" They helped sort it out. And this wasn't at election time. They're there for the students all the time, not just before elections.'

'Did you vote for Hamas?' I asked.

'No, I voted for Islamic Jihad because I think Hamas are more superficial. They're organized on the surface but Islamic Jihad, their strategies are better thought out.'

The Indiana students had appeared on the screen but there was still no sound. The two sides were communicating by writing messages on sheets of paper and holding them in front of the camera.

I introduced myself to the man on my left, a student I'd never seen before. His name was Rami, he said, and he was a business student. His English was limited but he wanted to take part and to tell the Americans about his own experiences.

'Westerners don't know what is happening in Palestine,' he said. 'I was in prison. For nothing. Last Ramadan I was in Huwara prison for twelve days. They accused me of connections with Hamas. I had done nothing, I had no connections.'

He told me how the Israeli special forces had burst into the flat he shared with other students in Nablus.

'They came at 2 a.m.. They broke the door down. They took me. At first I wasn't afraid because I knew I had done nothing wrong. I told them I had nothing to do with Hamas or Islamic Jihad. But they tortured me. They beat with their fists and with weapons. They put me on a chair and forced me into a very painful position with my hands underneath it chained to my legs. I was questioned by Captain Talal. He is very famous here. He is the Israeli intelligence person in charge of students from An Najah. When I denied the accusations Captain Talal would put me back on the chair in a tighter and more painful position. I thought I would never get out because they seemed so sure of themselves. I began to think they could say anything and make it stick, that I wouldn't be able to defend myself. I was afraid I would never get out, that life was over for me. But after twelve days, I don't know why, I think the mercy of God, I was released. I want to tell the Americans about those things that are happening here.'

In the end, no one was able to tell the Americans about anything. Ala held up a final message suggesting that they postpone till a later date. A message from Indiana appeared on the screen: We love you and hug you. The television was switched off.

In the evening I went round to see Camelia and her flatmates. We sat in the kitchen and ate a supper of fried cauliflower, stewed tomatoes, avocado mashed with lemon juice, yoghurt and bread.

The girls were discussing Abu Mazen's religious credentials. 'He believes in money just,' said Rana, the fifth flatmate. 'He mocked Yasser Arafat for reciting verses of the Koran about the rights of Muslims to Jerusalem.' She tore off a chunk of bread and dipped it into the stewed tomatoes.

'Hilda, what's the difference between Catholics and Protestants?' Iman asked.

I explained some of the doctrinal and liturgical differences. 'Communion, for example. Catholics believe that during the mass – that's the Catholic religious service – bread and wine are changed literally into the body and blood of Christ, whereas Protestants say it's just symbolic.'

'But how can they believe that? It's not possible.'

'Well, Catholics would answer this kind of objection by saying that it's a mystery. They would say also that it's not against reason, it's just beyond reason. It's something that we're not able to understand because we don't have the necessary mental powers. I suppose you could make the same kind of objection about Mohammed's night journey to Jerusalem when he went up to heaven from the Temple Mount and came back down again. That seems equally impossible.'

It was becoming difficult to sustain the discussion as there were now several different conversations going on at once. The girls tended to get over-excited once they were inside their flat and there was a lot of yelling, running around, bashing each other and brandishing things.

Noises from the landing outside added to the hubbub. Camelia ran to the door and looked out.

'There's a quarrel,' she gasped.

'Ooh, wow, let's go and see.' The others rushed out and down the stairs. On the floor beneath a terrific row was going on with girls screaming, hitting each other, running up and down the stairs, in and out of the other flats.

'They're calling each other bad words,' Camelia said.

It quickly fizzled out and we settled back down at the kitchen table, the atmosphere calmer as if the tension had been vicariously released by the violence of the neighbours.

'The violence of the occupation is overflowing here,' said Fida.

Camelia made tea. We moved through to the sitting room and huddled round a small heater, a kind of grill fixed to the top of a bottle of gas. The girls started swapping prison stories interspersed with worries about an upcoming exam. 'We've got just three days to study *A Midsummer Night's Dream*,' Rana complained. 'All of it.'

Camelia's father had been with the PFLP and had been in

prison in the 1970s. 'When he was in prison the chief in charge was sympathetic because his own son was in prison but the authorities discovered he sympathised with the prisoners so he was moved.'

Iman told a gruesome story about a cousin. 'He was put naked in a cell and they put hungry dogs in and you can imagine what happened. He had a fiancé but he couldn't marry her after that because, you know...'

Fida whispered the embarrassing details to me.

Rana had a cousin who died in prison. 'His family brought his corpse back to Palestine. It's important that a Muslim is buried in his homeland. If a prisoner dies before the end of his sentence his body is kept in a refrigerator till the end, even for years.'

'Last December Israeli tanks invaded Tulkarem and there was a curfew,' Fida said. An eight-year-old child was playing near a roundabout, playing with a ball. A sniper shot him in the heart. I saw the bullet. I knew the family. He had no heart any more, you could see right through his body. I saw it on television.'

Camelia told a story about a student who shared her brother's flat, a story which I had already read in a document published by the PR department. 'He was travelling to Nablus in a group with other students. At the checkpoint the soldiers told him to kiss one of the girls. He refused. He's very religious. The soldiers beat him up. The girl was very upset, she was terrified. The boy was all beaten and bloody, so she went over to him and she said: "It's OK, you can kiss me. I'm like your sister." The boy went to the girl's family to talk about it and explain. In our culture it's different. Maybe in the West you can't understand this. The boy left An Najah because of it.'

Fida had been chatted up by a soldier who detained her for several hours at a checkpoint. 'He was teasing me about being my boyfriend. And you know what boyfriend means in their culture. You go to their apartment and dada dada dada. I said to him: "Are you nuts? I'm a Palestinian girl, a Muslim." He gave me a new name, Dana. He said: "We can become friends, dada

dada dada. I will take you to Jerusalem in my jeep.'"

'It was good that you were able to remain confident during this time,' Iman said. 'If I'd been you, I don't know what I would have done.'

There had been a lot of laughing and shrieking while these stories were being told, and interruptions as sub-conversations about Chomsky, Middle English and *Waiting for Godot* cut across the conflict talk.

'You know, Hilda,' Iman said, looking serious, 'sometimes we tell these stories as if they were jokes. But they are part of our life.'

Rana spoke again. 'Hilda, did you know that my brother was a martyr?' Everyone looked serious now and gave her all their attention. 'He was working in a village. He woke up in the middle of the night to prepare the Ramadan *suhur* and he heard shooting. He went out to see what was happening. He saw a building surrounded by about eighty soldiers. My brother and the other men wanted to get away from the place, they didn't have any weapons. They got into their car and the soldiers started shooting at them. My brother was killed with three other men from my village. Two others were injured. There were a lot of helicopters flying over the place. We could see them from my village. My parents were trying to call my brother. There was no reply, he was already dead. We turned on the television about 5 a.m. and we saw the news. My mum started screaming. I couldn't believe it. We had the funeral that day, four families in the village, it was a very great disaster for us. My mum, when she sees things on television about martyrs the same age as my brother, she starts to cry. What really bothered me when I saw his corpse in front of me was that they took it away suddenly. I couldn't say goodbye to him. My brother and I had a great relationship between us. The most difficult thing is, you won't see this person for the rest of your life and I might live for another fifty years or more.' Rana was crying. 'When I see an Israeli soldier I just want to take a gun and kill them all because I feel that every one of them killed my brother.'

'You know, Rana, you shouldn't cry,' Iman said comfortingly. 'He's a martyr.'

Camelia took hold of her hand. 'He will book a seat for you in heaven.'

We gathered closer to the heater, chaffing each other's hands to keep warm.

'You know, during the 2002 curfew in Nablus, when so many people were killed, the hospital morgue was full,' Fida told me. 'Bodies had to be buried temporarily in the hospital grounds and even in people's gardens. When you see children playing they're usually funeral games, or about Jews and Palestinians fighting each other. Any child can talk about our issues. Even a five-year-old can talk about who is right and who is wrong. And wherever we go we are not respected because Israel and America don't like us. To them we are terrorists.'

'How did you feel about 9/11?' I asked.

'We were happy,' said Iman. Then she backtracked. 'Well, when I saw the events I was happy at first but when I saw the people throwing themselves out of the windows I was unhappy.'

The girls were inclined to believe in the conspiracy theory, that the Americans had set the whole thing up to discredit the Arab world.

'The American government at that time was interested in executing prior plans and wanted an excuse to do so,' said Fida, swiping vigorously with a broom as she cleaned the floor. 'It's the spirit of hegemony, we can't fight against it. The US is the only superpower since the end of the USSR so they are able to get away with much more than before. The Israelis do the same kind of thing. They set up Monica Lewinski to weaken Clinton's position at a time when he was helping the Palestinians.'

'What about Saddam Hussein?'

'I like Saddam very much,' Iman said. 'He supported the Palestinians, he gave money to the martyrs, he was the only one who said no to America.'

'But he tortured and terrorized his own people,' I pointed out.

'Yes, that's true,' Iman agreed. 'So if the Iraqis had killed him that would have been OK because he was a dictator but we don't like what America is doing there.'

The conversation turned to marriage. Iman said her parents hadn't met until their wedding day. Fida said her father saw her mother sitting on a wall, liked her and asked her parents if they could marry. I asked Fida if she could take the initiative if she saw a man she liked and send her parents to talk to the man's family.

'No,' said Fida. 'Only the man can do that.'

Iman disagreed. 'In Islam that is OK. Prophet Mohammed's first wife sent her servant to ask Mohammed if he would marry her.'

Fida didn't believe in the concept of romantic love. 'I think people should get married because of compatibility. Emotions should play no part in the decision.'

'Don't you sometimes feel attracted to a man?' I asked.

'Not at all. I'm totally in control of my emotions. In any case, I don't want to get married. I don't want to be dominated.'

The others believed that love grew later.

'I'm not thinking about it yet but it must begin with admiration from both sides,' said Iman. 'And before this admiration develops into love I'd like him to be acceptable to my parents. If my parents refuse, I won't act against their wishes.'

The girls found western norms of sexual behaviour incomprehensible.

'Hilda, sex is a holy, spiritual thing,' said Fida, almost accusingly, as if I was on trial for all the iniquity of the West. 'How can people have relationships with more than one partner? How can they have children without being married?'

I talked about cultural differences but felt that I was cutting very little ice.

[4] Democratic Front for the Liberation of Palestine

CHAPTER 8

I had heard that Ahmed Masri, a boy I'd met in Balata refugee camp, had been shot. I went to visit him in Rafidia hospital.

The walls of the ward were covered with posters of martyrs stuck on with Elastoplast. Ahmed, his arm encased in plaster, sat up in bed surrounded by the faces of dead militants.

Ahmed was nineteen, a pleasant-looking boy with even features under thick, straight eyebrows. He was studying for the *tawjihi* exams and had been working at Zatara checkpoint, helping to load and unload trucks being searched by the army. A few days previously he had been standing in line waiting to show his ID to the soldiers to get the go-ahead to start work.

'I heard the sound of bullets,' he told me. 'A lot of bullets, like the sound of a train. I looked down and I saw my arm was bleeding. I didn't feel pain immediately. A soldier told me to sit on the ground. I was bleeding for thirty minutes without any help. The pain was like something boiling. The jeeps started to come. They were shooting here and there. Maybe there were Palestinian shooters, I don't know. The Israelis shoot at random. My friend here,' he waved his hand towards the boy in the next bed, 'he was shot in the leg. The soldiers said to us, "Wait, wait. We will bring the ambulance." After thirty minutes the soldiers made the first aid for us. My friend had said, "Please, by your God and by your religion, please help us." I was overwhelmed with pain. Blood was pulsing out. I tried to stand up but I couldn't. I fainted. They helped us very gently and it was very nice, but not so much as they care for a soldier or somebody important. I don't say they didn't care. They cared, but not as much as for one of them.'

Ahmed was lucky. The bullet had passed clean through the lower part of his arm without causing any bone damage.

His friend had got off less lightly with two bullet wounds in the thigh. It was the third time he had been shot by Israeli soldiers.

A small boy called Nasser, wearing a track suit and with a towel draped round his neck, limped over carrying a catheter bag in his hand. He sat on Ahmed's bed smoking. He had been shot in both arms, one leg and the abdomen, Ahmed told me.

I asked Nasser what had happened.

'I was going home at about half past nine. Some other boys in the village were throwing stones at a jeep. The soldiers saw me. They shouted at me to go over to them. I was afraid to go. I ran away. The soldiers shot me.'

Nasser tossed his cigarette end on to the floor and ground it under his heel. He lit another one.

A Palestinian ambulance had come for him, he said, but it was stopped by the soldiers who had shot him. They kicked him and punched him, then choked him for two minutes, stopping only when he began to pass out. His father, who was with him by this time, tried to intervene, shouting at the soldiers to stop, that they were killing Nasser. The soldiers hit him and told him to shut up. An Israeli army doctor tried to take one of the bullets out of his leg, handling him roughly. Nasser was screaming, demented with pain. 'The soldiers said, "He's just pretending, not really injured." And they said bad words about my mother and sister.'

As I scribbled down the details of his story I felt that it would seem unbelievable. Yet I believed it because I had heard so many others that were similarly outrageous and aberrant, and also because of the matter of fact way in which he spoke. It was nothing special to Nasser or the others in the ward. It was just part of the daily Palestinian grind.

Ahmed passed round a packet of biscuits I'd brought him and tossed the wrapping into one of the overflowing rubbish bins. He introduced me to the man in the bed opposite who was lying with his leg in traction. He too had been shot, as had the man next to him, Ibrahim, who had five bullet wounds in his legs. It was Ibrahim's second spell in hospital; the previous time he had been shot in the stomach.

Every patient in the ward was there as a result of Israeli-inflicted injuries. Even the visitors had all been shot.

Abdel Mowaz, an eighteen-year-old, had recently lost four fingers. The stump of his hand was still bandaged. He pointed to a scar along his left jaw, the result of a previous shooting, and then pulled up his shirt to show me bullet wounds in his chest from a third incident. On each occasion he had been throwing stones at soldiers. I asked him how, after experiencing the atrocious pain of the first shooting, he had continued to run the risk of it happening again.

'He offers his soul and his body for Palestine and Al Aqsa,' Ahmed translated for me. 'He wants to be a martyr.'

Sami, another young man, had been shot in the thigh while throwing stones but no longer did so. His father forbade it.

An older man had been shot three years previously and still had the bullet lodged in his back. Another, only twenty-one, had already been shot four times.

'Many of my friends, at least fifty per cent have been shot,' Ahmed said. 'Now me. Soon it will be one hundred per cent.'

A man in his mid-thirties joined us round Ahmed's bed. His name was Fowaz. He had just come in an ambulance from Tulkarim with his cousin who had been shot by soldiers in a passing jeep while he was walking along the road. The cousin, Mohammed, was in the operating theatre having surgery on his thigh and his hand. While he waited Fowaz recounted the catalogue of injuries and imprisonments suffered by himself and his family.

Mohammed had previously been shot in similar circumstances, caught in the crossfire as a band of Israeli special forces gunned down a group of men in the street. Fowaz's brother had been shot and lost an eye. Mohammed's sister was serving seventy-five years in an Israeli prison. A student at An Najah, she had been accused of assisting with a suicide bombing in Netanya.

'I myself was in prison for three and a half years,' Fowaz

said. They took me from my house. I was nineteen then. I had been throwing stones. It was during the first *intifada*.' He talked about the many prisons he had been in, the bad food, the cold in winter.

The others started reminiscing about their own experiences of arrest and brutality.

Ahmed Masri had woken up one morning surrounded by eight soldiers, one of them pointing a gun at him. He spoke in the same calm voice and with the same beatific expression that he always had. 'They beat me, they kicked me in the ribs. They searched the house, they broke everything in my room. Three or four soldiers were punching me in the face, another one was hitting me with his gun. They have to practise, it is like a sport. They said, "We will kill you like a dog, we will come again." My younger brother – he was only thirteen – he had a toy gun he had made himself. The soldiers hit him and kicked him because he had this gun.'

Mohammed's bed was wheeled back in from the theatre. He was unconscious, wearing the same bloodstained T-shirt he had arrived in, with an old grey coat thrown over him. The orderlies parked his bed over a patch of floor strewn with bits of newspaper, cigarette ends and empty drink cans and left him to come round.

I asked Ahmed how he imagined his life would be if there wasn't the conflict.

'I would be studying, preparing for a career, enjoying myself with my friends, instead of lying in hospital with gunshot wounds.'

CHAPTER 9

In mid-December I finished working at An-Najah University. I planned to spend some time in other parts of the Occupied Territories.

I went first to visit Rasmiya's family again. In the pharmacy I found Shatha with several crises on her hands. A woman with an unwanted pregnancy had been ringing her for the past few days, begging for an abortifacient. 'I can't,' Shatha told me. 'It's against the law.' She had asked Shaddi to check the religious position with a sheikh. 'He said it was OK up to forty days because there is no soul till then. But it's still against the law. I can't help her but she keeps on calling me.'

Another woman had phoned asking Shatha to give her some medication which would make her ill. Her husband was having an affair and she wanted to lure him back by making him feel guilty. Again Shatha had refused but had invited her to come to the pharmacy so that she could talk about her problems.

I left Shatha waiting for the abandoned wife. Rasmiya had asked me to go with her to a funeral in a neighbouring village. A young man, a student in Nablus, had been killed the day before by the Israeli army.

When we arrived in the village we found the street outside the house decorated with Hamas banners and posters. A line of five or six young women, all with the green and white Hamas scarf round their necks, greeted us at the gate. Inside the sitting room was packed with women sitting on mattresses on the floor. Rasmiya and I sat down amid the subdued murmur of talk about Ihsan, the dead man. One of his sisters knelt beside his mother wiping tears from her cheeks. Another handed round a tray of cakes. I took one but couldn't eat it in that grief-laden atmosphere. I put it in my pocket.

The Israelis had taken Ihsan for no reason, the women said. He had already been in prison, for no other reason than that a friend of his had been wanted by the army. The friend, who was his flatmate in Nablus, had been killed by the Israelis, and now, in what they saw as the inexorable consequence, Ihsan too had been killed.

I wanted to know if anybody knew what Ihsan was supposed to have done to justify being shot to death. I asked Hadi later that evening.

'He belonged to Hamas.'

'But thousands of people belong to Hamas. It isn't a crime.'

'Let me tell you something, Hilda. When there is a suicide bombing or a military action the Israelis are enraged. They have to take revenge to satisfy all the angry people. Five Israeli soldiers have just been killed in Gaza. So, they have to kill Palestinians.'

I was watching television with Hadi and Shatha. We had just seen a programme featuring suicidal Japanese people who were contacting each other through the internet with a view to meeting up and killing themselves together. This triggered a conversation about the psychology of Palestinians throwing stones at Israeli soldiers. It seemed to me that they were playing a kind of Russian roulette. Yet the Palestinians, with their social cohesiveness and close family bonds, were surely in far better emotional health than the isolated and alienated Japanese we had been listening to. So why did they dice with death in this way?

Shatha acknowledged the difference but maintained that the Palestinian attitude was understandable. 'They make a realistic assessment about what life has to offer them and decide it isn't enough to go on living,' she said.

Despite the apparent closeness of their relationships Palestinians did not talk readily about emotional problems, Shatha said. 'I have very few patients on medication for anxiety and depression. There's a lot of bedwetting in children but that's all. We don't have special doctors for this kind of thing.'

She told me the story of a psychiatrist who opened a clinic in the West Bank. 'Nobody came because of the stigma attached to mental illness. He discovered that the only people working successfully in this field were sheikhs, holy men. So he tried to give the impression he was a sheikh, growing a beard and suchlike, and the police arrested him. He decided that as Palestinian society is like this, it is not the place for him and he left the country.'

A couple of days later I left to spend Christmas in Jerusalem. I took a bus first from Nabi Elias to Ramallah. We passed through two checkpoints en route. At each one the man I was sitting beside made a point of telling the soldiers that I was British. 'They will be more polite with us if they know you are here,' he explained. 'They are frightened when there are foreign observers watching them.' From Ramallah I took a shared taxi to Qalandiya checkpoint, which marked the border between the West Bank and East Jerusalem, and then a bus into the city.

I checked in at the Jaffa Gate Hostel and went to the restaurant next door, overlooking the square. The walls of the restaurant were covered with posters for a course in psychomedicine, the words in both Hebrew and English. The tablecloths continued the message. *Teach your mind its map and put your mental life back on track*, I read as I picked up the menu. *Knowledge of the mind upgrades unknown higher ideas and a non-standard life into a standard fulfilling life.* An easel in a corner displayed a rural scene with a man and woman dressed as ancient Romans, with a second woman naked and full frontal.

The restaurateur, a small, taut Palestinian, was not in a good mood. He railed against the other Arab countries for their lack of support as he laid my table.

'All the prostitutes in the world are in their palaces,' he shouted, talking of the Saudis. 'All their money is being gambled in Las Vegas.' He changed tack. 'Who is our real enemy? Our real enemy is not Israel, it is America. We have to fight America.'

'How can you? How could Palestine take on a country like America?'

'Like we did in the seventies. We have to attack them on their own ground. Then they were paying us. The oil companies, the airlines, were paying us not to attack them, not to hijack them. They were paying hundreds of millions of dollars.'

'Who were they paying? The PLO?'

'Yes.'

'How do you know?'

'I know. Maybe you weren't aware. Maybe you know nothing about it.'

A squad of black-clad Hasidic Jews hurried by, heads jutting forward and with purposeful gait. The strains of *Silent Night* drifted over from a nearby tourist shop.

'In the West you criticize the Arab countries for their governments, sons inheriting from fathers. What about the Bush family? And did you know the Bush family were supporting Hitler in the 1940s? No? Well, you know nothing.'

He was stamping up and down in his anger, marching from one of end of the room to the other, flailing his arms as he struggled to get them into the sleeves of his bomber jacket.

I asked him why he allowed Israelis to advertise in his restaurant.

'I have no quarrel with Jews, only with Zionism.'

'You get to know Jesus Christ because he loves you, honey. The Church of the Holy Sepulchre, forget it, that's from the pit of hell. For you to be saved, honey, all you have to do is ask Jesus to come into your heart and mean it. Praise the Lord!' Ruthie clapped her hands. 'Hallelujah.'

I was back in the Jaffa Gate Hostel and had joined some of the other residents in the reception area. The hostel had no heating system and Ruthie, a little old American woman, was swaddled from waist to toes in a tartan blanket. With a fuzz of

127

white curls standing out round her head and an effervescent air she looked like a poodle fresh from the dog parlour. She and her companions – a youngish Puerto Rican called Rico and Dahleen, a middle-aged South African woman – were Messianic Jews, Jews who believe that Jesus Christ was the Messiah and follow his teaching. Ruthie had been ignorant of her Jewish blood until she was about sixty. During a previous visit to Israel she had the very strong feeling when she arrived in Jericho that 'these were her people'. She then did a search for her mother's name in the diaspora list and found that she was indeed Jewish. Rico, a second generation Puerta Rican, was able to trace his family back, via the Canary Islands, to Spain which had expelled all Jews during the Inquisition of the fifteenth century.

'I've got a DVD I'm going to give you. It's about a doctor who dies and goes to hell and comes back to tell us what he saw. Amen!' Ruthie continued. Dahleen and Rico in the meantime were discussing a book about the Ark of the Covenant and the symbolic meaning of the materials used for the priests' clothes. 'Praise the Lord, I'd like to read this,' Ruthie broke in. 'Hey Hilda honey, what brings you here anyway?'

I told them about my interest in learning more about the Palestinian perspective.

'That's good. You should see both sides,' said Ruthie.

'But it's not so easy to get to know the Jews so it's difficult to see both sides.'

'Oh no, it isn't,' said Rico. 'Not if you read the Bible. I could point you back to Genesis chapter 12 and show you where all this began. The fact that Israel is here proves that there is a God.'

'Israel is the sign for the nations that there is a God and he is going to come back and there is going to be a judgement,' Dahleen chimed in. 'Get into that Bible, honey, and study it, because you've got to know that Bible backwards and forwards for the last days.'

Ruthie backed her up. 'You've got to know the word of God like you've never known it before.'

The Palestinian manager appeared at the reception desk. They all stopped talking and turned their attention to the Ray Charles movie that was showing on the television.

'They're really nice guys here,' Ruthie whispered. 'We don't want to upset them.'

'But why are you all living in the Muslim Quarter,' I asked.

'Because it's cheaper,' replied Dahleen with a short sharp laugh.

The manager left and Rico started reading aloud from the Book of Revelations. 'And I stood upon the sand of the sea, and saw a beast rise up out of the sea, having seven heads and ten horns, and upon his horns ten crowns, and upon his heads the name of blasphemy.'

'What's the beast supposed to be?' I asked.

'It's the new world government,' said Rico.

'Read on, read on,' cried Ruthie.

Everyone started talking at once. Rico launched into an explanation of the Palestinian struggle that rooted it back in the Second Temple period, Dahleen told a story about a cat to prove that God is love, and Ruthie advised me to improvise a hot water bottle by boiling water in the kitchen upstairs and putting it in an empty coke bottle.

Dahleen came to the end of her story. 'He loves every animal, he loves every person. When the tree blooms you will know that the Messiah is coming back.'

'Explain to me how the Catholic church helped Hitler to kill my people,' demanded Rico, of no one in particular.

'The solution, it's easy. Christ is the solution. You don't need all that complicated ritual stuff,' said Dahleen.

'Nobody's right,' said Rico.

'You say nobody's right but you think you're right,' I said to Rico.

'That's right,' said Dahleen.

'The peace agreement, they were going to give Arafat everything he wanted, he didn't take it.' Rico was shaking his head in disbelief at his own words.

'You're self-righteous, that's your problem,' said Ruthie to Dahleen.

The next day I called on Ruthie in her room. It was stacked high with bedding, suitcases, kitchen equipment and plastic bags crammed full of pills and dietary supplements. 'You see, honey, I'm planning to rent a place where I can provide accommodation for Russian Jews moving to Israel. People have donated so much stuff.' She waved a hand at the bedding.

I asked her why she needed so many pills. 'Well, I don't know how old you are, honey, but every woman over thirty should take calcium supplement every day to protect her bones. Calcium, zinc, iron, lecithin and vitamin C. By the way what'ya doing for lunch, honey? I've discovered this lovely little restaurant, really cheap. Like to try it?'

'Sure.' So far I'd only eaten in Palestinian places and was ready for a change. And Ruthie, for all that I found her religious ideas eccentric if not downright dangerous, was fun. In fact, in a funny sort of way, with her I found it easier to talk about literal interpretations of the Bible and extreme political views without getting angry as she had a certain loveableness which disarmed me.

We went to Dishes, a small self-service place in Jaffa Street in West Jerusalem.

'Now listen to this,' said Ruthie between forkfuls of vegetable couscous. 'God told the tribe of Benjamin to destroy the Jebusites, every man, woman and child. But they didn't. They disobeyed God and that's why the Palestinians are still here today. This was back when God gave all of this land to the Israelis. God gave this land to the twelve tribes of Israel. Anyone who is not of the twelve tribes is trespassing. It's in the book of Joshua. It describes the territory. And even in Jordan, the half tribe of Menassa didn't come over the river, so that area in Jordan belongs to them. Beneath them in Jordan is the land belonging to the tribe of Reuben. All that will be returned to them just before Jesus the Messiah comes back. As far as the Palestinians go, you see, Abraham is the father of the Jews and he is also the father of the Arabs. They are half-brothers. Sarah, Abraham's wife, is the mother of the Jews, and the maid Haggar is the mother of the Arabs. So the Palestinians...

Hey, good to see you guys.' Ruthie broke off to introduce me to a couple who were sitting down at the next table, a cosy-looking woman with thick wavy grey hair and her less prepossessing husband whose face was a network of broken veins. 'Hilda, meet my good friends Don and Linda. They're here in Jerusalem doing the Lord's work.'

'Hi, where are you from? Do you believe in the Bible?' Don asked. 'I've got an article here.' He thrust a couple of photocopied pages into my hand without waiting for answers to either of his questions and turned his attention to his food. 'We thank you Lord for this wonderful food put in front of us.'

Ruthie took up her Bible lesson again. 'I've told my Arab friends, now y'all are half-brothers and you're killing each other. The Arabs have Saudi Arabia, they have Jordan, Syria, Iraq, they have the Gulf States. Do you mean to tell me that you can't give that little land of Israel to your half-brothers? You are being greedy, you are being unjust. It's the Arabs that are being unjust, unfair and greedy. That's the word of God. If anybody's in the wrong, they are. They're trespassing. This land belongs to the twelve tribes of Israel. In the Bible it says that all the tribes of Israel will be gathered together here before the return of Yeshua the Messiah. This peace that they're talking about, that could be the false peace prophesied in the Bible, the seven years of false peace. After half of it, true hell will break loose. Satan will show himself. Christians know this because that's what the Bible says. We sit and watch the news and we see what the Bible says taking place before our eyes. God says do not divide my holy city Jerusalem. The Road Map which gives East Jerusalem to the Palestinians is going against the word of God. And you don't go against the word of God and think you're going to win. No way.'

At this point Don butted in. 'Probably the greatest miracle this generation has ever seen was in 1948, the creation of the state of Israel.'

Ruthie nodded her head. 'Amen, amen.'

'That was the first sign,' Don continued. 'That had to happen before anything else could happen.'

'Let me ask you this,' Ruthie said to me. 'If you owned so much and your half-brother inherited just a teeny little bit, wouldn't you be terribly greedy if you refused to give him a teeny bit more? Wouldn't you want to give him that teeny little bit?'

'Well,' I said, 'I'd have to believe first of all that that person really was my half-brother.'

'But it's in the Bible! God says so. Praise the Lord! The Palestinians are just being greedy. Honey, do you know that the other Arabs won't let their own brothers come into their countries? That's why the Palestinians are so upset, because their own brothers won't let them in.'

'It's not that they're short of land,' said Don. 'There's plenty of land. We've seen the masses of empty land in Jordan, nobody living there. In Jordan, boy, there's money. They have houses like hotels.'

'And there was Arafat,' Ruthie said. 'He had twelve billion dollars and he kept it. He didn't use it for his people. Honey, he kept it all, except for a little bit that he gave out piecemeal. The Palestinians, they didn't know all this stuff but we know it. Hey, Eva, how're you doing, honey?' Ruthie turned to a woman who was sitting down at our table. Her lined face, framed by bobbed brown hair held back by an Alice band, quivered as she delivered her news.

'Have you heard that the Palestinians have fired a rocket at a settlement in Gaza? It hit a synagogue.'

'Wow!' gasped Ruthie. 'It's down to the wire now.'

'Road map!' spluttered Don. 'That's the stupidest terms that anybody's ever come up with. It's a road map against a covenant. Shimon Peres is Jewish but he's more Palestinian than Jewish because he's always doing what the Palestinians want.'

Ruthie took up her thread again. 'The Palestinians are in a difficult situation because their own people don't want them and they're trespassing here. Poor things. I do feel sorry for them. In Genesis chapter 12 – is it verse 4? I think it's verse

4 – God said if you bless my people, I will bless you, if you curse my people, I will curse you. These Arabs don't know what they're doing. God will curse them.'

'You see,' said Don, his mouth full of fish, 'Abraham was faithful to God, he was prepared to offer his son as a sacrifice. That's why God favours the Jews. The Jews were selected as a group to teach the rest of the world how to live.'

'And you know, honey,' said Ruthie, 'the love of God is so vast that anybody, Jewish descent or not, Hindu, Muslim, Greek, when they have accepted Jesus into their hearts, then they're grafted into the main root, into the Jewish tree. And that makes you Jewish in his eyes.'

Eva in the meantime was deep in conversation with Linda, lambasting Bush for being soft on the Palestinians. 'Why does he push through with these things?' Eva asked.

'If he read through his Bible he would know he was wrong,' said Linda.

'Pray for Tony Blair to repent of the British Mandate,' an elderly American woman called over our heads as she passed on her way to the counter.

'Hey, I thought you'd gone,' shouted Don.

'No, I'm still here. The Lord wants me to live here.'

After lunch Ruthie and I went shopping.

'You mean to say you haven't been to the Shouk, the Jewish market? Hey, honey, am I gonna show you something!' We walked through the wide, light arcades of Mahane Yehuda market – for Ruthie it was vastly superior to the Arab souk in the Old City – and dived in and out of the clothes shops in Jaffa Street. Ruthie was brimming with enthusiasm for everything. I bought a denim skirt.

'Oh honey, you look so cute in that skirt, like a little doll. God bless you.'

She bought a fleecy jacket. 'Now I'm going to be praying for freezing weather so I can wear it. Isn't it a bargain? Isn't it just too cute? Praise the Lord!'

She pointed to a pastry shop at the other side of the road.

'That used to be Sbarro, the restaurant where they had that awful suicide bombing. And up the road there was another one on a bus.'

We passed a group of rifle-carrying soldiers.

'God bless their hearts, they're protecting us,' said Ruthie. 'God bless them.'

CHAPTER 10

I went back to Nabi Elias to spend New Year with Rasmiya's family. The beginning of a new year is of little significance to Palestinians. This year in particular it was eclipsed by the presidential election which was to be held on 9 January.

The only serious competition for Mahmoud Abbas was Mustafa Barghouti although six or seven other candidates had put themselves forward.

On New Year's Day Shatha called me from the pharmacy.

'Quick, you must come down. Mahub's sister is here and she's going to see Mustafa Barghouti in Azzoun. She'll take you there.'

Mustafa Barghouti, a medical doctor, had recently co-founded Mubadarah (Palestinian National Initiative), a democratic opposition party. He was a prominent figure on the political stage and a leader of civil society. He was also widely popular.

Mahub's sister, Imtan, was a member of Mubadarah. She and a group of other female supporters were accompanying Barghouti on the campaign trail in the Qalqilya area. We drove together in a minibus to Azzoun town hall which was filling up with an audience that was more than ninety-five per cent male. Flashing coloured lights decorating the stage contrasted frivolously with posters of Barghouti striking a pose of exaggerated rectitude. Boys with red bands round their heads were distributing free cartons of fruit juice.

Barghouti, sober in a grey suit with a Palestinian flag lapel pin and a sheaf of handwritten notes stuffed into a pocket, came on and made a predictable speech committing himself to the right of return for refugees, the abolition of checkpoints, and the removal of the Wall. He spoke in praise of Abu Ammar,

Ahmed Yassin and Rantisi and called for unity between Fatah and Hamas. His manner was earnest and decent, but it highlighted what a hard act Arafat was to follow.

We piled back into the minibus and joined the cavalcade which was heading towards another small town, Kfar Tilit. A carnival atmosphere was developing, with horns hooting and men hanging out of the cars, waving banners and chanting slogans.

It was about noon by the time we reached Kfar Tilit. The sun beat down on the school playground where the gathering was being held. The Mubadarah women and I took shelter in the shadow of the van, and while Barghouti repeated all the things he had said in Azzoun the women told me about Mubadara and the reasons for Bargouti's appeal.

'I support Mubadarah because it is talking about the suffering of the people that no one is interested in, that no one is helping,' Imtan said.

'And it is talking about what the people need – all the people, not just one group of people,' said Falastine, an accountancy student. 'It is developing programmes to support the poor people and the disabled, and it is working to free all prisoners, not just one kind. It also has programmes to support women. It is concerned about social services.'

The next stop was Habla, a town of cement, breeze blocks, graffiti and rust – rusty gates, rusty satellite dishes, rusty vehicles, rusty garbage. A stage was set up in front of the mosque, a new building of whitish stone with a wooden entrance structure shaped like a Swiss chalet. Barghouti was clearly popular here. A big crowd had turned up. The area in front of the stage was full, as were the roofs of the surrounding houses. I went for a walk in the nearby streets as the audience sang the national anthem, observed a minute's silence for the martyrs, and listened to Barghouti's speech. Wherever I went people pressed fruit and drinks on me. A group of young teenagers yelled at me, pulling at each other and giggling as they asked me what my name was and where I was from.

'Who do you like best?' I asked them,

'Abu Mazen or Mustafa Barghouti?'
'Mustafa Barghouti.'
'Why?'
'Because Abu Mazen is a collaborator.'
They ran off, chanting political slogans.

Back at the minibus Imtan told me that we were now going to Qalqilya where we would have a get-together with Barghouti at the Mubadarah headquarters. We drove off at the head of the cavalcade to a flat in the town centre. We sat around for a while, drinking coffee served by men in white waistcoats with Barghouti's face on the back. After about half an hour Imtan reported that Barghouti wouldn't be coming after all. He'd slipped away from the cavalcade and gone to have lunch in Selfit.

I said goodbye to the Mubadarah people and got into a taxi for Nabi Elias. Straight away I found myself caught up in one of those Palestinian travel problems that make you feel as if you're involved in some kind of fiendish topological puzzle in which you're trapped inside a boundary without having crossed a boundary to get there. To get back to Nabi Elias I had to go through a checkpoint. By some cartographic quirk, nowhere on the circuitous route we had taken that morning had we encountered a checkpoint, so I hadn't realized till now that I didn't have my passport on me. I asked the driver what I should do about it. He didn't want to know. To a Palestinian, being without your passport is an automatic prelude to trouble. He dumped me on the Qalqilya side of the checkpoint, pocketed his fare, and squealed through a three-point turn in his haste to get away.

The only thing to do was to phone Rasmiya and ask her to bring my passport to the checkpoint. The passport was in one of my bags. The trouble was, I had three bags, not much different in size and colour, and in one of them was a bottle of vodka I had bought in Jerusalem – not the kind of thing to be harbouring in a devout Muslim household. Rasmiya would surely be appalled, I thought, if she came across it while rummaging for my passport. But there was no alternative. I made the call, described the bag in as much detail as I could in an agitated jabbering, so anxious was I that she shouldn't look in the wrong bag. Then I walked up to the checkpoint to explain to the soldiers that I was waiting for someone to bring my passport. Without giving me a second glance one of them simply waved me through. Ten minutes later Rasmiya drew up beside me, amazed to see me on her side of the checkpoint and with no sign of her having uncovered any contraband.

The Israelis had announced that travel restrictions would be eased in the West Bank for the period around the presidential election to facilitate voting and to allow access to international observers. I took advantage of this to go back to Nablus for a few days.

For the first time, I would be able to enter through a checkpoint. I took a shared taxi from Nabi Elias to Beitiba. Rain was coming down in sheets when I got out of the taxi, and I queued shivering with several hundred others while it drenched us all. As soon as I got to the flat in Al Makhfia I took off my wet clothes and then discovered that I had no dry ones to change into. The rain had got right inside my bag, soaking everything. 'Now you know what we have to go through,' said Camelia briskly when I told her about it later.

On 6 January Abu Mazen was campaigning in Nablus. In the morning he visited the university. I talked with some of the students about their preferences while we waited for him to arrive. On the whole they took a pragmatic view.

'Let's be honest,' said Tarik, an engineering student. 'Bush wants Abu Mazen. The key to the solution here in the Middle East is in his hands.' Tarik wasn't happy about the influence wielded by Bush. 'But we have to live with it,' he said. 'This is the real world.'

The students were concerned about the effect the election's outcome would have on their futures.

'The youth here in Palestine, there is no hope in the West Bank,' Tarik said. 'After I graduate what am I going to do? Here there is nothing. Before the second *intifada* there was money and jobs. It has all been destroyed. We hope that if Abu Mazen is elected he will make peace and that things will return to the way they were before. We hope that Abu Mazen will stop the suicide bombers and the rockets.'

'How will he manage that?' I asked sceptically. 'How do you expect him to succeed where others have failed?'

'The only way is by speaking to the people who want to do these things, not by arresting them. It's the only way.'

His friend Lutfi agreed. 'He has to try to convince them. It is time to take a break.'

'Even Hamas and the Jihad people are saying it's time to take a break,' Tarik added.

'They have to learn from their experience and see the wrong things they did,' said Lutfi.

The boys were less optimistic about Israel's commitment to finding a peaceful solution.

'Even if Abu Mazen wins, I don't think Israel will give him anything,' said Sabih. 'Israel does not want a solution and as the US supports Israel there will be no solution. I am not hoping a lot from this election so I'm not going to vote.'

They believed that the fault lay more with the Israeli government than with the Israeli people.

'I've spoken to Israeli soldiers my age,' Tarik said. 'They say they don't want this. They just want to be back in their homes with their studies. At the checkpoints they say: "Our place is not here." I find that many Israeli soldiers hate Sharon. Sharon does not want peace.'

A Hamas supporter who had stopped to listen laughed and stuffed a torn-up picture of Abu Mazen into Tarik's pocket.

Several groups of students were processing around with banners and flags and pictures of prisoners and martyrs, but on the whole there were relatively few people and little enthusiasm. It was very different from the days of the student election. Outside the university several hundred soldiers were on duty in readiness for the arrival of Abu Mazen. He arrived accompanied by three ambulances and a long line of official and military vehicles. It was all in marked contrast to the rag, tag and bobtail retinue of Mustafa Barghouti. Didn't this give him an unfair advantage in terms of image, I asked.

'Well, it's normal,' said Iman who had joined us with her friend Jamila. 'He's the leader of the PLO and of Fatah, and his life has been threatened. He needs all this security.'

Neither Iman nor Jamila would be able to vote as they were both going to be working as interpreters with international observers on election day.

'But if you could vote?' I asked.

'I think I'd vote for Mustafa,' said Iman. Because of all the work he's done with Palestinian Medical Relief. There's something humane about his job. And I like the guy.'

Jamila felt that the fact that he didn't have the support of America and Israel was a point in his favour.

She had also been impressed by a recent incident in which soldiers at a checkpoint had manhandled Mustafa Barghouti and hit his bodyguards. 'He said on television, "It's an honour for me to suffer like the other Palestinians suffer." I highly appreciate this.'

Generally the students felt that Abu Mazen would win, in view of the head start given him by his high profile.

'But we all respect and love Mustafa,' Tarik said.

'Me too,' said Fowaz, his brother. Fowaz was only fourteen but already realistic about possible ways forward. 'I love Mustafa but if I could vote I would vote for Abu Mazen, to stop the killing and because Israel and the Americans like him.'

The city centre was jammed with military vehicles. Abu Mazen was visiting the Old City. Coughing and croaking with a chest infection I had developed since my drenching at the checkpoint, I dropped by to speak with Waddeh. He made up a bag of herbs for me, taking a pinch from each of a variety of jars. 'You take one teaspoonful in a glass of water three times a day and soon you will feel very, very best.'

I asked him what he thought of Abu Mazen.

'He is the new Dracula. After two or three months you will

see… He will say hello to Sharon. How will that help us? Hhh, I want to have something for the families of these martyrs.' He waved his hand at the gallery of posters on his walls and then turned to serve a woman who looked about sixty-five. After she had gone he told me she was only forty-two, that her periods had stopped some time ago and that he had now managed to get them started again with his herbs.

I left Waddeh filling up little pots with pink cream from a big jar and moved deeper into the souk where I got caught up in a swell of movement as people, jostling with international press teams laden with recording paraphernalia, pressed round a procession of vehicles inching slowly forward through the narrow alleys. Despite the crowds – and the narrowness of the alleys must have made the numbers seem greater than they were – the atmosphere was fairly low key, the mood being more one of polite curiosity than of political fervour. Abu Mazen sat on the roof of the leading car, packed between security men. Squeezed up against a crate of turnips, I watched from the threshold of a shop as he approached, raising his arms to the crowd and looking avuncular. Once outside the souk, the cavalcade took off at high speed, sirens blaring.

The next day I passed through the checkpoint again, with no more than a nod from the soldiers. I was on my way to visit Amjad, a student who had invited me to his village which lay about eight miles to the north-west of Nablus. He wanted to show me the ruins of Sebastia, a city dating from the ninth century BCE and once the capital of Israel.

Before the *intifada* Sebastia, with its temples, palaces and colonnaded streets, had been one of the main tourist attractions in the West Bank. It was home to the biblical Jezebel who worshiped Baal and turned the city into a centre of idolatry, incurring the wrath of the prophet Elijah. The head of John the Baptist is believed to be buried there.

Amjad and I stopped at a coffee shop at the entrance to the ruins. The owner, Abdul Rahman, sat with us as we drank tea.

'You are the thirty-first visitor since the beginning of the *intifada*,' he told me. 'Before, we had between two and three hundred a day.'

At that time Sebastia had been a stopping point for tour buses traveling from Jerusalem to Galilee. Amjad's father had a souvenir shop and a restaurant which had once done thriving business. They were now closed.

We wandered through the ruins – remnants of successive occupation by Israelites, Assyrians, Persians and Romans – with Amjad interspersing archaeological information with political comment as we walked.

Amjad studied chemical engineering and this caused him problems.

'People here have a picture of chemical engineering students as people who make bombs, who blow themselves up. So at the checkpoint when they ask me what I study I say civil engineering. Once I said chemical engineering and they held me for three hours. Once when I was looking for a flat, the owner said to me, "What are you studying?" I said, "Chemical engineering." He said, "I am very sorry."'

Amjad thought that Abu Mazen would win the election because the Americans and the Israelis supported him. He himself supported the DFLP candidate. Like the PFLP, the DFLP had its origins in Communism but differed in that they aimed at a Palestinian state built along the 1967 boundary, whereas the PFLP took the more hardline stance that it should be defined by the 1948 boundary.

'But we must all deal as one,' he said. 'We must have just one leader, although for those who have prisoners or martyrs in their family it will be hard when they see Abu Mazen shake hands with Sharon.'

Despite the difficulties of the occupation Amjad felt that in at least one respect Palestinians were in a better situation than those in other Arab countries – they were free to vote as they wanted. 'I am against the PA and I am against Hamas. But that's OK. It's no problem for me.'

Before I left Amjad took me into his father's shop, an area

about the size of a tennis court, its shelves crammed with all manner of souvenirs, ranging from labelled antiquities to picture postcards. Next door was his restaurant, with seating for seventy. All the chairs stood upended on the tables. Both shop and restaurant had a still, abandoned air. No client had set foot in them for four years.

On the day of the presidential election I was back in Nabi Elias. In the morning I went to the polling booth in the village school with Rasmiya and Shatha. After they had voted their thumbs were marked with indelible ink to ensure that they wouldn't be able to vote again. As we were leaving, a carload of Israeli women from Machsom Watch arrived. We spoke with one of them, Ruth, who told us that they were extending their usual checkpoint activity to the election to make sure that there was no Israeli obstructionism blocking Palestinians from their electoral rights. She suggested we might meet up some time and gave me her phone number.

I spent the rest of the day on a visiting spree with Rasmiya. We started with her friend Afaf, one of the few remaining members of the only Christian family in the Qalqilya region. I was curious to know what it was like being part of such a vanishingly small minority group. It was no problem, Afaf said, offering as proof the fact that she had just been elected to the town council with the second highest number of votes. She pressed *halwiyat* on us and gave us each a plate with five pieces of fruit on it.

Our next visit was to the house of man who had just been released from prison. He had an interesting story about being set up by a collaborator, said Rasmiya, and she wanted me to hear it. We sat stiffly on straight-backed chairs in a very cold room with his wife and other family members but the man didn't put in an appearance. Again we were given *halwiyat* and a plate with five pieces of fruit. After waiting an hour, we moved on to a household of Rasmiya's nephews and nieces who plied us with stuffed olives soaked in brine, the tart taste a welcome change after so much sugary *halwiyat*. The last visit was to an aunt whose husband had just died. Other mourners were already there, sitting on the floor, their legs covered with blankets. We joined them. The widow was worried because she had no children and feared that the children of her husband's first wife would now take the house from her. Her guests murmured advice and reassurance.

No one had seemed very interested in the election, perhaps because the result was pretty much a foregone conclusion.

Back at the house later we watched as the results were dissected on television. Abu Mazen soon emerged as the winner. 'He will be assassinated within a year,' predicted Shatha.

The relaxation of travel restrictions continued for another couple of days. I took advantage of this to try to visit Azzoun Atmeh, a village about six miles from Nabi Elias and strictly out of bounds for curious foreigners.

Azzoun Atmeh lay two miles to the east of the Green Line and was therefore within the West Bank. But it also lay close to several Jewish settlements, and the Separation Barrier, which cut into Palestinian territory in many places to bring such settlements back into the territorial embrace of Israel, also snaked round to the east of Azzoun Atmeh. The village was thus completely cut off from the rest of the West Bank, the only access to it being through a checkpoint. Entry and exit were controlled by the Israeli army between six a.m. and ten p.m.. The village residents could come and go during this time; anyone else – friends, family members – needed special permission. The rest of the time the gate was closed, the residents banged up overnight like prisoners in their cells. The village was isolated from its homeland like a strangulated hernia.

I had got to know Ashraf, a young man from Azzoun Atmeh who worked in a shop in Nabi Elias. He offered to take me to the village.

We took a taxi first from Nabi Elias to Azzoun where Ashraf had to leave his car every day – because of the usual kind of board game obstacle connected with zones, he wasn't allowed to take his car into Nabi Elias. When we arrived at the Azzoun Atmeh checkpoint Ashraf quickly jumped out and spoke to the soldiers before they could come round to me. A few minutes later he got back into the car, having convinced the soldiers that I was an international observer on election business, and we passed through the gate.

About 1,500 people lived in Azzoun Atmeh. The houses were mostly greyish beige in the older cuboid style. As we drove in Ashraf pointed to a stretch of modern houses along the periphery. They belonged to the settlement of Sharei Tikva and shared their back fences with the gardens of the Palestinians.

Azzoun Atmeh had previously thrived on its main activity which was vegetable cultivation. It had first lost much of its farming land when it was appropriated for the building of Sharei Tikva. More recently it had been affected by the logistical difficulties involved in cultivating the crops and getting them to market in the restrictive circumstances. We stopped to talk with Majid, Ashraf's neighbour, in his greenhouse. He had one and a half dunums of land. Previously he had another eight dunums which had been taken for the settlement.

Driving on we came to a pile of boulders which blocked the road. At the other side of the boulders, at right angles to the village road, lay a highway which led to Sharei Tikva and was for the sole use of the settlers. At the other side of the highway lay nine Palestinian houses, cut off not only from the West Bank like their fellow villagers but from the village itself. Their only access was by foot. The highway had in the past been the villagers' direct route to Nablus, with a journey time of thirty-five minutes. Now they had to use an inferior, circuitous route with a journey time of one and a half hours.

Four young men who had been lounging around in the back of a pick-up came over to talk to us. They crowded round eagerly. They were all unemployed. The sight of a foreigner in their midst was probably their highlight of the week. 'Is Azzoun Atmeh a beautiful place?' they asked me. What could

I say? One of them introduced himself as Osama and pulled up his shirt to show me his battle scars – bullet wounds on both sides of the chest and in the stomach. He claimed that he had never engaged in any kind of militant activity, not even throwing stones. He had simply been caught in cross-fire. They had all voted for Abu Mazen, they said, and were hopeful that his election heralded peace.

After we had left, Osama came running after us. He had forgotten to show me something, he said, and pushed aside his hair to show me a bullet wound in his head.

On the way back to the checkpoint we passed a demolished building, a heap of stone and concrete bristling with twisted reinforcement bars, a warped bath sitting atop it all. A young man was poking about in it with a hammer. Ashraf stopped the car and we got out. 'This is Omar,' he said to me. 'This is his house.'

Omar was one of a number of people in the village whose houses had been demolished by the Israeli army, having fallen foul of yet another of the zonal traps. Although the village was in Zone B, the edge of it was in Zone C in which Palestinians needed a permit from the Israelis if they wanted to build. With no more land available in the Zone B area of the village, and with permits not being forthcoming, some people had gone ahead with construction – following which the Israeli army arrived with bulldozers and knocked the houses down. 'The soldiers came,' Omar said. 'They told us to get out. They didn't give us any warning, they didn't let us take anything, they just knocked the house down.' He was now trying to get in to rescue his belongings. It was a fruitless task. The pile of stone and concrete was impregnable. We left him hacking disconsolately at it with his hammer.

CHAPTER 11

After the election I went back to Jerusalem to spend more time there. I was beginning to find the Palestinian lifestyle claustrophobic and monochrome. I booked into a hotel in East Jerusalem, near the Mount of Olives.

Shortly after I arrived I met up with Ruthie again for lunch in Dishes. We got our food and sat down.

'Give me your hands, we're going to pray.' Ruthie grasped my hands in her own and bowed her head. 'I thank you Lord for sending Hilda and for bringing her here today, and we thank you for this food set before us and we wait here in your own blessed city for the return of the Messiah. Amen.'

'What do the Palestinians think about Abu Mazen?' she asked me. Without waiting for an answer she gave me her own thoughts.

'Abu Mazen is the best person to carry out God's plan. God said there would be a false peace of seven years and Abu Mazen will help to bring this about. But in the middle of it, all hell's going to break loose with war.'

I wondered how there could be a peace for seven years if war was going to break out after three and a half. Ruthie carried on. 'Abu Mazen fits in with God's plan but he doesn't know it because the Palestinians don't know the word of God because they're in a false religion. By the way, did you know there's a demonstration outside the Knesset just now? People sleeping in tents to protest about withdrawing from the settlements in Gaza?'

'No, I didn't. I haven't heard anything about it on the news.'

'I know, they don't tell you this sort of thing. You see, the Jewish people are descended from Isaac so they are meek and mild. They're more peaceful than the Arabs because the Arabs are descended from Ishmael. That doesn't mean that God doesn't love them,' she added hastily. 'He does love them all. I understand both sides and I feel sorry for them both. Read Isaiah chapter 28, verses 14–18, about the leader yielding to lies. It's about him now, Sharon, because he's yielded to this lie that the Road Map is the way to peace, even though it divides Jerusalem. It won't lead to peace, it will be a false peace, and after three and a half years Jerusalem will be surrounded by armies of all nations. Read Hosia chapter 4, verse 6. God says there my people are destroyed from lack of knowledge. Let's face it, the Jews are peaceful because of Isaac. Ishmael had to be rough and tough to survive in the wilderness so he was born with that nature and so are his sons, the Arabs.'

Ruthie had been shooting off at several different tangents. I brought her back to her claim that Jewish people were meek and mild. I had more often found that the Israelis were not very approachable, unlike the Palestinians who were almost invariably friendly.

'Well, yeah, I guess, sometimes they are. I spoke to an Israeli about that and he said, "Lady, if you'd been bombed as often as we have you'd be suspicious too." But generally there's no problem. Once I was going to Bethlehem and I forgot to take my passport. At the checkpoint I said to the soldier, "Oh honey, I've forgotten my passport." And the soldier said to me, "Well, I guess I'm gonna have to shoot you then." Wasn't that cute? So you see, there's good in everybody.'

Ruthie had moved out of the Jaffa Gate Hostel and was now living in a guest house run by the Church of Scotland. She was keen to show me her upgraded circumstances. We went back there after lunch.

The two double bunk beds of her room were strewn with all the paraphernalia of her previous one, plus some extra stuff that she had acquired in the interim. As soon as we entered she laid her hands on my head and started an impromptu prayer. 'Repeat this after me,' she ordered. 'Lord Jesus, I invite you into my heart, I believe in you, I believe you will come again to reign over heaven and earth, I believe that the last days are near...' She reeled off a list of things I was supposed to believe in, thankfully without waiting for me to repeat any of them. She changed gear. 'I ask you, Lord Jesus, to drive out of her every devil, every hex, every curse, every voodoo. I ask you to mend her of a broken heart, to bring her to your bosom, to bring to her the light of understanding, so that she may be gathered into heaven with the righteous and worship you for all eternity. Amen.'

I'd been feeling increasingly uncomfortable with all this. As she finished I gave a forced laugh. 'That sounded very nice,' I said lamely. She gave me a roguish look. 'The Lord's been talking to me about laying hands on you.'

The next day I went to the Knesset to talk with the protesting settlers. The road outside was lined with tents. Inside the tents people seemed to be running classes of some sort.

I approached several people and asked if they spoke English. They all said no and didn't show any interest in communicating by trying, for example, to find someone who did.

In the queue at a refreshment stall I finally managed to speak with a young Russian woman who lived in a West Bank settlement. She had come from Russia eight years previously, immediately after finishing school. She came, she said, because Israel was the only place where a Jew could live life fully. She was pleasant and willing to talk, but her English was too limited for us to be able to explore her ideas further.

At the other side of the road I saw a woman carrying a sign written in English. I went over to her. She turned out to be Australian. On her head was a paper hat with the words: *Sharon's solution – missile-proof headgear.* She was pushing a toddler in a stroller bearing the words: *Sharon's solution – missile-proof strollers.* The signs, she said, were a response to Sharon's advice that the Gaza settlers should strengthen the roofs of their houses to resist Palestinian missile attacks. 'This is not the solution. He has to stop terrorism itself.'

She had come from Australia fifteen years previously and

loved the life in the settlement despite the restrictions. 'We have a very full life. There's lots to do. Most people go to work in Israel every day anyway.'

Her belief in the biblical stories about God giving the land to the Jews was absolute. I put to her the difficulties that arise in taking biblical accounts literally.

'How do you explain, for example, that people in Genesis supposedly lived for hundreds of years? Adam's son is said to have built a city but where did the inhabitants come from if Adam and Eve were the first human beings?'

'Some of these things worry me,' she conceded, 'but I think there is another dimension of understanding that can explain them. It's just that we don't at present have access to it.' She gave me a farewell nod although I hadn't indicated that I wanted to bring the conversation to an end. 'Enjoy your stay.'

Later that day I sauntered down one of the lanes in the Christian quarter of the Old City. A voice rang out as I passed a falafel café. 'Hi baby, hey, come in.' It was Ruthie. She put her arm round me. 'Hilda, this is Samir. He makes the best falafel in the whole of Jerusalem. He's a Christian, he's one of us. Sit down and join us. We're watching this video of Benny Hinn. D'ya know Benny Hinn?'

I didn't.

'Aw, honey, you gotta get to know Benny. He's a preacher, a healer, a real miracle worker. Born in Jaffa. He came to Tel Aviv last year. Samir went to see him. Now just you watch this.'

We sat on metal stools at a formica table. The café was about the size of a horse box, the air thick with the smell of stale cooking oil. From the television high on the back wall Benny Hinn worked himself up into a paroxysm of religious fervour.

'Samir goes to the Church of England,' Ruthie told me. 'Praise the Lord!'

I tried to ask him if he believed what the Bible said about the land belonging to the Jews but he evaded the question. 'We're all waiting for Jesus the Messiah to return here,' he said. 'You want to know what I think of the Palestinians?' He bent to whisper in my ear. 'They are crazy.'

I tried my questions about the literal interpretation of the Bible on Ruthie.

'Ruthie, surely you don't believe that Methuselah and all these people lived for hundreds of years.'

'Yes, I do, honey. They had to live for a long time then to populate the earth. That's why.'

'What about Adam's son's city then? How could there be enough people to populate a city when there was nobody in the world but Adam and Eve and their children?'

'Well, you see, honey, Adam and Eve lived for a long time so they produced enough children for a city. They had to create all the population of the earth so they had lots of children and these children all married each other and had lots more children. That's how it happened. It's the word of God. That tsunami, that was God's judgement on those who don't heed the word of God. The Trade Centre, that was God's judgement. The four hurricanes also. That's God saying: You get down on your knees to me.'

'How do you know this isn't just an idea generated inside your head?'

'Because we know God's word. It says in the Bible, the Holy Ghost will teach you all things and bring them to your remembrance. Amen. Amen.'

The next morning I took a minibus to Hebron to visit the mosque Ibrahimi. The mosque is built over what is believed to be the family burial ground of Abraham and, as such, is sacred to both Muslims and Jews. The building is divided into two parts, one for Muslims and the other for Jews.

As I got out of the minibus in the centre of town I asked a young man for directions to the mosque.

'I'll take you there,' he said. 'Come with me.'

He took me down a side street and then into another minibus. I was a bit puzzled because I'd thought that the mosque was within walking distance. I grew even more puzzled when I found that the minibus was taking us away out into the suburbs of Hebron. In the meantime Iyad was telling me the story of his life. He was twenty-six, married to Shaddia who was four years younger, had four brothers and one sister, and worked nights in a bakery in Jerusalem. 'Would you like to come home with me?' he asked. I hesitated. To refuse seemed churlish. On the other hand, I was by now in the middle of nowhere and had no idea if this man was telling me the truth. For all I knew he might be about to mug me. I decided to give him the benefit of the doubt.

We got off the bus and went down a narrow alley. He pushed open a gate, led me in, and there, to my relief, were his wife, his mother, his brothers and sisters, his mother-in-law and his grandmother. We all sat on mattresses on the floor and tea, coffee and cakes were handed round.

I asked them what they thought about their new president, Mahmoud Abbas. The grandmother, a tiny woman in a leopard-skin-patterned dress, black socks and brown cardigan, raised her eyes to heaven. The others were equally unenthusiastic. But other than a disenchantment with politics, they seemed to be untouched by the conflict. They had no problems with Jews or the army, they said, only the problems that go with having no work and not enough money.

Iyad said that he and his wife would go with me to the mosque. Shaddia put her coat on and we got into a taxi.

Security at the mosque was stringent. At the first barrier a soldier made a phone call to check Iyad's identity card. He rifled through Shaddia's handbag, took her perfume and makeup from her and stowed them away among the sandbags which formed a protective wall around the sentry post. We passed through a metal detector. Shaddia set off the alarm. She had to pass through several times before it was discovered that the source was the buckles on her boots. There was a second barrier at the door of the mosque. Although Iyad's ID had already been cleared, the soldier told him that it had to be checked again and that it would take some time. He ordered Shaddia and me to go into the mosque.

'No,' I said. 'These are my friends and they've brought me

here. We're all going in together. The ID has already been checked. What do you need to do it again for?'

The soldier ignored the question.

The weather was bitter. Iyad, who had been working all night and should have been in bed asleep at this time, looked tired, cold and wretched. We waited for about half an hour. A female soldier we had dealt with earlier, who had been joking with some Palestinian children and taking photos of them with her mobile, came by. I complained to her. She spoke to the aggressive soldier, then came back to say that Iyad could go in if he left his ID with the soldier. He refused. A Palestinian will never agree to being separated from his ID. The loss of it would cause too much trouble. As the mosque would soon be closing for prayers Shaddia and I finally went in, leaving Iyad shivering outside.

By the time Shaddia and I had taken off our shoes in the entrance hall Iyad had joined us, the soldier having finally capitulated. I put on one of the black hooded cloaks made available for unveiled females and we went inside.

In the central area, standing behind metal grilles, were the biers of Abraham and his wife and sons, covered in a black and gold material. At the further side were a second set of grilles through which the biers could be viewed from the Jewish synagogue. The biers were empty, the bodies being buried in caves far below.

I took some photos of Iyad and Shaddia standing in front of the grilles and then we said goodbye. I was going to visit the adjacent synagogue which they were not allowed to enter, and Iyad needed to get some sleep.

CHAPTER 12

Ruthie had suggested that I should meet a couple of people she knew, Grant and Barbara, Canadian evangelists who had been living in Israel for about thirty years.

'They hold a prayer meeting in the YMCA once a week,' she said. 'Just go along. They'll be able to tell you all you want to know about God and the Jews and the Bible.'

I went along and found them easily enough from Ruthie's description – a couple in their eighties, the man with a hook hand.

We settled down round a table in the dining room. There was just one other person, Dorothy, a Christian Zionist[5] I had already met in Dishes.

We ordered coffee and toasted cheese sandwiches. Barbara, a feisty woman with a thick hank of long grey hair, proceeded to tell me the story of their lives.

Barbara had been in Israel in the 1960s, working at the Canadian embassy in Tel Aviv. Back in Canada she started to study the Bible. 'The miracle of the creation of present day Israel convinced me that God was a miracle worker,' she explained. 'That was the beginning of my born-again Christian life. I wanted to seek God and I started a correspondence course on the Bible. I was working as a receptionist in a very fancy bar in British Columbia and I was trying to find God, sitting with the owner who was an alcoholic, and she was tossing back these scotch on the rocks because she could feel the presence of God as I was reading the Bible.' She quoted the Book of Joel about the Lord's army marching across the land and told me about a woman who had been cured of leukaemia and a motorcycle maniac whose troubled marriage had been healed, in both cases because they had been born again.

By this time she had met and married Grant who shared her religious and political beliefs.

'We were standing with the Jewish community in Vancouver when the UN declared that Zionism was racist. As Christians we wanted to stand up for the Jewish people and their rights according to the Bible. We took part in demonstrations. What was that song that we used to sing, Grant?'

'Oh bless Israel, Yeshua,' said Grant in his gravelly voice.

'Ah yes, that's right. I remember now.'

Barbara sang one of the verses and Grant started complaining about the wimpishness of those who were failing to stand up for the rights of Israel. 'Iran is the current danger for Israel. Here it is.' He pointed to an article in the Jerusalem Post which he had been reading while Barbara and I talked. 'Iran will be nuclear this year but the gutless left is preventing Israel doing what she did in 1981 when she bombed the nuclear facility in Iraq. God gave to Esther and the Jewish people the authority to kill all the people who would destroy the Jews. And when they have exercised this power they have succeeded and when they have neglected to exercise it they have suffered terribly.'

He told a string of anecdotes to illustrate the perfidy of the West during the conflict with Lebanon.

Barbara broke in. 'Grant, I think you're telling Hilda more than she wants to know.' Grant rambled on.

'The American State Department is the enemy of Israel. Israel should have told them to go jump in the Potomac but it didn't, it was trembling in its shoes. The yellow-bellied rascals who ran Associated Press didn't rescue Terry Anderson. The PLO were capturing random civilians in streets and draining them of all their blood for transfusions for their wounded fighters. Just rounded them up and took them in. Your British newspaper, *The Guardian*, it was captured by the KGB and used as a vehicle for Soviet propaganda. I suspect it's still owned by the communists.'

Barbara interrupted again.

'Hilda, why don't you come and stay with us for a few days? We'd love to have you.'

'Where do you live?' I asked.

'Ariel.'

I was amazed. Ariel is a settlement in the West Bank, one of the biggest. I hadn't imagined that non-Jews could live there.

Barbara put me straight. There was a community of about forty Christians and Messianic Jews in Ariel, she said. She and Grant had been among the first when they moved there about twelve years previously.

'They were very welcoming,' she said. 'It was a very young population and the children had no grandparents around because they were all in New York or Russia or Poland or wherever. They had been praying about this when we thought about moving there. And, you know, the Israelis know that evangelical Christians support them. So it worked out very well for everyone.'

Three days later I was sitting in Grant and Barbara's kitchen. Their house was in a terraced row called The British Cottages. 'Because of their style,' explained Barbara, offering me a plate of digestive biscuits and ginger snaps.

I had hesitated before deciding to take up their offer of hospitality. They had asked very little about my reasons for being in Jerusalem, assuming, I supposed, that I shared their views. Although they knew that I was planning to write a book, they had no idea that I had just spent four months in the West Bank. I wondered how they would react if I told them but I didn't want to take the risk. The opportunity to visit a settlement was too much of a godsend.

The journey from Jerusalem had been straightforward. A bus from the Central Bus Station in West Jerusalem had sped over the settler bypass roads, unhindered by checkpoints. Arriving at the *Merkaz* – the central shopping area in Ariel, I stepped off and into what could have been small town America. A short taxi ride through quiet suburban roads with well-tended gardens took me to the house.

'There was a strange-looking man on the bus,' I told Barbara and Grant later. 'He looked as if he might have been South-East

Asian, something like that. Brown skin, squarish face and kind of Asiatic features. But he was wearing a Jewish skull cap.'

'Oh, that must have been one of the Peruvian Jews,' said Barbara. 'There's a community of them in Ofra, that's a settlement not far from here. The Jewish Agency went over to Peru and brought them back.'

Anyone, it seemed, could convert to Judaism, thereby gaining the right to immigrate to Israel. Not surprisingly, a number of people living in less than satisfactory conditions in their own countries were taking advantage of this. The Jewish Agency, Barbara explained, sought out Jews from all over the world and encouraged them to move to Israel in order to bolster up the Jewish population. There was a fear that without this sort of measure the number of Arab-Israeli residents in the country would increase disproportionately, diluting the Jewishness of the state.

'You see, the Arabs have a higher birthrate than the Jews,' grumbled Grant. 'If nothing's done about it then Israel's going to be overrun with them. Out of the present Israeli population of five million, more than one million are Arab already.'

Barbara was no slouch when it came to networking.

'Now, Hilda, I'd like you to come with me when I go to visit Elizabeth this afternoon. She's a Christian from Alabama. She's been living here for two months and I think you'll find her very interesting. Then there's Jerry and Sylvia from New York. They're secular Jews. And there's a Ukrainian family we're very friendly with. We'll drop in and see them some time. Then on Saturday night there's the shabat prayer meeting at David and Leah's. You must meet David and Leah.'

I was surprised to hear that there were secular Jews in a settlement.

'Oh, you'll find there are a lot of non-religious Jews in Ariel,' said Barbara. 'They come because they can have a better life. It's cheaper. The air's better.'

'I think before you and Hilda go out we should say a prayer,' rumbled Grant. He and Barbara took one of my hands each and we stood in a circle.

'Thank you, Lord, for Hilda's visit,' Grant intoned. 'We beseech you to make it a fruitful experience for her and we ask you humbly to give her the help she needs so that she may further the cause of Israel and the works of the Lord.'

'Amen,' said Barbara.

'Amen,' I said, not wanting to ruffle my hosts' feathers by distancing myself from both the concept of prayer and the aims expressed in this one.

Grant heaved a great sigh and dropped my hand. 'You know, when I came to Israel I could look every Israeli soldier in the eye because I could say to him, "I am fighting with you in prayer just as you are fighting in the field."'

Elizabeth lived just up the road from Barbara and Grant in a block of flats inhabited mostly by Russians.

'Elizabeth has leukaemia,' Barbara explained as we walked along. 'But she's fine, all praise to the Lord.'

Elizabeth had not only leukaemia but also a very bad dose of the flu. Despite these two ailments she was full of energy and talked non-stop for several hours. Her only sign of physical weakness was a chalk-white face.

She was cock-a-hoop because the Lord had that morning revealed himself to her as the Keeper of Hearts.

'It started last night,' she said. 'I was out in the garden and I saw this delicate little bird, a tiny little bird, a hummingbird. It was the cutest, the sweetest, the most perfect little bird. And I said, "Oh Lord, don't you look at this hummingbird and feel pleased with yourself for having created it?" Then after that I had some smoked salmon for supper. It was the tenderest, the tastiest, the most delicious smoked salmon.' She smacked her lips and rolled her eyes. 'And I said, "Oh thank you, Lord, for having created this. Thank you, Lord, for all your wonderful creation." This morning I was thinking again about those wondrous things, the dainty little bird, the exquisite smoked salmon, the countless gifts that shower upon us from heaven, and I was thanking the Lord again, and that's when the Lord revealed himself to me as the Keeper of Hearts.'

'What did he mean by that?' I asked.

'God hates violent hearts. He means that he cares about the hurting, about those that cry out to him, but those who go in for violence and murder and hatred, here in his own chosen land, well... But I believe the gospel of Christ is now reaching out to the Arabs. The movie *The Passion* has affected Islamic people. They come away with questions about Jesus, this Jew. There's a shift in attitude in a positive direction. In the United Arab Emirates a cinema complex was so jampacked they had to shut down movies in the other theatres just to let in people who wanted to see it.'

We were straight away caught up in vigorous religious debate. I'd put forward an idea that I remembered from my Catholic education about evil being defined as the absence of good, the reason being that God had created everything and, as he couldn't by his very nature create evil, evil must simply be a kind of hole in the moral universe.

Elizabeth was having none of it. Her Bible lay at her side, the open pages liberally highlighted with every available shade of marker pen. She flicked through it.

'Here we are, Isaiah 54 verse 16: "Did I not create evil?" Satan is real! Satan was the praise and worship leader in heaven, he was covered in sapphires and lights, but he rebelled and he is at work in the world today, tempting us down with him into the pits of hell.'

Elizabeth was a Pentecostalist, one of the born-again Christians who believe that they have been baptised by the Holy Spirit, an experience supposedly accompanied by the gift of tongues. The idea stems from the New Testament story in which the Holy Spirit appeared as flames of fire on the heads of the apostles, transmitting to them the ability to speak other languages so that they could go out and preach to other nations.

'How did you know you had been baptised by the Holy Spirit?' I asked.

'Because I started speaking in tongues.'

'What language did you find you could speak?'

'Oh, it's not a known language. The Holy Spirit takes hold of you and puts words into your head. You don't know what you're saying, you just say the words you feel compelled to say.'

'So how did this manifest itself?'

'I'd been praying and praying and opening my heart up to the Lord and then I heard myself saying *shonda, shonda*. Over and over again. *Shonda, shonda*. And I knew I'd received the blessing of the Holy Spirit. I was speaking in tongues. I'd been born again. Thank you, Lord.'

The conversation shifted kaleidoscopically as Elizabeth leaped from anecdote to anecdote with the agility of a mountain goat: Pat Boone, the Washington Red Socks, her father's death, her 'divine' appointment with a circuit court clerk in Alabama – all were grist to her conversational mill, linked by the common thread of religion.

'God has a reason for you being in Israel,' she assured me. 'This is a divine appointment.'

I asked her how she had ended up in Israel.

'I first came in 1998. I wasn't interested in churches and suchlike, only the land and the people. I linked up with a religious tour group and we witnessed as we went. We were camping out, in a 5,000 star hotel, you could say.' She laughed. 'One day the tour guide said to me: "Everywhere we go you're taking photos of soldiers." I said: "My heart goes out to these kids, they're protecting the land." The guide said: "Why don't you volunteer then?" I said: "I can do that?" Her voice peaked in a squawk of amazement. 'The guide said: "Sure. Just call them."

'I fasted and prayed about it and then I decided I was going to volunteer. I called Sarel, the army volunteer people, and went to their office in Jaffa. I had to get a medical check and a recommendation. I was fifty at the time. I had leukaemia even then but the doctor didn't ask and I didn't say anything. Next morning I was in an army base. They asked me what I wanted to do. I said: "What do the soldiers least want to do?" They said, "The kitchen." I said, "OK, I'll take that."

'You're helping soldiers to do what they do. So if you work in a kitchen, for example, you're helping the kids. They're not going to put you in the line of fire in Nablus, of course. You're a guest. It encourages the soldiers, it's a good will gesture, sitting around at night drinking coffee and talking with people. American volunteers are very industrious and organized. The Israelis are more laid back. They're in a life and death situation all the time so they're not so concerned about non-essentials.'

Elizabeth had enjoyed the experience so much she enlisted again a few years later.

'I was here for longer that time, four months, so I worked in several different bases. I was in the kitchen at a signal jamming base, sorting uniforms that needed repairs at Tel Shamir, wiring radios for helmets somewhere else. I loved it. I remember sitting in a big huge mess hall and the soldiers opposite were looking at me, not very friendly. One said: "Are you paid?" I said: "No. Young man, I buy my ticket on El Al and they pay me no money. I'm here because I love Israel." You should have seen the change on his face. Then the whole bunch were friendly and smiling. "Are you Jewish?" they asked. "No," I said, "I'm Christian." "Why do you care?" they asked. I told them "Because I'm behind you. I want to stand with you."

'Do you see that army base up there?' She pointed to the top of a nearby hill. 'It was put there because suicide bombers were coming from an Arab village near here. There were two suicide bombers at the hotel in Ariel. I can see the base from my window here. I sit and look at it and pray for the soldiers. I love organization and military things. Even when I was a child, the fourth of July, all the military pomp, I loved it all.' She swung her arms in a marching movement. Then she picked up a photo from a shelf and handed it to me. It was Elizabeth in army uniform, surrounded by a batch of smiling Israeli soldiers. 'I love the Israeli army,' she said. 'They're my babies.'

Elizabeth had visited Ariel during her first stint with the Israeli army.

'When I saw the signs for Ariel and the mountains with the white rock, I was smitten. The neat way the city is put round the *merkaz*, the swimming pool for the kids, the bougainvillea. I just fell in love with the place. And over there in Shilo was the tent where God met with Moses and Abraham. There's a synagogue there now on the site. We went over towards Nablus as well. We couldn't go into the city of course, but the guide pointed out Jacob's well from a distance high up. I'm like, oh my gosh! You just can't believe all the Bible history here. And they want to give it away! They've got to be crazy.'

'But surely the secular Jews don't believe their forefathers were promised the land by God?

'Well they do, sort of. Jews are a very particular society because of the diaspora. There's this social Jewishness. There's this Jewishness of being descended from Abraham, Isaac and Jacob. The Arabs came through another line. You see, Abraham's wife Sarah was barren so she agreed to Abraham having a child with their maid Hagar. The child they had was Ismail and the Arabs are all descended from him. But after that Sarah got pregnant and they had Isaac, and that's who the Jews are descended from. So you see, all this trouble today with Islam stems from Abraham's relationship with Hagar, and Sarah agreed to it. Thank you very much, Sarah!' She jerked her head sharply in reprobation. 'The Bible is a history fact book, God's history of the world as he created it. It tells you what God wants us to know.'

The next morning, as it was Friday, Barbara decided we should go to the merkaz to see all the hustle and bustle of the pre-*shabat* shopping.

'We'll just wait till Sivka comes,' she said. 'I'd like you to meet him.'

Sivka was their landlord. He was coming to take some measurements. 'He's very talented,' Barbara said. 'His work is something to do with maths and science. He's very musical too. The first time he came to the house he picked up the guitar and started playing 1960s music. I said that I really like country and western and he started playing some numbers. Singing too. He knew all the words.'

Sivka was small and Arab-looking. He was a Yemeni Jew whose parents had come to Jerusalem in 1942.

We'd been talking about the Peruvian Jews in Ofra. I asked Sivka what he thought of them. 'They have foggy roots,' he said, shaking his head. 'Very foggy. To be Jewish means "next year in Jerusalem" all down the years. But, you know, even the Russians who come here, only about thirty per cent of them are Jewish.'

Barbara and I left Sivka and Grant and drove up to the *merkaz*.

The hustle and bustle Barbara had promised me wasn't particularly spectacular, and apart from the skull caps on many of the men's heads there was little sign of overt religiosity. We stocked up with fruit and vegetables and headed towards the bakery.

'Hey, shalom! What a coincidence!'

Barbara had stopped short at a table outside one of the cafés where an elderly American couple were sitting.

'Hilda, meet Jerry and Sylvia. Now isn't this convenient. We were planning to catch up with you guys over the weekend. Hilda, why don't you just sit down and have a chat with Jerry and Sylvia while I go and do the rest of the shopping.'

I sat down.

Jerry had been reading *The Jerusalem Post*. 'Did you see this?' he asked. 'Two Palestinian terrorists released this morning. It's not the Arabs I'm afraid of. It's the Israeli government.' He tossed the paper down on the table where it lay open at an announcement about a forthcoming demonstration against the withdrawal from the Gaza Strip. Sharon's minority government, it declared, was established as an act of wickedness for a single purpose – to expel the Jews, succumb to terror and suppress the will of the voter and of democracy.

Jerry and Sylvia told me that they had come to Israel on vacation in 1987 and decided then that they would move there. They finally did so in 1995 when they were both sixty-four.

'It was a spiritual feeling,' Jerry said. He stared hard at me through small round tortoiseshell glasses, his stubbly face shaded by the peak of a blue and white striped cap. 'A very deep and significant feeling. It was just a feeling that this is where we belong.'

'For me it was a political thing,' Sylvia said. 'This land belongs to the Jewish people, and if you want to make that happen you've got to be here.'

Jerry agreed. 'This is Israel,' he said, speaking not only of Ariel but of the whole of the West Bank in which it was situated. 'It is not disputed territory, it is not occupied territory, it is Israel. We feel it has been a rewarding experience, being able to contribute. We felt like pioneers. In New York financially speaking we were doing OK, we were well fixed, but we were terribly unhappy living there. We gave up quite a lot as far as materialism is concerned to come here, but it didn't matter to us.

'But you say that neither of you are religious, so why this spiritual feeling?'

'It's true that we were quite secular, in our families, in our childhoods. We believe in God but we don't pursue this belief in a religious manner, we don't attend the synagogue. But I feel one can become possessed by a strong feeling of duty, of belonging. When we came in 1987 we spent practically the whole month in Jerusalem, integrating ourselves with the people on a day in, day out basis. During that time Sylvia and I looked at each other and, it was almost a simultaneous feeling, we realized this was home, where we belonged.'

In 1997 Jerry and Sylvia had to go back to New York to deal with some business matter.

'We allowed six weeks for this,' Jerry continued. 'As it turned out, it was concluded in about ten days, which afforded us four weeks' free time. It was an astonishing experience in the sense that we had spent all our lives in New York, where you can find a multitude of enjoyment, yet we felt very unenthusiastic. We felt lost. We contacted the airline, changed our tickets and flew back to Israel immediately. We saw friends and family, but then there was a compelling desire to come home which superseded the other feelings.

'And there's something I want to say about family feelings here compared with the US. Here parents and children are more united, they're more bonded in Israel than in the US. In the US you almost have to make an appointment when married children see their parents. In 1987 we would spend evenings in Ben Yehuda mall, sitting in cafés, and you would see parents walk arm in arm with their children, a sight you never saw in the US.'

I'd been surprised to find that many of the people living in the settlement were not religious.

'You don't need to be religious to want to live in Israel,' Jerry explained. 'Ariel is secular. There are religious people here, there are synagogues, but some places may be open on *shabat*. You can drive on *shabat*. You don't find that in the religious settlements. There are stores in Ariel that sell non-kosher products because there is a large Russian population. You can even find pork. The older people in the Soviet Union couldn't get kosher stuff because there was no religion. In our language classes the teacher had to teach not only Hebrew but how to be Jewish. The Russian people didn't know what it was to be Jewish.

'Sylvia and I are not believers but many of our friends here are believers. We have accepted one another. Here people are very open. At the first holiday about six or seven people invited us. They knew we had no family here. It's the same every holiday. They just feel you shouldn't be alone. That's just how Israeli people are.'

'What sort of solution do you see for the Palestinians?' I asked him. 'How do they fit in with all this?'

'If he knew that he'd be prime minister,' said Sylvia. 'I don't see a solution.'

Barbara, who had just returned from the shops, chipped in. 'God has a solution.'

Jerry disagreed. 'We are beyond any answer, any solution, because of the unbelievable degree of violence and hatred here, because of the enormity of it. It's very difficult to conceive of any everyday way of life for both people. The hatred and violence have blocked us off from any reasonable reality. Just look at the way they celebrate. Normally when people celebrate they hug and they kiss, they dance, they partake of food and drink, but when you see Palestinians in a celebratory mood they are forever shooting guns in the air. It's a known fact that cannot be disputed that a Palestinian schoolchild is taught to hate Jews. Hatred is embedded in them from the moment they start school. Perhaps the answer is in the Bible where it says the Jews are God's chosen people. Perhaps one day that will be realized.'

When we got back to the house Sivka was still there. There was also a young couple with a small child. Sivka had put the house up for sale and the couple were prospective purchasers. Barbara's jaw dropped. This was the first she'd heard of it. Sivka assured them that there would be no undue pressure on them to move quickly. There were still several months of the lease to run.

'I am angry,' said Barbara after Sivka and the family left. She sat down. 'I am angry, I am angry, I am angry. We haven't been here very long, it's the fourth place we've had since we came to Ariel. If we have to move again, I'm going back to Canada.'

Grant rumbled some resigned and comforting comments. Barbara stood up abruptly as if she'd given herself a mental shake. 'I think we need to pray about this.'

We stood in a circle holding hands.

'We thank you Lord for the time we have spent in this lovely house and for guiding our steps in coming to Ariel. We ask you now to guide us in the decisions which we will have to take. We ask you to give us strength to cope with the trials which lie before us. If it is thy will for this young Jewish family to live here, then thy will be done.'

'Amen,' Grant and I chorused.

That evening Barbara and I went to a concert given by some of her Russian friends. The concert was held in their flat, in a small open-plan kitchen/living room which strained at the seams to accommodate the thirty or so people present, gathered round a white grand piano. The older ones had a kind of haggard look, raddled and careworn. On the wall were pictures of family friends of previous generations. 'That's Chopin,' whispered Barbara pointing to one of them. 'And that's Rubinstein. Henry comes from a long line of very famous musicians. All these people here tonight, it's the Russian aristocracy.'

Henry stood beside the piano, a tall man in evening dress with a soft voice and self-effacing mien, his shoulder-length black hair swept back from a high forehead. The concert, he said, was being held in memory of his father who had died twenty-five years previously. He sat down and crashed into the opening bars of a Rachmaninov piano concerto. A violinist from the Tel Aviv Orchestra followed, a man in his sixties, his bow dancing to the sounds of Paganini. Next was a series of duets with Henry's wife at the piano, a slim redhead dressed in black trousers and a black top which closed loosely at the back like a surgeon's operating gown.

Later we stood around with cake and drinks. I spoke with Anna, a chic young woman wearing a little black jacket, flared tartan mini skirt and black tights. She had come to Israel from St Petersburg when she was twenty-five. 'I couldn't stand it any longer in St Petersburg because of the anti-semitism,' she explained. 'Right from the time I was very little I was aware of it. At the nursery when I was just three I used to be taunted by a boy about being Jewish. I didn't want my daughter to experience that.'

'Are you a religious Jew?' I asked

'Well, I'm getting there.'

On the morning of *shabat* Barbara and I walked round to visit her Ukrainian friends. The names beside the doorbells of their apartment block were all in the Cyrillic alphabet.

Slava and Marina had been in Israel for eleven years and had two children, both of them born there. Slava was studying in Tel Aviv, doing a Ph.D. in fluid mechanics.

I asked why they had moved to Israel.

'Because life was very difficult in the Ukraine,' Slava said. 'Also because there was a lot of anti-semitism there. I couldn't study there. I didn't get into university because I failed one exam by one mark. My mother said to me, "You are Jewish so here in the Ukraine you will always fail by one mark." I've been back to visit the Ukraine just once but I wasn't happy when I was there. It was very distressing to see the poverty that they were still living in.'

Slava preferred Ariel to Tel Aviv.

'The air is cleaner here, it's quieter. But we may move later. When the children are older they will want more attractions.'

'What about crime?' I asked. 'I don't suppose there's much of that in Ariel.'

I was wrong. Slava and Barbara both had stories to tell of being burgled and Slava's car had been broken into. There was quite a problem with petty thieving, they said. Slava blamed the Palestinians. 'It's due to a drug problem. The Arabs in the villages around here, they sell drugs to young people in Ariel.'

Slava's son had been ill recently and had had to be rushed to hospital.

'Did he go to hospital in Ariel or in Israel?' I asked.

'This is Israel,' Slava said sharply, waving his arm at the land outside. He seemed irritated at my implication that Ariel wasn't in Israel.

I pressed him a bit on this. How, I asked, did he justify the Jews taking possession of this land.

'We lived here 2,000, 3,000 years ago. It wasn't our fault we had to leave. We have the right to come back.'

Barbara, sensing perhaps that the conversation was veering towards the confrontational, started telling a story about two tsunami survivors which had been emailed to her by a fellow evangelical as a demonstration of God's goodness to believers.

Speaking in a comical mixture of Hebrew and English for the benefit of Marina, whose English was poor, she told of the Malaysian brother and sister in Thailand who had felt compelled to sing a hymn about a great storm just before the tidal wave washed over them. The pair survived, suffering no more than the loss of the man's shoes. Slava and Marina, who didn't believe in any religion, appeared bemused by the story.

That evening we were to go to a *shabat* prayer meeting, the religious highlight of the week for Barbara and Grant and their co-religionists, celebrated on the Jewish sabbath rather than on the Christian Sunday.

'I have to drive over to Rosh Ha'ayin first to pick up Joanne,' Barbara said. 'Why don't you come with me?'

Off we went, speeding along the highway and into Israel after a friendly exchange of greetings with the soldiers at the checkpoint as we passed over the Green Line.

Joanne was American and had converted to Judaism when she married an Israeli in the early 1960s. Now divorced, she had switched to Messianic Judaism. Plying us with coffee and homemade brownies she filled us in on the latest details of a longstanding family drama as we sat at her breakfast bar.

We started back for Ariel, with Joanne in the front of the car beside Barbara talking nineteen to the dozen. 'Stop!' she cried suddenly. 'I want to witness. Stop! Stop!' Barbara rammed on the brakes and we skidded to a halt just in front of a group of Palestinians who were standing at the side of the road. 'I've got some leaflets with me,' Joanne explained. 'Whenever I see Palestinians I give them leaflets so that they can learn about the word of the Lord.' She brought a sheaf of papers out of her bag and opened the door. I jumped out after her, keen to witness this 'witnessing'. Joanne was thrusting her leaflets into the hands of the Palestinians, speaking to them in English about the love of Jesus. They appeared not to understand a word of what she said but accepted the leaflets politely.

Back in Ariel we picked up Grant and drove round to the flat where the prayer meeting was held. Barbara introduced me to everyone. The hosts were David, a Puerta Rican Pentecostalist pastor, and his wife Leah who was a Messianic Jew. There was also Leah's niece Tikva who was half Chinese, three Russian women, two Belgian men and Jerry and Sylvia who, although they weren't religious, came along for the social side of it.

After an opening prayer there was a singalong with Leah playing a guitar and the group singing from hymn sheets which had the words in both English and Hebrew. I shared a hymn sheet with Grant who was beside me on the sofa.

'Now this is the point at which we are all invited to give testimony,' David said when the strains of the last hymn had died away. 'I'd like to start off the testimonies this evening by telling you about an important piece of news.' Everyone looked at him expectantly. 'Last week I received a phone call from a Palestinian man in Norway. When I first met him he was with Hamas, they were training him how to use explosives, he was ready for action. They were preparing him to be a suicide bomber. They took him to a disco in Tel Aviv to show him what paradise would be like with the seventy virgins promised in the Koran. I gave him the Bible. He took it home, started reading it and right away he saw the light. He became a believer. He told his family and he was thrown out of his village, he was threatened with death, a fatwa was put on him. Then he was told that if he would go back to Islam he would be given a job with the Palestinian Authority, he could go back to his village, to his family and that would be the end of the matter. He refused and he managed to leave the country and get to Norway. He's travelled all over Norway. He travels three hours every Sunday to get to church. And he warns them about Islam. "Do you know, David," he said to me, "they don't understand about *jihad*. I tell them it means killing people."'

There were nods of assent from the group and some negative talk about Islam and about the Koran being difficult to understand because it was written in poetry. 'Anyway, the good news he had yesterday,' continued David, 'is that he's got permission to come to Israel to get his wife and take her to Norway. So she's going to be able to take that thing off her head,' David mimed throwing away a *hijab*, 'and go shopping for, oh, Calvin Klein.'

'Praise the Lord, allelujah,' cried the group.

Tikva then spoke for a few minutes about some thoughts she'd had triggered off by a passage she'd been reading in the Bible. Nobody else had anything to say.

'Well, then,' said David after a short silence, 'I'd like now to invite the sister from Scotland to say a few words to us about how she was saved.'

'Well actually, I haven't been saved. I'm just a visitor.' I quailed, thinking I was going to be either shown the door or subjected to a barrage of proselytising.

'Oh, that's all right,' said David. 'Welcome to Ariel.'

We moved on to the next item on the agenda, with David reading from the Bible and providing his own interpretations.

For the grand finale we all stood in a circle for more hymn singing. 'Tonight,' David announced, 'I'm going to invite Grant and Barbara to lead us in praising the Lord with a number that they've performed on television, on the 700 Club, on CNN, and on the BBC.'

Grant and Barbara straight away burst into exuberant song in a blend of strong contralto and gruff baritone, swinging their arms and swaying their torsos. The others followed their movements in an improvised hokey-cokey of religious fervour. In the crescendo of spiritual enthusiasm Barbara, despite her eighty-plus years, was practically break dancing.

When the singing came to an end we gathered round the table where a buffet supper had been laid out. I spoke with one of the Russian women while we queued for the salad. She was Russian Orthodox and used to attend the Russian Orthodox church in Jerusalem. 'I had to stop because of these Arab people on the road,' she told me. 'It's too dangerous to travel. So now I come here.'

I loaded up my plate and joined Tikva, a pleasant-looking girl of about nineteen or twenty. She had been in Ariel for eighteen months, living with David and Leah. She had first come to Israel through the Birthright programme, a project whereby any young Jewish person anywhere in the world can have a free visit to Israel. After this first visit she decided to leave the US and settle in Israel. She spent five months in Jerusalem following an absorption programme for Jewish immigrants and was now studying at the College of Judea and Samaria in Ariel.

'What was it that made you want to come?' I asked her.

'Well, I loved it here. I think I can have a good life, and I've got my aunt who's living here. But most of all it's to do with the fulfilment of the prophecies, about the Jews being scattered among the nations and being brought back to Israel. I feel part of that, and it's such a wonderful feeling.'

Hans, one of the Belgians, joined us. He had been staying in Ariel for a few months with his friend Peter whose wife was Jewish. Peter was a morose-looking man in a leather hat, of the type that Australians wear with corks hanging from the brim. Hans had been 'saved' only a few weeks previously. It had been through his contact with Grant and Barbara, he told me, and he was now receiving instruction from them.

We drifted back into one group, lured by stories that David was telling about miracles he'd seen on the 700 Club. 'There's no limit to the power of healing,' he said. 'There's nothing that's beyond the power of the Lord. There was this man whose head was almost cut off in an accident.'

Leah interrupted. 'No, that's not quite right. His skull was separated from his spinal cord.'

'Whatever. The man was believed to be a hopeless case. Now he's playing baseball again. Then there was this other man. Something sliced through his skull and his brain, now he's an A student. Same thing. The work of the Lord.'

'David's just called,' Barbara said when I went down for breakfast the next morning. 'He and Leah want us to go over and have lunch with them today. I think you'll enjoy that.'

'Yes, of course I will.'

'And Joanne phoned too. One of her grandsons is in hospital, in a coma. He was suddenly taken very ill last night and they don't know what it is yet. It was like flu or something. Anyway, he was very feverish and then at one point his father swore. Jews don't have swear words so when they swear they use Arabic swear words. When the child heard that his eyes rolled and he went into a coma.'

She laid a boiled egg in front of me. 'I get these from Hamid who lives in one of the villages near here. He has lovely eggs, with yellow yolks. The eggs here usually have pale yolks, but his are very yellow.'

I wondered how Barbara came to be consorting with a Palestinian, but Grant was already saying grace and straight afterwards plunged us into another exercise in biblical exegesis so I didn't get the chance to ask.

The three of us drove over to David and Leah's. Over lunch David told me about their life as Christians in Ariel. Originally a dental technician, he had become a pastor after being 'born again'.

'We came here twenty years ago. We bought this apartment and then the people in Ariel wanted us out. They said we wanted to convert everybody. They tried to get our children removed from the school but the headmaster refused to go along with this. Then some of the religious people, the rabbi and his associates, came to see me. They threatened me. The rabbi said he was going to make so much trouble I wouldn't know what to do with myself. The mayor, Ron Nachman, wrote to me saying he wouldn't allow any violence in the town. We had the mayor and the rabbi and other people demonstrating outside our home. Most of the residents in the building signed a petition demanding that we be forced to leave. Then some Christians came to visit as tourists. They heard about it. They went to the mayor and said, "You're causing trouble for these people." After that people came round. We were accepted. When we came we were the fifth Christian family. Now there are more than fifty. Most of them are Russians. Some were

Christians before they came, some not.'

Although not an Israeli, David had served as a reservist in the army for fifteen years. He described being in Nablus during the invasion of 2002.

'We were sent to form a gate outside the city, a group of soldiers and a dog. The Palestinians were throwing stones and bricks at us. The dog was more scared than we were. It was whining. We said, "Next time don't send a dog with us." My two oldest sons are in the army right now. One of them's in charge of the soldiers at the checkpoints round Nablus and the other's in the dog unit.'

After lunch David invited me out on to the balcony to see the views. He pointed to an area of construction on the edge of the settlement. 'This is new housing that's going up for a group of Orthodox Jews from France. It's separate from the rest of Ariel because they want to maintain strict observance of the Jewish religious laws. Things like not driving on the Sabbath and so on.'

The wall of the balcony was inset with stones from the Dead Sea and shards of pottery which the family had collected from biblical sites. On top of it perched a wooden bird table with the Israeli flag on it.

'Hamid built this,' David said, pointing to the bird table. 'Barbara may have told you about him. He's one of our converts. He's done a lot of odd jobs for us.'

'Yes, Barbara did mention someone called Hamid. But how come that you, as Christians and living in a Jewish settlement, are involved with Palestinians?'

It turned out that David's ministry extended far beyond the handful of Christian families living in Ariel. His work focused mainly on proselytising among the local Muslims. Although not able to move freely in and out of the Palestinian villages, he had nevertheless, he claimed, been able to establish a burgeoning network of converts to Christianity. He had met Hamid when he drove into a village once to take a sick person to a clinic.

'When I came out of the clinic I saw that my car was surrounded by a bunch of aggressive-looking men. There was a bit of an altercation. Things were starting to get ugly. So to appease them, I offered to give them some books, and very gingerly, stretching out my arms to show them I had no hidden weapons, I opened a box of Bibles that I had in the car and I distributed them. A few days later I was driving along the road and Hamid stepped out in front of me and waved me down. He wanted to learn more. After he converted he was arrested by the Palestinian police. They told him Muslims can't convert. They tortured him, they hung him up for thirteen days. The man next to him died, his spinal cord separated from his brain. I got on to the American Embassy about Hamid. They put the pressure on and the police let him go. Four of his brothers converted. They too were arrested and tortured. One of them was whipped with a rubber hose till his stomach was coming out in pieces. Another one was made to sit on a bottle. It ruined his insides and made him sterile.'

Hamid was married with ten children. Although his wife and children remained Muslim, they were all ostracised, David said. 'In their society the house is regarded as a Christian one. The oldest daughter is twenty, but nobody is allowed to marry her. Hamid was all set to go to El Salvador. Barbara and Grant had it arranged with a friend there, but his children didn't want him to go to South America, they said they would miss him too much, so he didn't go.'

'How many Muslims have you converted around here?'

'We now have more than 150 who have become believers. In the past year we've had three more Hamas members who became believers. People who were very active in Hamas – throwing stones, shooting, killing other Palestinians who didn't see it their way. The first change I see is that the hate and anger are no longer there, they develop a respect for their wives for the first time, a desire to have a relationship with their wives as people, and a desire to love unconditionally. Hamas are very different from the Fatah people in character. The Fatah are crooked and corrupt. The Hamas people are very honest.'

'Isn't it dangerous for you to be evangelising in this way?'

'I have to be careful. They started shooting at me in a refugee camp in Nablus. I was there with a Nigerian guy, Kwami. We were there to witness. There was an echo and the shots were going ping, ping, ping, all around us. I said, "Kwami, somebody's shooting." Kwami said, "Oh good, how exciting, something to tell my mother." They beat me up only once, that was in Hamid's village. Just a minute, I've got some stuff I want to show you.'

David took a file out of a drawer. It was filled with letters and articles about his evangelical activities. 'I travel a lot,' he said. 'Germany, Norway, Hungary, Greece. I've been to all these countries and all over the US. I know a lot of senators. I give lectures about the Islamic mentality. I've been on Israeli television. I'm going to Morocco soon. I've been invited by the King of Morocco to advise him about relations between Muslims and non-Muslims. They've been having a lot of problems since 9/11 with Moroccans being badly received abroad because they're Arabs.'

He showed me a few of the letters, and also an article in *Time* magazine which he passed over very briefly.

'Hey, would you like to meet Hamid?' he asked.

'Yes, sure.'

'No problem.'

David picked up the phone, dialled a number and spoke briefly.

'OK, we can go now.'

'Where to? We can't go into the village surely?'

'He'll be waiting for us in an olive grove outside the village. When we get there he'll get into the car.'

Grant wanted to go straight home but Barbara said she'd come with us. Before we left, I asked David if he had a copy of the *Time* article he could give me.

'Sorry, I don't have any copies.'

'Could we take it with us then and get a photocopy made somewhere in the *merkaz*?'

'Wait a minute, maybe I've got a copy somewhere.'

He disappeared and came back with a folded sheet of A3. 'You can have this.'

We drove out of Ariel, past the gate guards and on a few miles further. 'There he is,' said David, pointing to a man lurking in a clump of trees. He braked sharply and the man hastily climbed into the back of the van beside me. The van had curtains. Hamid tugged at them to make sure that they were tightly closed. We did a quick U-turn and drove back the way we had come. David drew up at the side of the road and parked near a petrol station at the entrance to Ariel.

David introduced me to Hamid, a well-built man of about fifty, and explained to him that I wanted to hear his story. David spoke no Arabic and Hamid spoke only a little English so it was agreed that the conversation would be in Hebrew, which they both spoke, with David interpreting for me.

'I'm sorry I can't take you to my house,' Hamid said. 'It ruins my honour that I cannot honour you by bringing you to my house but I'm under threat. And, first of all, you must not identify me so they won't come and remove my head from my shoulders.'

I asked him why he had converted to Christianity.

'I read in the book of Matthew, come unto me all that are tired of working and I will give you rest. I received the light of Jesus. Those that have problems and have heavy things on them, they should come to him. Even though I've been to jail twice and it's very dangerous for me at this point, I believe it's a test, to test my faith. But the trials, the difficulties make my faith even stronger.'

'Were you religious before your conversion? Were you a devout Muslim?'

'You could call me eighty per cent Muslim at that time.'

'And why did you think Christianity was better?'

'Islam was supposed to be everybody caring for one another but it turned out to be like a mafia, everyone killing and torturing one another. In Islam you were supposed to help other people. This is what it says, but it was different. When

I was in jail my children were persecuted because of me. My European friends, Norwegians, built a school in the village. It says in front of the school, a gift from the Kingdom of Norway. Yet my children were not allowed to sit with the other kids, they had to sit in a corner with a hat on them to identify them as infidels. When I was in jail I evangelized. I told seven men about my faith in Jesus. Two of them were killed when they left, one in Qalqilya, one in Nablus. They were killed by men sent by the Palestinian Authority to execute judgement. Their widows and children don't eat very well, they are going through a very difficult time.'

'How is life for you now in the village?'

'You know, my life is in danger, and my family also. If there was a way for my family and me to leave the village, to be safe, it would be good. My children were beaten up because of me. The UN gives the village funds for a summer camp for children. My children are not allowed to participate. I have ten children, small and big, all at home. I receive some help for food from the believers. We have no electricity because I haven't paid the bill. My wife doesn't leave the house except to go to the doctor. She has cancer of the ovaries. She's not a believer but she is still ostracized. The mosque announced over the loudspeaker that I am an infidel. This has weakened her immune system.

'The Bible says that if people do harm to you, you still have to love them. One day I believe that they will be sorry for what they have done to me. When Jesus was on the cross he said, Father, forgive them for they know not what they do. He came to deliver us from the power of the devil and to deliver us to the power of God. The book of Luke says when you go into difficult times be patient. This is what I do. Through the Bible we learn the words of Jesus. I read it to my children. I'm telling them the truth. I'm afraid to read to them now because of the trouble they're having from the village. In school I'm afraid for them. The teachers ask questions about what their parents are doing in the house. The teachers ask them to spy on me. For two weeks they didn't go to school because of the problems. The Palestinian Authority has said to me, "If you renounce Christianity, we will give you back everything. We will give you a job."'

'What do you think about the biblical prophecies and their relevance to the present political situation?'

'According to prophecy the Al Aqsa mosque and the Temple Mount will be destroyed. The Jewish people believe that this land belongs to everyone. You can see yourself that in places like Haifa and Tel Aviv they allow Arabs to live there. In the Koran it says: Look, oh Israel, the land is given to you. The Arabs believe that the land of Israel was given to the Jews but the Hamas people say God brought the Jewish people here to make it easier for the Arabs to kill them. We have no other choice but to live together. We are Arabs, Jews and Christians in this land, we have to learn to live together. We have no other choice. If there was peace we could all make a living together, we could all have food in our homes, but that's not the case today. Everybody's just for themselves. I have hope and I have faith because in the Bible Jesus tells the parable of a man who inherited ten kingdoms because he had patience. We can see how Jesus multiplied the bread and the fishes and there was bread and fish left over because there was the blessing and mercy of God. If everyone would do according to the words of Jesus, everyone would be living in prosperity.'

'David told me you'd been tortured in prison. Can you tell me about this?'

'If you notice I can't sit down straight. They handcuffed my hands behind my back and put me on a pulley so that my feet didn't touch the ground for thirteen days. I had no food. It was good for me because I lost weight. I was too fat.' He laughed. 'I'm just kidding but I have to see the humour in these things.'

During all this we had been sitting outside the petrol station where one of the Ariel suicide bombings had happened. We drove in to look at the memorial, a stone slab inscribed with the names of the five people who had died. In a box in front of it a single candle burned.

We turned round to take Hamid back. Hamid said something to David.

'He wants to pray for you,' David said.

Hamid laid his hand on my shoulder and prayed aloud all the way to the olive grove.

Back at Grant and Barbara's house I opened up the paper David had given me.

Inside it was blank. The other side showed only the first page of a *Time* article published in June 2003. It showed a photo of the inside of David's van with curtains tightly closed, the back of a *keffiya*-covered head and a hand holding a Bible. The title read *Missionaries under Cover*, the sub-title *Growing numbers of Evangelicals are trying to spread Christianity in Muslim lands. But is this what the world needs now?* Below this the introductory paragraphs to the text that David had withheld suggested that the answer to that question would be no.

I had been profoundly disturbed by my meeting with Hamid. There was no doubt in my mind that what David was doing was wrong. By proselytising in this way he was creating conflict within the Palestinian community. Muslims generally regard apostasy as a very grave matter and here it was aggravated by the fact that Hamid and others like him were seen to be associating with the enemy; they would therefore be treated as collaborators. If David's motives were purely religious I felt that he would surely see that his missionary work would be better carried out in an environment where it was less likely to make victims not only of those targeted but of their families too. I had no doubt either that if he had been trying to convert Jews to Christianity he would have found himself bundled onto the first plane out of the country.

All this increased the feeling of discomfort that I already had about being in Ariel. I felt guilty about not being upfront with Barbara and Grant. As with Ruthie, I was fond of Barbara despite her extreme views. Grant was less likeable, but there was no doubting the sincerity of either. I had been there for five days and didn't feel able to talk freely because I'd taken the decision from the beginning not to reveal that I'd been living in the West Bank. I felt sure that people like Tikva and Anna had little idea of what life was like for Palestinians and that they would be horrified if they did. Jerry and Sylvia, Slava and Marina and the others probably had an equally distorted view but I couldn't say anything. David, for all his super-smooth miracle-working tele-evangelist style – or probably because of it – was a more dubious character. It stuck in my craw that I had to listen to his accounts of conversion in silence. Added to all this, I had just phoned Ruth, the Israeli human rights activist that I'd met on election day. We chatted for a bit, then I told her where I was. 'Oh,' she said with a sharp intake of breath, 'for us, that's the lion's den.' It was time to leave.

The next day I went back to Jerusalem. Grant and Barbara were going there for their weekly prayer meeting so we went together. We bowled along the highway to the tune of religious music from the car's cassette player. 'In all our trials, Lord, in all our trials, there is one place of refuge.' Barbara hummed along with it while Grant held forth about the sedimentary limestone rock which predominates in the geology of Samaria.

'Do you see that hill there?' Barbara pointed to the left. 'That's Shiloh. That's where the Israelites installed the Tabernacle after they took over the land of Canaan. That's where they housed the Ark of the Covenant containing the two stone tablets on which the ten commandments were written, the stone tablets that Moses brought down from Mount Sinai. See these little houses.' She pointed at some ruins. 'They're Bible houses, from biblical times. On the inside they were plastered, on the outside they were covered with mud. It was a beautiful comfortable home.'

We passed a Palestinian village, the houses the usual greyish-yellowish cubes with a couple of newer houses in the modern style.

'And here are the poor Palestinian houses,' shouted Barbara scornfully. 'When everybody is crying about their poor conditions this is where they're living.' She started clapping her hands in time to the music. 'Oh I need you Lord. I need you like the summer rain, like the river that flows in the desert, bringing light to a weary land.'

'It was somewhere near here that Abraham pitched his tent, between Ai and Bethel. Bethel, the house of God, is right over that hill. Ai is the hill up ahead. It's where Joshua came in and razed it to the ground. I was on an archaeological dig there and I was scraping ashes from that time.'

The next hymn was a catchy number. 'Glory to the great I Am, worship him with all your might, so fear God and give him glory, glory to the great I Am.' Barbara gave Grant a great thump on the shoulder that nearly drove us off the road and cried out, 'Give him glory, Brother Livingstone. Worship the lord Jehovah.'

As we entered Jerusalem Barbara pointed to one of the settlements that had been built around it. 'That's Pisgat Zeef. The Israelis had to build these here. It's a line of defence. And there's Tel al Ful. It was Gibeah in the Bible, the first capital of the kingdom of Israel. That unfinished summer palace up there was started by King Hussein of Jordan. The Arabs building it destroyed the Jewish foundations that had been there from Saul's time. This is what happens when Islam comes in. They take over other religious sites, Jewish and Christian, and destroy them. Now keep your eyes open. Just ahead the Mandelbaum gate is coming up. It was the border crossing point till 1967. Amen. Now Jerusalem is united. Thank you, Lord, Thank you, Jesus.'

We dropped Barbara off at the YMCA. Grant offered to drive me to my hotel on the Mount of Olives.

We spun round the walls of the Old City and across the Kidron Valley. 'Now here,' said Grant, nodding towards the valley, 'is where we will all be standing on the last day. This is the valley where the Last Judgement is to take place. Up on the left there is the Russian Orthodox Church of Saint Mary Magdalene. You see those gold onion domes that it has?' He gazed up at them. 'They're supposed to represent the tongues of flame that danced on the heads of the Apostles when they received the Holy Spirit.' There was a sharp squealing sound as Grant wrenched the steering wheel round, just missing a traffic island. At the same time we felt a dragging and a bumping. We had a puncture.

Grant opened the boot and got out the spare wheel and the jack. He lay down on the road and set about changing the wheel. With only one arm it was a slow, laborious job but he refused my help. He was still struggling to get the car jacked up when a Palestinian stopped and offered to do it for him. This time Grant accepted. We got chatting to the man while he busied himself with the wheels. His name was Iyad and he said that he worked just across the road.

'Where? What do you do?' I asked.

'I'm the gardener in the Garden of Gethsemane.'

It seemed unreal. The Garden of Gethsemane had such powerful resonance for me, evoking so much that was at the heart of my religious upbringing. Iyad's claim to be the gardener there seemed as incredible as if he had said he was the keeper of the Golden Fleece. Grant took it all in his stride. He fumbled in the glove compartment of his car, pulled out a booklet about Jesus Christ, and pressed it on Iyad as a thank you for his help.

[5] Christian Zionists believe that the return of the Jews to Israel is in accordance with biblical prophecy and is necessary for the second coming of the Messiah

CHAPTER 13

As I planned to spend another six weeks in Jerusalem before I left the country, I decided to rent a flat. I found one advertised in a tourist office in the Muslim part of the Old City. It belonged to a Palestinian called Mike, and was part of his house, also in the Old City. He took me to see it, down a cobbled alleyway past boys playing with marbles, a candy floss vendor whipping up clouds of pink froth, and men in a coffeeshop sitting with backs to the wall, puffing on *arguilas* and staring solemnly ahead like patients in a dentist's waiting room. We stopped at a big studded door. Mike opened it and we entered a vaulted hallway floored with massive flagstones. We climbed a narrow stone stair to an open courtyard which was surrounded by the living quarters. A further stair led to a flat roof.

The flat was a room with a kitchen and bathroom. Although it was on the upper floor, the rooms were like dungeons. The walls were a couple of feet thick, puddles from the leaking roof had accumulated on the kitchen floor and a white ferny fungus sprouted out from between the wall tiles. But it had character – plus satellite television and an internet broadband connection. I took it.

Mike told me a bit about the history of the neighbourhood and the current situation. The Muslim part of the Old City was within East Jerusalem and was therefore Palestinian. However, in 1967, at the time of the occupation of the West Bank and Gaza, Israel went a step further with East Jerusalem and annexed it. Since then its status had been in dispute and its residents in an anomalous position in relation to both Palestinians in the Occupied Territories and Arab-Israelis in Israel.

As in the settlements of the West Bank and Gaza, Jewish

people were setting up home in East Jerusalem, particularly in the Old City area. Those who did so were generally extremely religious. Unlike the settlements which drew many people for environmental or economic reasons, the attraction of the Muslim quarter was its proximity to the Western Wall and the site of the Temple.

Mike explained to me how, by a complicated system of Islamic inheritance law which I found hard to follow, it was theoretically impossible for property owned by Muslims to pass into non-Muslim hands. But ways of circumventing this were often found, enabling Jewish families to move in. At the same time, Muslim families were being harassed, either by the enforcement of Israeli laws similar to those resulting in the house demolitions in Azzoun Atmeh which made it difficult for them to renovate and extend their properties, or by persecutory behaviour on the part of Jewish neighbours.

To illustrate the kind of thing which could happen, Mike took me up to the roof where he had another two studio flats. The original building had included rooms at this level which had deteriorated so he had knocked them down and built new ones. However, the new construction covered a bigger floor area than the old one. This contravened the law because the work had been done without a permit which, Mike said, would have been impossible to obtain. His Jewish neighbours reported the matter to the authorities. As a result Mike had to demolish the flats and build them again according to the old floor plan.

We went downstairs again where Mike introduced me to his wife and left us to sort out the bedding and the kitchen equipment together.

'Can I help you, sister?' The voice was American, the figure was ample and shrouded in veils.

'No, I'm OK , thank you.'

'Oh, I thought you looked lost.'

That wasn't surprising. In the area where I was now living I kept on having the illusion that I was experiencing a time slippage, like the two Edwardian women who caught glimpses of Marie Antoinette and her friends when they visited Versailles. Frequently I stood stock still as I watched Jewish men, women and children in long, black clothes, apparently from a long-gone era, scurrying along, oblivious to all non-Jewish occupants of the walkways, as if they were in a parallel universe. No wonder the woman thought I was lost.

We got talking and discovered that we were near neighbours. Her name was Maria and she invited me to her house. 'I'm going out now but come round later. Any time.'

I called round that evening. The flat was on the ground floor and consisted of three large vaulted rooms clustered round a small courtyard like the hallways of a baronial castle. The rooms had no apertures apart from the doors and several small side windows opening onto the courtyard.

Maria was cooking dinner. I sat at the kitchen table while she prepared chicken and mashed potatoes and told me about her family.

Maria was half-Paraguayan and was born a Catholic. Her mother had been a nun in Paraguay for seventeen years but had left the convent because of health problems. She married a Palestinian and had two children. After living in the US for a few years, they moved to Jerusalem where her husband's family lived. When Maria was nine, she converted to Islam, a decision entirely of her own choosing, she insisted. Her mother, by this time, was afflicted by severe bouts of manic depression and was spending a lot of time in a mental hospital in Bethlehem. During one of these episodes she kidnapped Maria and her younger brother and took them back to Paraguay. Her husband followed up the trail and snatched them back again six months later. Back in Jerusalem Maria became engaged to a cousin and was married to him at the age of fourteen. With her husband she went to live with relatives in the US where she finished her schooling. She had her first child when she was fifteen. 'At school I referred to my husband as my boy-friend,' she said. 'That was the more normal situation in the States. It was OK having a baby at that age, but not being married.'

Now, some twenty-seven years later, she had ten children. She clarified. 'I had ten and the tenth one died but now I've got ten again because my husband has had a daughter with his second wife.'

On that cliffhanger the conversation came to a stop as Maria wanted to go and pray.

Maria's oldest daughter was married and lived elsewhere. The second was Aisha, a post-graduate student of *fiqh* (Islamic law). Like her mother, Aisha had an American accent, having been educated mainly in the US. She was highly articulate, forceful and fervently religious, with something of the Germaine Greer about her.

'Most Palestinians support Hamas,' she told me as we sat in the sitting room after dinner. 'It's got nothing to do with Islam. My grandmother was a Christian and she supported Hamas. She was more extreme than us.'

Aisha had a friend who had been engaged to a suicide bomber.

'He called her the day before and said he loved her and they were going to be together for the rest of their lives. He had become more religious in the previous few weeks, praying more, giving more to the poor, encouraging his fiancé to do charity work, teaching kids to read the Koran, and always to be kind and nice to people. The last time I saw her she still had her engagement ring on. I asked her why. She said it was for him, that she wouldn't ever love anyone else.'

'How did she feel when she heard about the bombing?'

'She was completely delighted. She was sad too but at the same time delighted about what he had done and she considered him a hero. He was very kind and loving and loved children very much.'

'How do you reconcile what you say about him loving people and children with the fact that he attacked civilians, including children?'

'The way they would answer this is, our intention is not to

harm the children and they have nothing to do with this but it's the only way we can retaliate. And as regards attacking civilians, well, civilians are supposed to be unarmed. Yet these people, each and every single one of them, has to serve in the IDF[6], so each and every one is a warrior.'

Another of Aisha's friends was in prison. She had been arrested for belonging to a women's group whose members had been on call to help with militant activities.

'She'd been married for two months and even her husband didn't know about it. She used to say that she wanted to have children to have them all as suicide bombers.'

'How could a mother have such ambitions for her children?'

'Their belief in Islam.'

Aisha said that she herself was against suicide bombings as they did more harm than good but she felt that the media gave the wrong impression of the bombers. She poured scorn on the idea that suicide bombers were tempted to catapult themselves prematurely into paradise because of the seventy virgins that were waiting for them there.

'For the West, it's always seen as something to do with lust.'

I told her the story that David had told me about the Hamas man being taken to a disco in Tel Aviv to show him what awaited him after death. She laughed. 'This is completely ridiculous. If it's a question of lust, go sleep with seventy women right now. Why wait for heaven? Just go to the disco place. No, it's for a higher reason.'

We talked about the stories that were emerging about the ill-treatment of prisoners in Guantanamo Bay, the way in which attempts were being made to break the men down by exposing them to prostitutes.

'If it was western prisoners they would say, hey thank you very much.' She laughed again. 'They would say, hey, I wish I was all the time in Guantanamo Bay.'

I tried to explore further with Aisha the question I had asked Shatha, the ways in which Muslim men deal with their sexual urges.

'Well, some of them may be going with women, I guess, or they may masturbate or watch porno movies. But, you know, Hilda, something that helps many people is that the moral system here does not induce the expression of sexuality. Even inside homes women are not dressed in an immodest way. That's not necessarily because Palestinian society is a religious one, it's more a cultural thing. In fact, although adultery is forbidden by our religion for both sexes, culturally it may be permitted for men, or at least the punishment is less.'

One morning Maria called me and asked if I would go to the dentist with her. Aisha was at the university and she couldn't go alone as the dentist was male.

We walked through the fruit and vegetable part of the souk, past women sitting on the ground surrounded by their baskets of produce. Maria, who knew some of them, described their circumstances. They came every day from beyond the checkpoints. 'This one carries her stuff herself. It's not too heavy,' she said, pointing to a woman selling bunches of herbs. 'This one with the cauliflowers and cabbages probably pays for a truck to bring them, or maybe her husband helps her, but generally the husbands don't help. It's the women who cultivate and carry the stuff to the market and the husbands just sit in the coffeeshops smoking *narguila*.'

In the dentist's waiting room Maria took up again the story of her husband's second wife.

'He said he needed a second wife because he might otherwise be unable to resist doing something *haram*, committing adultery. I was unhappy about it at first but Aisha persuaded me. She was doing a course in Muslim women's rights at the time and she made me understand that Islam approved of polygamy, that it was a husband's right and that it was my duty as a Muslim to help him. Once I had agreed, he went to see many candidates and settled on a woman from the Hebron area. They got engaged, he gave her presents of clothes and gold jewellery, and then two days before the wedding he changed his mind.'

Maria, who had been so resistant to the idea at first, was now shocked at his treatment of the woman and tried to persuade him to go ahead with the marriage – to no avail. He was adamant.

'He said to me, "When I see her I see the devil in front of me."'

The clothes and gold were taken back and he had to pay her 10,000 shekels in damages. Soon after that he found Khawlah, a young divorcee in Ramallah. The fact that she was a divorcee made her more acceptable to Maria. She saw it as an act of Islamic charity as women who have already been married don't generally attract proposals from men who are single. This time the marriage went ahead and Khawlah now had a daughter about two years old. She lived in Abu Dis, at the other side of the Wall in Palestinian territory. The husband, Yahia, divided his time between the two households.

It puzzled me that Aisha could be talking about women's rights while at the same time encouraging a situation which deprives a man's wife and children of fifty per cent of his time.

'It's not really like that,' said Maria. 'Husbands spend most of their time at work or in coffeeshops with their friends. When he takes another wife it's just as if the husband was out at work. They don't see all that much of him anyway. Another wife can be a good thing. For example, if the man doesn't work or spends a lot of time in the house, he butts in where he shouldn't be butting in. Just now Khawlah is away at her family's house so Yahia is at home more and I'm getting fed up of having him around, getting in the way. For a woman the most important relationship is with her children. When a man wants another wife it's always because of sex.'

'Doesn't it cause financial difficulties when a second wife is taken?'

'At first it did a bit. He was always on my case, saying I was spending too much. Now it's OK.'

'Perhaps it's easier for wives in arranged marriages to accept other wives than for women who have chosen their own husbands and been in love with them,' I suggested.

'No,' said Maria, 'because love grows after marriage. And you know, I always used to think I wasn't pretty. But since he married again I've stopped thinking that. I know I'm the first.'

Later in the week I went to the university in Abu Dis with Aisha. She wanted me to meet someone called Ghassan Muhaibesh who, she said, would be able to explain to me everything I ought to know about Islamic inheritance law and its tortuous relation to property ownership. I felt that I had already been exposed to more information on this topic than my brain could process but Aisha pressed on with her usual single-mindedness.

We got a bus which took us as far as Ras el Amoud in East Jerusalem where the Wall cut through the urban fabric. At the other side lay Abu Dis. To get there we were going to climb over the Wall. In this area the construction was still underway and there was a point at which it could be crossed with a bit of effort. A cairn of stones had been placed to provide a foothold, and bits of reinforcement bar jutting out served as handholds. The temperature was below zero and a drizzle of sleet had been falling all morning. I threw my umbrella over first and then heaved myself up with fingers too cold to get a firm grasp of the bars. Aisha, hampered by her *jilbab*, struggled up after me.

Landing on the other side I found that we were in someone's garden. 'The owner leaves the gate open at the other side so that people can pass through,' Aisha explained. 'But this is causing him a lot of problems. The Israeli army is threatening him and Palestinians have been using the garden for drug dealing and dating. The route will probably be blocked off soon.'

We passed out of the garden and crossed a sloping area of wasteland, slithering in the wet mud. Arriving at the road we were forced to walk in the way of the traffic as the Wall had cut off the pavement at the other side.

At the university Aisha introduced me to Ghassan. As I had expected I followed little of what he said about documents dating back over centuries, property changing status, and British mischief-making. He called in a colleague who showed us a book he had written about the history of his village, with the names of his ancestors who had lived there and plans of the village dating from the fifth century CE.

'The history of this village goes back to the time of the Canaanites,' said Ghassan. 'The Jews can't say nobody lived here before them because in the Old Testament it was the land of the Canaanites. Most Palestinians here now are descendants of the Canaanites. Can we Muslims claim that we own Spain because we lived there for 500 years? Of course not. If the Jews claim that they have archaeological evidence of their right to live here, where is it? Money is with them, power is with them, the EU is with them. Most of all, America is with them and today the world is controlled by America.'

When we left Ghassan, Aisha suggested that we visit Khawlah as she lived nearby.

Khawlah's flat was very different from the family's home in the Old City. It was on the ground floor of a small block, basic and not very homely. Yahia was there with Khawlah and their two-year-old daughter, Sara. We sat on a mattress on the floor.

Khawlah, at twenty-six, was not much older than Aisha, but looking at the rather colourless young woman I could see why Maria believed that she herself came first.

As we sat with them, Aisha talked about her own ideas about polygamy. She was a keen advocate of it, and not just because of the many men killed and in prison which made it a practical solution in a society where women increasingly outnumbered men.

'I myself would be very happy for my husband to have another wife,' she said. 'It would be useful if I had someone to help me to cater for his needs. I want to be free to pursue my own interests, to continue with my education and to work at spreading the teachings of Islam. I try to encourage my friends to think like this. Just recently I persuaded a friend of mine to become a second wife and now she's very happy.'

'Hey, you want to meet Yousef el Khattab,' Aisha said to me after we had climbed back into East Jerusalem. 'He's this Jewish guy that converted to Islam. He was a really extreme orthodox Jew and now he's a Muslim, very fundamentalist. You should go meet him. He's got a perfume shop in the Old City. Why don't you drop by?'

'Just a minute, I think I know this man,' I said, thinking back to my first day in Jerusalem and the perfume stall with the inflammatory slogans about 9/11 and the perfidious Americans. 'Does he have a booth in the Via Dolorosa, near the corner of Al Wad Street?'

'That's right.'

I followed up Aisha's suggestion and dropped by. The booth had had a makeover. Gone were the slogans and inside the walls were covered in brown hessian with sprays of artificial flowers pinned all over them. I'd felt a certain trepidation at the thought of bearding Yousef in his den, remembering his belligerent manner with the Russian tourists. I needn't have worried. He seemed to have had the same kind of makeover as his shop front and it was a much milder Yousef that I introduced myself to, mentioning that I was a friend of Aisha's.

'Welcome, come on in.'

Yousef raised the counter which separated him from the street and pulled out a stool for me. I told him that I was interested in learning more about the Jewish take on things but hadn't found it easy to make contact. I described my abortive attempts to talk with the demonstrators outside the Knesset.

Yousef settled himself down again. 'Well, you know, these people aren't big thinkers,' he said.

Yousef had been brought up in a secular Jewish family in America. He started to tell me his life story as he served a young woman who was sniffing at a variety of different bottles. 'I was about eighteen, working in a VCR store, so I'd go to work, go home, watch a video, that sort of thing. That was about it and I asked myself, is this what life is all about? So I began to look deeper into Judaism and I came to a Talmudic school in Jerusalem to learn the basics. When I went back to the States I wanted more of this environment so I moved to Brooklyn and started wearing the Hasidic dress and the side curls and everything.'

The customer had made her choice now. Yousef syringed some perfume up from a large bottle and squirted it into a phial. I asked how his family had reacted to his changed lifestyle.

'My family were OK about it. American families are happy if their kids don't become burnouts so that in itself is an accomplishment.'

In 1998 Yousef moved to Israel. He lived in a settlement in Gaza and worked in a software store.

'But, you know, when I came here, honestly, every Jew I met was a liar. The whole attitude of the people was disgusting. Then I met a Muslim in a computer chat room, I started learning about Islam and that was it.' He handed over the perfume to the customer, put the money in the till and rinsed out his syringe.

By the time of his conversion to Islam Yousef was already married to a Jewish woman.

'At first she was horrified. She said, "I was born as a Jew and I'm going to die as a Jew." But a friend advised me just to act as an example of what a Muslim can be and within two weeks she took the *shahada*, she was reading the Koran and she loved it.'

Yousef's wife embraced not only Islam but also a co-wife.

'My second wife was a good friend of my wife. She was divorced and we tried to find her a husband.' He pointed to a photo on the wall. 'We introduced her to this brother – he's in jail now – but his family wouldn't accept a divorced woman. So I discussed it with my first wife, one thing led to another and here we are.'

Yousef already had four children. The oldest, Abdul Rahman,

was eight at the time of his father's conversion.

'Didn't he have problems? Losing his friends, changing school?'

'No problems, he loved it. Muslims are inclusive, not exclusive. They took him in. They said, before you were our cousin, now you are our brother.'

I asked Yousef why he had removed the Happy September 11 sign.

'After thinking it over I decided it wasn't an effective way of getting the message across. The sign made it more difficult for me to talk to Americans even though they brought it on themselves. Jesus drove the moneylenders out of the temple and Muslims flew a plane into the Trade Centre.' He said it matter-of-factly, as if the two acts were more or less equivalent.

We spoke about the Wall. Yousef saw this as a barrier round the Israelis rather than round the Palestinians. 'We think the wall is a good thing because there will be no safe place for the Jews in this world except the ghetto they've built for themselves.'

We spoke too about the biblical promises. Muslims, like Christians and Jews, revere the Bible. How did Yousef square this with the claim that, according to the Old Testament, God had promised the land of Israel to the Jews for ever?

'It's like, say you rent a property in London, say you take a lease on a bookshop for all eternity, and you agree this with the landlord. And then you set up a peep show in the bookshop. In that case the landlord has a right to say to you that you can't keep the premises any longer, that he's going to take the place back and give it to somebody else.'

'And what's the equivalent of this peep show in Jewish history?'

'They killed prophets. They refused to accept Christ. So they no longer had a right to the land.'

I'd noticed a lot of perfume shops in Palestine. The reason, Yousef explained, was that the Prophet Mohammed liked perfume very much. 'Mohammed loved three things: prayer, women and perfume. So perfume is very big in Islam.'

Yousef imported the essences from France and mixed them with alcohol. 'It brings out the smell and makes it lot cheaper,' he said.

The use of alcohol seemed unIslamic. No, said Yousef. As long as it wasn't drunk, alcohol was permissible.

Despite his fighting talk Yousef was not optimistic about the outcome of the conflict. 'The Jews are going to win here. That's the way it is. Because they control the media and the banks. Judaism has raped the world and has it believing in everything they want it to believe.

He glanced at breaking news which was appearing online on his laptop. 'Hey, Charles and Camilla are going to marry.' He laughed. 'Now there's a real love story.'

I left Yousef reading up about the royal fairy story.

Not far from my flat I had noticed a building which had a constant stream of ultra-Orthodox Jews going in and out. It was also inhabited by Palestinian families. It seemed an unlikely ménage.

Aisha knew one of the families in the building. They had been her grandparents' neighbours. She took me to visit.

The Jewish people coming and going belonged to a charitable institution called Chaye Olam. Their premises were on the top floor, overlooking the courtyard areas of the Palestinian flats beneath. The courtyards were covered over with fine wire mesh.

Aisha's friend was Umm Mohammed, a woman in her late sixties. She lived in a three-roomed flat with her three daughters, two sons and several grandchildren.

From what Mike had told me, relations between Jews and Palestinians in this sort of situation were very bad. Umm Ahmed told us about some of the problems they had while one of her daughters served us with tea.

The Jewish organisation had moved in to the top floor shortly after the 1967 war. At that time, terrified by all the shooting and killing that were going on and by rumours of even worse to come, many Palestinians had fled their houses which later came under an absentee rule, enabling the properties to be taken over. According to Umm Ahmed, her Jewish neighbours had been trying to get the Palestinian families to leave the building. She told us stories of the Palestinians being spat at, having stones and bottles thrown at them, and of the children being kicked and punched. The wire mesh over the courtyard had been put in place to stop the Jews throwing rubbish down onto them.

So keen were these Jews to have more property in the Muslim quarter, they were prepared to pay the Palestinians far more than the market value of their houses. Umm Ahmed said that they had often come to her with cheque books, telling her that she need only name her price.

Given the intolerable conditions in which they were living, I wondered if they had never been tempted to take the money and go.

'No,' said Umm Ahmed. 'Our dignity is worth more than all this money they're offering.'

'But how can you bear to live in such a climate of hostility?'

'It's enough for me that I'm living so close to Al Aksa Mosque.'

I asked about the effects of such an environment on the children. Aisha didn't translate the question. 'She doesn't understand these psychological things,' she said.

After leaving Umm Ahmed's house we dropped in on another Palestinian family in the same building. Here the conditions were far worse. Umm Nasser lived in one room with eight of her nine adult children. A kitchen area was screened off by a wardrobe and a curtain. A stack of thin mattresses was piled high against a wall. There was only one small window, set above the door. The toilet and shower were outside.

We sat on the floor with Umm Nasser and three of her children, none of whom worked. The stories the family told us were similar to Umm Ahmed's.

Tahani, one of the daughters, said: 'Several times they

came and offered us money to leave. A Jew came into the flat, where you're sitting now, with a blank cheque and said: "Put whatever price you want. Look at you, you're living in complete ruin."' She waved her hand at the mouldy walls and leaking ceiling. 'My father said: "I wouldn't even sell a handful of soil from this house. I was born in it and I'm going to die in it."'

Her mother took out an old newspaper and showed me a full-page article about the family, written in 1986. The accompanying photo showed them in the same room, sitting on the floor in the same position as we were now. Nothing had changed except their ages.

Round the corner we visited another family. Houriyah, a widow of seventy, lived with one of her daughters, Muna, in the remains of a house which had been blown up when a bomb being prepared by her son had gone off prematurely. All that was left of what was originally a five-roomed house with three kitchens and three bathrooms were two rooms and one kitchen and bathroom.

Houriya was in bad health, suffering from diabetes, high blood pressure, rheumatism and a lung problem. She lay in bed linked up to an oxygen cylinder. Muna's husband lived in Jordan and was unable to get a permit to enter Jerusalem.

Shortly after we arrived a second daughter, Salwa, burst in, very large, full of life and talking nineteen to the dozen. Salwa was a journalist. She plunged straight into a story about having just come from a meeting with an American film maker who was planning a documentary about three Israeli women (a settler, a peace activist and an 'average' woman) and three similarly diverse Palestinian women losing weight together in a kind of Big Brother reality show. The idea was that they would live together for two months in Canada Park, a recreational area in Israel, where they would follow a diet and exercise programme, being filmed round-the-clock to monitor how they related to one another. Salwa had been interviewed as a possible participant. I suggested that the strain of being on a diet would exacerbate existing tensions between Palestinians and Israelis. Salwa disagreed.

'I think the director is very clever. Sure, the conditions will be difficult, but maybe there is unity in diversity. Maybe the settler and the pious Muslim will sneak off to get food together. Maybe they will sympathise with each other. I thought at first it was a crazy idea. I said to the American woman, "You're mad." She said, "It's to direct hope. Why do you want to lose weight," she asked me. I said, "Because I want to be an attractive woman. I'm a good journalist, I'm successful, but I'm fat. I hope to be thin." She said, "That's it. I direct your hope."' Salwa roared with laughter.

Salwa was preparing a new show for Palestinian television in which she would be comparing headlines from Palestinian and Israeli newspapers and holding phone-ins. She also worked with a Palestinian-Israeli peace organisation.

She talked about the brother who had died in the bomb blast. 'Hanni was a handsome man. All the girls liked him. But inside he was like a volcano. I think he had a struggle inside himself because he was feeling somebody was going to take our house. He was preparing a bomb to put in a settlement. But things have changed now. Before we thought we had to have all of Palestine, from Jaffa to Jerusalem. Now we are willing to accept less but we need good living conditions.'

The women said that they had no problems with the Jewish people living in the neighbourhood. They had no contact with them but neither was there any friction. They seemed merely to be indifferent to them. This was yet another example of the lack of personal animosity towards the Jewish people on the part of the Palestinians that I found so difficult to understand. I often tried to press them further, almost putting words into their mouths in my search for sentiments I was sure I would feel myself if I were in their position, but they didn't bite.

One of the rooftop flats above my own was occupied by a young English theology graduate called Andy. Andy was working at the time with Sabeel, a liberation theology organisation active among Palestinian Christians. In its wider international remit, it worked with Christians abroad in campaigning against the Israeli occupation of Palestine.

Andy invited me to a weekly get-together and lunch which they held in their centre in East Jerusalem.

We started with a religious service led by Sabeel's founder, Canon Naim Ateek, an Anglican priest. It was very informal. We stood in a circle – the centre staff and a few visitors – and introduced ourselves with a few words about why we were there or some relevant anecdote, rather like participants at the opening of a motivational seminar. Then we sang a few hymns, said some prayers and passed round the bread and wine of communion.

After the service we went back to the office where a spicy vegetarian buffet cooked by an Indian guest was laid out. We helped ourselves and Andy introduced me to several of the Sabeel staff. We were joined by a German man, Martin, who had been living in Jerusalem for some years. He had come as a Christian peace activist with an ideology similar to that of Sabeel, but had since converted to Christian Zionist beliefs so I was surprised to find him there. As a Zionist he must surely be fundamentally at odds with the members of Sabeel who believed that the Bible taught justice and equality for all people. I challenged Martin about this, asking how a God corresponding to the usual concept of monotheistic religions – loving, omnipotent, omniscient – could get involved in the kind of petty favouritism of the God of Zionism? How could such a God allow the Palestinians to suffer as a result of this partiality?

For Martin there was no question of God being unjust. 'The Palestinians are having a bad time now but God will see that they're all right in the longer term. I too want to work towards this. I consider that my role here is to act as a bridge between people with different viewpoints. That's why I'm here today at Sabeel.'

During my visit to Sabeel I learned more about Christian Zionism. Previously I had considered that Ruthie and her friends and the Christians living in Ariel were no more than a freak phenomenon, representative of a tiny, deluded minority. I was wrong.

Sabeel had recently hosted a conference about Christian Zionism, addressing in particular its association with right-leaning ideologies to the detriment of Palestinian human rights and, most importantly, the question of how it had become a potent force in the making of US Middle East policy.

One of the concerns expressed by Canon Ateek was that the mainstream churches had failed to take Christian Zionists seriously, shrugging them off as a fringe group. A further concern was that by lowering their guard in this way, the churches had allowed some sections of mainstream adherents to be seduced by the Christian Zionist beliefs.

The Christian Zionist movement is based on a literal interpretation of those parts of the Bible believed to deal with events leading up to the end times. According to these interpretations, the Jews will return from exile, the forces of good and evil will confront each other in the battle of Armageddon, and Christ will return to earth.

Already flourishing in nineteenth-century Britain, Christian Zionism influenced the thinking of politicians such as Lord Shaftesbury and Lord Palmerston, and later Lloyd George and Lord Balfour, the man so bitterly decried by the Palestinians as responsible for their plight. It gained momentum first after the establishment of the state of Israel in 1948, and again after Israel's occupation of the Palestinian territories in 1967, both events being seen as the fulfilment of biblical prophesies.

Although the US had lagged behind Britain in its support for Christian Zionism it moved ahead in the second half of the twentieth century with the rise of fundamentalism in American Christianity, particularly in the Bible Belt and the Mid-West. Adherents were vociferous in their demands for US support for Israel and active in subsidizing its settlements, believing that this would hasten the second coming of the Messiah.

During the presidency of Ronald Reagan in the 1980s, the Christian right began to make common cause with the

Jewish lobby. Reagan himself was heard to express belief in Armagaddon and to entertain the possibility that it might come about in his lifetime. At the same time Israeli prime minister Menachem Begin and his right-wing Likud coalition were beginning to foster what would become a long-term relationship with prominent fundamentalists such as tele-evangelists Jerry Falwell and Pat Robertson. Falwell received the prestigious Jabotinsky Award for Zionist excellence, the first non-Jew to be honoured by Israel in this way. The Israeli government also gave him a Lear jet for his personal use.

By the time George W. Bush became president in 2000, American evangelicals numbered well over 100 million, at least a quarter of them Christian Zionists. With Bush himself being a convert to Christian fundamentalism – and surrounded by politicians and community leaders who shared his convictions – the influence of the Christian Right increased. (One example was House Majority Leader Tom Delay, of whom former Mossad chief, Danny Yatom, commented: 'The Likud is nothing compared to this guy.') This influence was strengthened by support from the neoconservatives who, although not necessarily subscribing to the religious doctrines of the Christian Right, were committed to the pursuit of its political agenda and eager to court its voters.

In one well-documented incident, Bush received over 100,000 angry emails from Christian fundamentalists when he tried to remonstrate with Ariel Sharon for invading Jenin in the West Bank in 2002. Bush immediately dropped his protest, leading Jerry Falwell to claim in a televised interview: 'The Bible-Belt is Israeli's safety net in the United States'[7]. When Bush spoke out against the attempted assassination of Hamas leader Abdel Aziz Rantisi in 2003, the White House was deluged with thousands of emails generated by the Christian Right. A central message of these emails was the threat that failure to drop the criticism of Israel would result in the senders withholding their election votes. Bush promptly backpedalled. Following his announcement of support for the Middle East Road Map peace plan, Christian conservatives sent 50,000 postcards of protest to the White House. Bush backed down.

As George Monbiot had pointed out in a *Guardian* article[8], the majority of Americans have little interest in their government's Middle East foreign policy when they go to the polls, while for the fundamentalist Christian minority it is a matter which affects them personally. Bush therefore stood to gain more support by encouraging Israeli aggression, support which was all the more welcome as it chimed with his own personal religious inclination. The Christian Right, in fact, was overtaking the Jewish lobby in the extent to which it was promoting hawkish support for Israel in the Middle East conflict.

I met up with Andy again later that evening. He had invited me to dinner in his flat with Mordecai Vanunu, the Israel nuclear technician who had been jailed for eighteen years for revealing information about Israeli nuclear weapons developments to *The Sunday Times*. Lured to Italy from the UK by a female agent of Mossad, the Israeli Secret Service, he was then kidnapped, smuggled out of the country and taken back to Israel. Mordecai, who was a convert to Christianity, had been released the previous year and was now living in St George's Anglican Cathedral in East Jerusalem which had given him refuge.

Andy had told me that Mordecai never tired of talking about his case – his work on the nuclear weapons programme, his imprisonment, and his present circumstances in which he was prevented from leaving the country and forbidden to communicate with the media or talk to foreigners.

Despite the restrictions, Mordecai spent much of his time talking to journalists and foreigners. Whether because of this, or perhaps because he had been held in solitary confinement for much of his sentence, it was difficult to engage in a two-way conversation with him. He dealt with each question deftly and then waited, poised, ready for the next one, like a politician giving a press conference. He showed no interest in directing the conversation himself or turning to subjects other than those related to his own history.

Mordecai had always been a black sheep, first for his support of the Palestinian cause which resulted in him losing his job in the seventies. 'I was very concerned about the refugees,' he said. 'I was against the Zionist ideology and I criticised the government for this. I thought it was wrong that Jews, like my family who came from Morocco, were able to come back here after 2,000 years, yet the Palestinians who were forced to leave in 1948 were not allowed to come back.' His next offence was his conversion to Anglicanism, a decision taken because he wanted to divorce himself completely from Judaism which horrified his orthodox Sephardic family.

While working in the Israeli nuclear centre Mordecai had been able to gather information fairly easily. He had been overseeing the production of plutonium and had been working on the hydrogen bomb. 'Because I was a Sephardic Jew, they assumed I was totally loyal,' he said. He had been appalled at the build-up of nuclear weapons, believing it to be a threat to world peace. He was equally convinced that Iraq had no nuclear weapons and that it was unlikely that Iran had any either.

No sooner had we swallowed the last of the rice and lentils and the syrupy red wine that I'd managed to winkle out of some corner of our teetotal Muslim neighbourhood than Mordecai jumped up. He had another appointment to go to.

[6] Israeli Defence Force
[7] "Zion's Christian Soldiers", *CBS-Sixty minutes, 5 October 2002*
[8] Their beliefs are bonkers, but they are at the heart of power - US Christian fundamentalists are driving Bush's Middle East policy
George Monbiot - The Guardian - 20th April 2004

CHAPTER 14

A priest friend in Jerusalem, knowing that I hadn't seen much of Israel, arranged for me to join a group of Christian Arabs on a parish trip they were making to Galilee and the Golan Heights.

A bus was to pick us up just outside the walls of the Old City at 6.30 a.m.. Only two people were already waiting when I arrived, a couple of women in their sixties who were talking to each other in French.

'*Les musulmans sont de vrais sauvages,*' said one.

'*Je préfère mille fois les juifs,*' said the other.

I introduced myself and we chatted until the bus and all the others arrived.

As the first snatch of conversation had indicated, Simona and Alexandra seemed eager to dissociate themselves from the Palestinian nation. Both were of mixed Lebanese/Palestinian origin and Simona, who had been married to a French man, claimed to be French.

There was something of the *Coronation Street* character about them. I could imagine them both seated in the Rovers Return of the 1960s, drinking milk stout with Ena Sharples and Minnie Caldwell, Alexandra in her mid-calf black pleated crimplene skirt and black jacket spattered with foodstains, and Simona, less dowdy but more raddled, in trousers and high heels with a lacy blouse.

The bus filled up and we set off, with the passengers chorusing the Lord's prayer in Arabic as we headed out towards Jericho. Simona handed round sesame seed bread and falafel, and Alexandra, who was sitting beside me, showered me with crumbs as she ate. After a while she fell asleep. Behind us a small boy vomited into the stairwell at the back door.

At first the landscape was pure ochre desert, shading to green as we drove further north. Five hours later we were climbing snowclad slopes, stopping finally at the Mount Herman ski resort in the Golan Heights. The group leader told us to be back at the bus and ready to leave in two hours.

The main attraction for the group was the ski-lift which you could take to the top of the mountain, from where you could look down into Syria. I looked at the swaying and lurching of the chairs as they passed over our heads and decided to give it a miss. Simona and Alexandra went off to join the queue for it, leaving me their bags to look after.

I walked over to the foot of the ski slopes. It was the first time I had seen Jews and Arabs[9] together in a recreational environment. Despite the snow, the temperature was high, with a hot sun in a clear blue sky. Skiers sailed down the mountainside, some in tee-shirts, some wearing *hijabs*, some with rifles strapped to their backs. Jewish parents played with their children. Many of the men wore black trousers, waistcoats and *kippas*, with long side curls framing their faces. Their wives, in 1950s style suits with hats and court shoes, floundered in the snow.

While I waited for Simona and Alexandra to come back, I talked with two Arab-Israeli women about life as part of a minority group within a larger Jewish society. They had no problems, they said. They worked with Jewish people, they got on well together.

By the time the others got back from their trip to the mountaintop it was just about time to go. The heat of the sun was already fading and the air was chill. After a quick snack in a fast food outlet we all piled back into the bus.

I had assumed, as this was a church trip, that the visit to Galilee would take in some of the places associated with the life of Christ. The area was dotted with milestones of religious history: the site of the Sermon on the Mount, the Church of the Multiplication of the Loaves and Fishes, Capernaum, where

Christ taught in the synagogue, cast out devils, cured a leper and a centurion's servant, and of course the Sea of Galilee itself, on which Christ, according to the Gospel, walked.

But this was not to be. In the early evening the bus stopped at a restaurant just outside Tiberias, a resort on the shores of the lake. It was functional and utilitarian, the kind of restaurant you might find on a motorway. We had been booked in advance, the choice of food already made. As soon as we sat down, waiters brought us copious amounts of the usual Arab starters (hummus and salad), followed by fish. 'From Lake Galilee,' said the waiter as he put it in front of me. 'Saint Peter fish.' I marvelled at the thought that I was eating fish from the same stock which Christ and his disciples had fished two thousand years previously. But why? I had long since discarded the beliefs of my strict Catholic childhood. It meant nothing to me now. Yet still I had the feeling that the meal I was eating, here in what felt like a company canteen, was almost sacramental.

After the meal we drove into Tiberias where we were to stop for an hour or so.

'Come with me, sister,' said Tawzi, an oldish man with the balding head of a tonsured monk and a diamond-patterned cardigan. 'I will show you everything.'

We walked round the harbour area which was dotted with trendy little restaurants. Out on the lake the sounds of music came from a couple of tourist disco boats sailing by.

In contrast to the frozen slopes of the Golan, the air here was soft and mild; because, Tawzi explained, we were now more than 1,000 feet below sea level.

We came to an embarkation point where some of the other members of the group were buying tickets for a boat trip. Tawzi, who by this time had given me a potted version of his life story (he had recently retired after years of chauffeuring for the Greek Patriarch in Jerusalem) suggested we join them.

With a hoot of its horn the boat cast off. Standing at the rail Tawzi pointed out to me clusters of lights on the receding land, identifying the various churches. Behind us a DJ started the music and strobe lights streaked across the deck. Tawzi took my hand and led me to join the other parishioners on the dance floor. We swayed fast and sinuously, hands above our heads. I quickly wore out but Tawzi was just getting into gear. He pulled at Simona who protested half-heartedly before giving in. I stood watching them until a voice piped up at my shoulder: 'Do you want to dance?' It was ten-year-old Jessica, practising her English.

The setting was surreal. Or rather, the setting was real, it was the action that was surreal. Deep within me was a sense of outrage, at some visceral level I was scandalised, I felt that we were profaning a holy place, that we were behaving sacrilegiously.

How could I feel like this when the New Testament was of no significance to me? At most it was a compilation of myths and metaphors for those who had a psychological need for the kind of God portrayed in the Bible. My own attitude to such a God was summed up in Lawrence Ferlinghetti's poem *Sometime During Eternity* in which he has Christ claiming that 'the cat who really laid it on us is his Dad.' Yet I couldn't shake off the feeling that I should be reverencing this place.

Then I remembered how, in the Muslim Quarter one day, I came across a group of American Catholics following the Stations of the Cross. As they walked they sang, over and over again, a plaintive one-line hymn: *Jesus, remember me when you come into your kingdom.* The group bore a large wooden cross, taking it in turns to carry it. Still singing, they progressed up the Via Dolorosa, past Yousef's perfume shop, under a swaying sign for the Holy Rock Café (another profanity which had somehow disturbed me) strung between the buildings on either side, and into the small chapel of the Seventh Station. I had felt mesmerised by the procession and followed it all the way to the Church of the Holy Sepulchre.

It was completely irrational. For me, the current status of the Jesus story was, as described in the last line of Ferlinghetti's poem, 'real dead'. I could only suppose that, just as blood is thicker than water, so our religious/cultural origins are more emotionally binding than subsequent belief systems arrived at by a process of reasoning. And if I, an 'observant atheist', felt like this on the Sea of Galilee and in the Via Dolorosa, how much more so would Jews feel about the lands of their religious history, Muslims about Al Aqsa Mosque, even Grant and Barbara about Shiloh and Ai and Bethel?

A few days later I dropped in to see Mikail, a Russian-Jew who was doing a doctorate in Jewish history. I had met him in the bookshop where he worked.

Mikail had immigrated to Israel fourteen years previously, living first in Tel Aviv and now in a settlement near Jerusalem. In addition to his first language (Russian) he spoke Hebrew, Arabic and several other languages. He also spoke English with a range of expression and a subtlety of nuance rarely found in native speakers, never mind those for whom it is a foreign tongue.

I had been perplexed about the degree to which secular Jews were attached to the land. Mikail had referred to secular Judaism. Wasn't this a contradiction in terms, I asked him.

'No, it's a cultural thing, it's several thousand years of history. It's our Bible, our history, our land. For most Jews the Bible is still meaningful even when they're not religious. There are even people who claim the Bible was made up in the Hellenistic period, who say the kingdom of David and Solomon never existed, that the stories of the patriarchs were invented in the sixth century BC. But even if they're right, they're still myths and legends which reflect the times. The stories of Abraham, of the Red Sea dividing, the Babylonian exile, I still enjoy them. David and Goliath is maybe a myth but the place is real. Secular Israelis grow up with these stories. Israelis, even the secular ones, know the Bible stories much better than Christians.'

After my Galilee experience I felt I had a better understanding of what Mikail was telling me.

He himself was secular.

'But I'm a Zionist,' he added. 'I love this land.'

He spoke of the ever-present feeling of insecurity.

'A few years ago it was terrible, there were so many suicide bombings near here, shooting in the streets.' He pointed down the road towards Zion Square. 'You couldn't get on a bus without thinking that you might not get off it again.'

Mikail rented his house in Ma'aleh Adumim, a settlement just outside Jerusalem, being unwilling to buy because of the political uncertainty.

'This is my home,' he said. 'I think we have a certain right to it. People claim this is our historical homeland and this is true. But as regards ignoring other people's historical rights, it's clear now that this is not going to work out. The historical consciousness of the semitic people, and this includes Arabs as well as Jews, is much greater than that of other people. It is part of their education, their cultural baggage, it shapes their identity. We have to face the problem realistically and we have to be reasonable and humane. I don't think that a Palestinian somewhere in Nablus, for example, who has the graves of his grandfathers going back thousands of years, I don't believe he has any less rights than me. Some people say the land was promised by God. That's their idiosyncratic faith, OK, but this argument doesn't work in that they can't convince other people of it. The Muslims say that it's not their fault and that's true. The only solution is two states. The majority of Jews want peace and they are willing for the Palestinians to have an independent state. Many religious Jews will also agree with this. The reasonable ones are in the majority.'

After speaking with Mikail I contacted the Israeli human rights organisation, Machsom Watch, and arranged to go to a checkpoint with them. Their system was that each person did one morning or afternoon shift a week in a group of three or four people. Julia, a neat, brisk, white-haired woman, picked me up at Jaffa Gate and we drove into West Jerusalem to collect Rina, Rose and Hannah before making for the Bethany area where we would cross the Wall into Abu Dis in Palestinian territory.

Rina's view was that the Israelis had over-reacted in building the Wall and that they had simply created more enemies for themselves in doing so. 'The Palestinians must deal with their own dirty laundry and we'll do our own washing.' She complained that not enough was heard about those Israelis who supported disengagement, who she claimed were 'the silent majority'.

The conversation quickly turned to other things. Julia, Rina and Rose were of American origin and Hannah was German. They had all moved to Israel years previously but I might easily have found myself among a group of well-off retirees in Florida as I listened to their talk of orchids, champagne, yoga, pilates and bridge. Rose mentioned that there had been an article in the Israeli newspaper *Haaretz* about transcendental meditation being used in schools and that children who meditated for ten minutes a day were less violent. Julia said she'd just seen *Vera Drake* and that it was a wonderful film. Rina took out her diary to pencil something into it. I saw that every morning, afternoon and evening had some kind of activity marked. I contrasted this with the barrenness which blighted Palestinian lives, the monotonous round of tea drinking, the difficulty of going anywhere, the lack of anything to go to.

We parked the car at a petrol station in Ras el Amoud in East Jerusalem. A couple of Palestinian boys ran up and threw some dirt on the windows. 'They're doing that so we'll pay them to clean it,' said Rose. Sure enough, as we walked away from the car the boys ran after us asking for money to clean the mess they'd made. Hannah chided them gently in Arabic. One of the boys yanked at her scarf and threw it up into her face.

We were near the area I had been in previously with Aisha but this time we were going to cross into the West Bank by an easier method. At the point we were at, the Wall terminated at a monastery. As soon as the Wall was built, Palestinians started using the monastery garden as a route between East Jerusalem and Abu Dis. They knocked a hole in the garden wall at the Abu Dis side and passed through the monastery gate at the East

Jerusalem side. That was where we were heading now. 'At first the gate was kept closed,' Rose said as we passed through, 'but the monks were driven so mad by people constantly ringing the bell that now they just leave it open all the time.'

We walked through the monastery gardens and negotiated the broken stonework at the other side. A Palestinian with an old transit van was waiting to take us to the checkpoint which lay a couple of miles away. Samir was a new driver, Rina told me. The previous one, Ahmed, had been murdered by a cousin in an argument about a mobile phone. 'The cousin went to the bakery where Ahmed worked and cut his throat,' Rina said as we bounced along a narrow, rough-surfaced road. 'Then he fled to Jericho or Ramallah or somewhere. Ahmed's widow is pregnant and has three young children. One of them is going to have to avenge his father when he grows up. There's going to be an almighty family feud.'

When we arrived at the checkpoint the queues of cars were long and static. It looked as if there might be some kind of problem. Hannah went to investigate. In her tweed skirt, 'sensible' shoes, socks and leggings, a woolly hat pulled down over bobbed grey hair, she looked more like a supporting character from *The Sound of Music* than a champion of Palestinian rights. Coming back she reported that the hold up was due to a change of guard and that the traffic would be on its way shortly.

We stayed for an uneventful hour.

'For two months now it's been going very smoothly,' Rose said. 'There's less tension. They do random checking of the IDs, that's all.'

It hadn't always been as easy as this. Rina described chaotic scenes of people being hustled, harried and abused, old people being forced to clamber over rocks, babies being handed from one person to another, men and women being detained for hours for no apparent reason.

'The soldiers manning the checkpoints hate it,' said Rina. 'The conditions are terrible. They can be on shift for twelve hours. Those who are sensitive don't want to demean and harass the Palestinians. But they're put in a position of power, and when there is power there are abuses of power. These are young kids scared out of their wits, bored to distraction, and hating every minute of it. So of course, out of boredom they can do terrible things, and nobody wants to be seen as a soft touch. There's this macho thing, you've got to prove yourself.'

'I'm from Germany and I've seen the Berlin Wall come down,' Hannah said. 'I believe this wall will come down too. It doesn't solve any problems, it just makes more difficulties. God is with all. We must learn to accept others. Accept is the key word. We don't know much about what other people believe. There is a lot of misunderstanding. Christians now in America are supporting the Jews and speaking with so much hate against the Arabs.'

I asked what proportion of Jewish Israelis were religious.

'It depends on how you define religious Jew,' said Rina. 'Is it observance of dietary laws, wearing black hats, wearing the *kippa*, attendance at the synagogue? And then you have the secular ideologues.'

'What's their ideology?'

'That the land of Israel belongs to the Jews, but not necessarily God given.'

'What do you think about the Jews living in Jerusalem's Arab quarter?'

'It's unnecessary provocation. If I had my way, the city would be an open city and anybody could live anywhere they wanted. But that's utopian.'

'But as things are, how can they be happy living there where they're not wanted and are only creating ill feeling?'

'Because they're fanatics living in a fantasy world.'

'What's the content of this fantasy world?'

'That they know what God wants and that they're carrying out God's will. This belief gives them a kind of security. Just like the Palestinians who are proud because their sons are blowing themselves up.'

The women decided there was no point in staying any

longer so we got into Samir's van and drove back to the hole in the monastery wall.

'Have you heard the one about Bush, Putin and Sharon going to the Almighty?' asked Rose. 'Bush spoke to the Lord saying, "Oh Lord look at the problems I have. There's Iraq, there's Iran, there's North Korea. Will there ever be peace?" The Lord said, "Yes, my son, but not in your term."

Then Putin said, "Oh Lord, what about my problems with Chechnya? Will there ever be peace?" "Yes, my son, but not in your term."

Then Sharon spoke. He said, "What about us, Lord, and our problems with the Palestinians? Will we ever have peace?" And the Lord said, "Yes, my son, but not in my term."'

The desert stronghold of Masada is the ultimate in Jewish symbols of defiance in the face of attack. Built on a high plateau in the Judean Desert near the Dead Sea in the first century BC, it was occupied by some 900 Jews fleeing the Roman suppression of 66 AD. Besieged by 15,000 Roman soldiers, the Jews held out until it became clear that their defences were about to be breeched. At this point, in a mass suicide pact, ten men chosen by lot killed all the others and then each other, with the last one dispatching himself.

I went to Masada one day with Monique, a French friend from Jerusalem. The bus dropped us off at the bottom of Masada's sheer ochre-coloured cliffs. We decided to forgo the hiking route to the top in favour of the cable car.

The reverence with which the Israelis regarded this national shrine hadn't been translated into the design of the visitor complex which had the ambience of a multi-storey car park. Monique and I made our way through vast featureless corridors to the cable car terminal. As we were boarding the car someone pointed to a lone bag lying on the floor of the terminal. One of the staff wandered off, presumably to do something about it, without giving any impression of urgency. In the cable car I felt increasingly panicky as we waited for it to start. I was already nervous about being in the cable car, having no head for heights. I became convinced there was a bomb in the bag, and that it would explode when we were half-way to the top and break the cables. Fear gripped me. I wanted to get out of the car. But if I did, wasn't I more likely to be killed in the terminal? At least in the car there was a chance that we would get to the top before the bomb went off. A process of subconscious actuarial calculation impelled me to go for the more likely chance of dying instantaneously from bomb blast in the terminal than the less likely one of plummeting to earth in the cable car, and I leaped out. Overexcited and barely able to express myself I jabbered out my story to the ticket collector, while the other passengers, who probably hadn't noticed the bag, stared at me in perplexity. 'No, there's no problem.' said the ticket collector. 'Get back into the car.' He pointed to the bag, where the owner was now sitting beside it. I slunk back into the car feeling very foolish.

Although we are constantly exhorted to be on the lookout for suspicious-looking objects and to report them, I tend to feel that I'm over-reacting when I do draw attention to anything. But it made me reflect on how nervous and agitated Israelis, particularly soldiers, must feel.

'*Shalom*,' said a couple of boys sitting on the walls of the citadel.

'*Shalom*,' we replied.

They offered us their bags of crisps.

'Thank you.'

The boys were wearing shorts and T-shirts and had rifles slung across their backs. They were soldiers halfway through their three years of national service and on a week's holiday in the Red Sea resort of Eilat. The trip to Masada had been organized for them as a morale booster. They had been in action in Nablus and Jenin. I tried to talk to them about their experiences there, to get a view from their perspective. Their English was too poor to allow any meaningful communication but their frank friendliness and relaxed demeanour suggested a different species from the tense and glowering soldiers I was accustomed to seeing at checkpoints.

Parts of the fortress were being restored. We stopped to talk with a young American-Israeli man working on rebuilding the walls. He had been a theatre stage designer in America and had made aliya two years previously. To be living in Israel, to be working on Masada, was for him like a fairy tale come true.

It was my last Sunday in Jerusalem. I decided to go to a service in the Church of the Holy Sepulchre.

This was easier said than done. Built on what is believed to be the site of Christ's death and burial, the Holy Sepulchre is probably the most significant church in the whole of Christendom, revered by all sects. Yet it is this very universality which makes it seem more like a fairground than a place of worship. Different sects control different parts of the church where they conduct their services in different languages and according to different rites, each guarding its own patch with a jealousy which often gives rise to squabbling and open warfare. Perhaps this was why Ruthie had said it was from the pit of hell.

I went to the Roman Catholic chapel where a priest was shouting from the pulpit in a vain attempt to make himself heard above the singing from the nearby Greek Orthodox chapel. When the sermon ended, a choir of brown-robed Franciscan monks stood up and took their revenge by drowning out the Greeks with a crescendo of Latin chant. The three concelebrants, in chasubles of salmon pink brocade, huddled together on the altar, preparing for the consecration of the bread and wine.

I wriggled through a procession of candle-bearing, hymn-singing, Spanish pilgrims, past the shrine housing the tomb of Christ where a monk with a tall black hat bossily herded people in and out in groups of four, and on to another chapel where a Syrian Orthodox priest preached in Arabic to a handful of people sitting on benches ranged against the wall.

I left and walked up to join the service at the Anglican Christ

Church near Jaffa Gate which I knew to have Christian Zionist leanings. The first evidence of this was in the porch where a notice proclaimed that it had no connection with Mordecai Vanunu, that it wanted to distance itself in this respect from the Anglican church of St George which was harbouring him, that it did not approve of his disclosure of Israeli nuclear secrets, and that it was concerned about his opposition to the state of Israel.

Inside, the service had already started. The congregation numbered about sixty, most of them Western. The building was stark and simple compared with Catholic and Orthodox churches – plain stone walls, wooden ceiling, with only a few of the windows in stained glass. The seven-branched candelabrum of a Jewish menorah stood on the altar.

A pastor dressed in a white surplice was preaching. 'I want to give you a little lesson in aerodynamics,' he said, walking over to an overhead projector which was beaming an aircraft wing onto a screen. He described how the pattern of airflow over the wing led to a difference in pressure, giving lift. 'Now here, you see,' – he bracketed the angle between the wing and the horizontal with his hands – 'we have attitude. The greater the attitude, the greater the lift. We can find this idea right back in scripture. "They shall rise up with wings of eagles," the Book of Isaiah tells us. "They shall run and not grow weary." Attitude determines our approach to life and our relationships with people. Often the only difference between success and failure is attitude. Let us remember the words of Golda Meir: "All my country has is spirit. We don't have dollars, we don't have support, only spirit." Attitude at the beginning of a task will affect its outcome more than anything else. Are we going to adopt an attitude that's going to give us lift and enable us to fly? Or are we going to nosedive?'

He was a good speaker with a well-paced delivery and his approach was practical and down to earth. Without the religious surroundings I could have imagined myself at a cognitive behaviour therapy seminar.

The sermon was followed by some rather beautiful hymn-singing led by two women with spine-tingling voices and with a grand piano in place of the usual church organ. Members of the congregation started to raise their hands and burst into spontaneous prayer. I looked through the service leaflet. 'We want people to be free to express themselves within reason, so long as it is genuine,' I read. 'We should not distract others from their worship. If you wish to be more expressive than clapping or raising hands, please go to the left extension of the church and express your worship in that area of the building.' It sounded quintessentially English in its restraint.

The pastor ended the service with a few final words. 'Before we leave this week I want to ask every one of you to treat every person you meet as if they're the most important person in the world and see how it changes their attitude towards you.'

I wondered how many of them would meet any Palestinians and, if so, how they would treat them.

[9] Arab-Israelis, resident in Israel

CHAPTER 15

On a bus in the West Bank I had recently met an American woman. Originally from Las Vegas, she was now living in Jaffa. Her mother was Jewish, from an Orthodox family, and her father was Muslim. She considered herself primarily Jewish. 'We're not all bad,' she said as she told me how she had spent the last year travelling around the West Bank, staying in villages and compiling a photo diary of Palestinian life.

She had just been to the Selfit region around Ariel where the lives of the Palestinian villagers were seriously impacted by the activities of the settlement. I told her about my own visit to Ariel.

'You should go visit Hares,' she said, mentioning a village in the area. 'The land for Ariel was expropriated from the people in that village. The International Women's Peace Service have a project there. They provide non-violent support for the Palestinians and monitor human rights abuses. They've got a flat in the village and there are always several internationals living there. Here, take their phone number.'

I called the number and spoke with Rene, an Australian woman. She said she would be in Jerusalem the following day and suggested I travel back with her. She and another international, Catherine, were going to document the story of a man who had been attacked by settlers and she wanted me to join them.

I met up with Rene in East Jerusalem and we travelled by bus to Tappuah Junction, near Ariel. Yasuf, the village where we were to meet the man attacked, lay a couple of miles further on, along a minor road. The entrance to it was blocked by mounds of earth and chunks of rock. We took a minibus as far as the road block. At that point all the passengers had to get off, clamber over the obstacles and continue on foot.

Catherine was waiting for us at the other side with Nasfat, a local man who liaised with the IWPS. We drove to the house of Maruuf, the man who had been attacked.

Maruuf, a tall man in his late fifties wearing a grey *jellabiya* and a red and white *keffiya*, took us into a sitting room with pale yellow walls. We sat down on yellow brocade sofas. Sunlight filtered hotly through closed yellow curtains creating a curiously sick-room atmosphere.

Catherine explained to Maruuf the kind of information she needed for her report. Maruuf lifted the *keffiya*, revealing stitched up wounds to his forehead and scalp and a jagged tear just behind the ear.

'I was ploughing my land and six settlers came towards me, young men, early twenties. They surrounded me, they beat me on the head with a stone. Then they pushed me to the ground and ran away.'

'Did they have guns?' Catherine asked.

'No, I don't think so. I didn't see any guns.'

'What happened next? Did you report the incident.'

'A Palestinian shepherd came along. He took me to the guard at the gate of the settlement. The guard called the army and a jeep took me to Tappuah Junction. An army ambulance took me to Huwara and there I was transferred to a Red Crescent ambulance which took me to Rafidia hospital in Nablus. When I was in the army ambulance they told me to go to the police station in Ariel to make a report.'

Maruuf showed Catherine a paper with the details of this appointment.

We drank some tea, chatted a bit more and then left. Catherine and Rene had appointments elsewhere and Nasfat was taking me to his house in Marda, a village of about 2,000 people lying just below Ariel.

Nasfat worked with an NGO and had a four-wheel drive. In it we were able to get round the road block by navigating the precipitous and bumpy terrain to the side of it.

We drove to Nasfat's house, a villa just recently built, and had lunch with his family. Marda had started losing land to Ariel in 1978, Nasfat told me. 'The military gave orders to confiscate land in a hilly area for the military. Then they started building houses on it. This is the way Israel does it. First they say it's for military purposes, then it becomes something else. We have insufficient water, but the settlement has a swimming pool. They take the water from our land. We always have problems with water. For the whole village we are supposed to have only 70 cubic metres per day and we don't even get that.'

'What about settler aggression?' I asked. 'Do you have the kind of problems we saw today in Yasuf?'

'A few years ago a child was killed by a settler in the main street here. He ran him over with his car. The boy's brother saw it happening. The Israeli police asked for the name of the settler and the number of the car. The family didn't have it. So the police said we can't do anything for you. But if anything happens to a settler, the area is put under curfew. Nobody can move and police do everything to catch the culprits. Sometimes when the farmers from Marda are picking olives near the settlement the settlers shout at them, they throw stones and threaten to shoot them if they don't go away. Sometimes they burn the olive trees. Some settlers attacked a Palestinian farmer from Marda. They put a knife to his neck and said, "If you come back we will kill you." During the first *intifada* settlers entered the villages, they attacked houses at night, they burned the outside areas, they shot at windows. Some of the settlers are now pumping their sewage water over the olive tree areas, so there's a very bad smell in summer and insects spread disease. They try to prevent farmers from reaching their land.

'People here, I can't describe how they feel. The settlers are the enemy, they stole our land and they want us to leave. You see me laughing and playing with my kids but you don't know what is inside my head, what I'm feeling inside. Sometimes you can't take your kids to the doctor because you're scared of meeting a settler or a soldier. The soldiers and settlers are uprooting a lot of olive trees. In this village they've uprooted more than 500 olive trees – because of nothing, for no reason. At night the soldiers enter the village, shouting and making a noise to frighten the kids, to frighten everybody. We have a centre here for agricultural training, the Marda Permaculture centre. Four years ago the Israeli soldiers destroyed it: the windows, the doors, the seed banks, the nursery. For no reason. Just because the centre was helping people to cultivate and be independent. With their system of roadblocks the whole region of Selfit is divided into three clusters, and then into subclusters, making it difficult to travel, to get access. Marda is alone because no other village is connected to it. The only exit road is to Zatara. Sometimes even that is closed to Palestinians. During a lot of nights, settlers are shooting in the direction of the village from the main road to make a horrible environment and to make people afraid. In Zeita village a woman wanted to go to hospital, she was in labour. Her husband told the soldiers his wife was in labour, and the soldiers shot him and injured his wife. Palestinians were not supposed to be moving outside the villages, but what could they do? Another woman had to give birth at a checkpoint. She had twins. They both died.

'There was a blind man from Marda who forgot his ID. Soldiers caught him, and his brother came to me for help. I took the brother there in my car. The soldiers attacked me and put me in jail in Huwara for eight days. Why? Because I tried to help this man.

'These soldiers who came into the village just now, why did they come? Because they want the children to throw stones. They want to provoke them. Then they can arrest them or shoot them.

'The wall, they say it is for security. It's not true. It's to confiscate more land, to separate villages, to destroy districts. The land is the main source of food for the Palestinians. They want to take it away from us.'

CHAPTER 16

I spent the night at the IWPS flat in Hares, the upper storey of a village house furnished in a surprisingly IKEA kind of style. The next morning I headed back to Jerusalem. I took the bus to Ramallah where I got a shared taxi for Qalandiya checkpoint.

As the taxi drove out from the centre of Ramallah we passed a horse-drawn caravan. Several people were sitting in the driving seat, with a number of others accompanying them on foot. On the sides of the caravan were written the words: Roulotte pour la Paix, Peace Caravan.

I stopped the taxi and went back to meet them. As I approached, a man jumped down from the caravan. It was Arafat, a Palestinian journalist I had met previously in Ramallah. He introduced me to Amit, an Israeli Jew, and his French wife, Aude, who had travelled in the caravan from France on a peace mission. Their two-and-a-half-year-old daughter Annabelle was with them, asleep inside. Their dog Zaza, a black and white mongrel, had trotted alongside them all the way.

They were just drawing up outside a restaurant for lunch. Aude woke Annabelle, Amit shook out a bag of hay for Loupio, the horse, Arafat introduced me to the other people in the procession, all of whom were from an Israeli peace movement called Middle Way, and we sat down.

The journey had taken two years. Their only big problem had been at the Turkish border. 'There we had problems with the horse,' Aude said. 'Big, big problems. We had to wait one week at the border and then they refused to let us in so we had to go back to Bulgaria and continue through Greece and get a boat to Haifa. Then we crossed Israel and entered the West Bank at Jenin.'

'How did people react to you in Israel?'

'We had only good reactions. We met only a few people who spoke badly, not about us but about the Palestinians. A lot of Israelis are afraid of Palestinians. They say you are crazy to go there, you will be murdered, they are terrorists. In Palestine people have been very nice. They want to know if many other Jewish people have Amit's ideas. The action of citizens in Israel is very much needed. Politics will not do it. But if the Israelis will wake up and realize that they have to do this, then they can do it.'

'How did you manage at the checkpoints?'

'We've been working all the time with Middle Way. They help us to get special permission from the army to get through the checkpoints. But we're only allowed to travel through Zone C areas.'

'So how did you get into Ramallah? It's in Zone A.'

'We really wanted to go to the *Maqata* and we were lucky. We waited till there was nobody at the checkpoint and just walked through. We visited the *Maqata* this morning, we saw Arafat's tomb, but they wouldn't let the animals in. The caravan had to stay outside.'

Amit gathered together some of the leftover food and put it down for Zaza, then scooped up the remains of Loupio's hay and put it back in the bag.

We set off again. Amit and Aude planned to enter the outskirts of Jerusalem that day and rest for a few days before finishing their journey with a grande entrée into the city.

I walked beside the caravan with Ghers, an eager, bubbly talker with curly hair.

'Here it is so easy to kill. The people, they have gasoline in the head and it comes out in flames. First the Palestinians but it contaminates everybody, the fanatical people from both sides.'

'How do you extinguish the gasoline?'

'Instead of water you put love.'

Ghers had moved to Israel from Columbia nine years previously. 'I wanted a better environment for myself and my family. But when I arrived I began to suffer from the environment, the conflict.' He chattered excitedly about a peace organization called Noah's Ark that he was involved with.

Gaby, a garrulous sixty-year-old, caught up with us and started telling me about the philosophy of Middle Way. 'It's influenced by the thinking of Gandhi. We can achieve things by non-violence, by tolerance. We are striving for peace in a peaceful manner.' Loupio bent his head and licked Gaby's arm. 'Did you see that? This horse just licked me. He heard me talking about non-violence and he was sympathetic to me.' Gaby patted Loupio's nose. 'This horse gives me a lesson in staying calm. He's curious but he's not like this.' He made a jerking movement. Loupio plodded stolidly on. 'We can learn a lot too from the zen masters. I believe in an engaged Buddhism, not just individual meditation. There are techniques from this that I use for dealing with things when we have problems at checkpoints.'

Gaby had been born in Israel. 'My father was from Vilna in Lithuania. His first language was Hebrew. Vilna was called the Jerusalem of Lithuania because there were so many Jews there. He moved to Israel in 1935. My mother was born into a Russian family in the United States. She moved to Israel in 1939. She and my father met because they were in the same kibbutz.

'I think we are responsible for a lot of what is going on here but I would ask other people to try to relate to our anxieties, to our frustration about the situation. Many Israelis are not in a position that they can change the situation. Once every four years in the elections, but there are other things that influence the elections. They want change but they don't know how to achieve it. I would like Europeans to relate more to the different shades in the Israeli society, the different opinions and attitudes. Me, I was against the occupation from the start. I knew that basically this land should be divided. You know, an enemy is someone whose story hasn't been heard. This is the fundamental principle of the compassionate listening developed by Gene Hoffman[10]. In the Middle Way we try to implement some of this. We get together with people from both sides and listen to each other's stories.'

'We went with Arab friends to do this in Gush Katif, that's a settlement in Gaza,' said Shai, who was walking alongside us. 'We did a listening circle with the settlers, each one speaking from his own point of view. I was surprised to see – because sometimes it's difficult to stay patient – that the settlers were fully listening and keeping peaceful. They didn't freak out. We felt very welcome, the Jewish people in our group that is, but our Arab friends didn't feel welcome.'

'What justification do the settlers have if they're not religious?' I asked.

'For some it's just practical. It's a cheaper life, they get subsidized houses. It was too short to really understand and go deep into the dialogue.'

Shai, in his orange drawstring trousers, rainbow-striped mohair jumper, red woollen hat and long crinkly red hair and beard looked the quintessential hippy.

'I was born Jewish but I don't feel too much Jewish,' he told me. 'I feel we are human beings and I try to see the humanity in each of us. To come for a day on this walk was so important for me, to be touched by the energy and to feel the fear and the stress. "There is no way to peace, peace is the way." Do you know this saying? It was Gandhi.'

We were approaching Qalandiya checkpoint now. A long line of vehicles extended before us, waiting to be processed by the soldiers. Alongside us a row of vendors displayed their good on stalls improvised from blocks of concrete: boxes of glasses, crockery, socks, *hijabs*, beauty products, crates of fruit and vegetables, bags of peanuts, stationery, toys and a host of other items. Over the next hour we edged slowly forward. Zaza rooted around in the mounds of rubbish. We fed Loupio handfuls of carrots and bought coffee from a vendor wearing a fez and gold-embroidered baggy red trousers. An arrangement like a three-branched brass candelabra was strapped to his back with artificial flowers cascading from the tips, an incongruously touristy sight in the bleak and unlovely landscape. Clumps of barbed wire lay on the ground decorated like Christmas trees with coloured scraps of plastic bags and other litter that had stuck to the barbs. Music blared from the car in front, joined by the shriek of a siren as an ambulance zoomed up to the head of the queue. The soldiers checked it and waved it through. A handcart piled high with mattresses followed. The co-ordinator of the West Bank taxis climbed into the driving seat of the caravan and shouted 'Jerusalem, anyone for Jerusalem?'

As we neared the soldiers, we wondered what sort of obstacles were going to be put in front of us. Amit and Aude didn't have permission to pass through Zone A. The Israelis in the group didn't have permission to be in Zone A either. Being found there normally incurred a 1,000 shekel fine. As a Palestinian, Arafat was not allowed to pass out of the West Bank without a permit.

Aude trained her video camera on an argument between a soldier and an old man who was being turned away. A soldier moved away from his colleagues and made for Loupio. He started stroking his neck and laughing. It was a good sign. Amit spoke with him while the soldier continued to canoodle with Loupio. An agreement seemed to be reached. Amit came back and told us that no one was allowed to go through the vehicle checkpoint on foot so we were all to get inside the caravan. We piled in and drove past the soldiers with Amit and Aude in the driving seat, the soldiers turning a blind eye to the passengers inside. No IDs were asked for.

'This is a moral victory,' said Ghers.

Arafat, having accomplished his part in the moral victory, said good-bye and turned back into the West Bank. The Middle Way people, apart from Shai and a man called Dany who were planning to stay with the caravan for the rest of the day, headed back to Israel.

Amit and Aude now had to find a place with suitable grazing for Loupio where they could put up for a few days. Within about five minutes of crossing the checkpoint, amid the welter of people milling around, Amit had got talking with a Palestinian who had a stud farm in East Jerusalem. The typical Arab 'my home is your home' offer of hospitality was extended forthwith.

We swung out into the tangle of traffic enclosing the Qalandiya roundabout and veered off into the road to Jerusalem, with the ten-metre concrete slabs of the Wall within touching distance on our right. Aude and I sat in the driving seat with Annabelle between us. I marvelled at her bravery in setting out two years previously with a six-month-old baby.

'Weren't you worried?' I asked.

'Maybe I wasn't aware of what was ahead. But, in fact, it wasn't too difficult. Only now, since we entered Israel and she's a bit older, every day she says she wants a house. It's difficult for her always changing friends. She needs now to be stable.'

As Loupio clip-clopped onwards, bystanders waved greetings and gaggles of children tagged along. Still the stud farm was not in sight. It seemed that every fifteen minutes Mohammed, the owner, said that it was just another fifteen minutes. Amit was worried that Loupio was getting tired. I got down to lighten his load. The road was hilly. We positioned ourselves round the back of the caravan, pushing with all our might. Children and bystanders joined in. A final steep slope took us up to the farm. Amit unharnessed Loupio and hosed him down under the flaring nostrils of half a dozen Arab thoroughbreds ranged in stalls.

Mohammed had phoned ahead to tell his wife he was arriving with guests. When he led us into the house she was already laying out steaming platters of chicken and rice. We sat down, three Jewish-Israelis and two Europeans, guests in a Palestinian household.

Mohammed told us about some of the problems he had had with the Israeli authorities. They were the usual things – land expropriated, business license refused.

'So why do you welcome us into your house?' Amit asked him.

'Because you are for peace and I too am for peace.'

But it was more than that. There was a feeling of complete ease, an absence of resentment or even discomfort. Not for the first time I thought that, no matter how anti-Zionist Palestinians may be, there seems to be not a trace of anti-semitism among them.

Aude contrasted their behaviour with those of a settler they had met in the West Bank who invited them to visit his settlement. When he found out that they had a Palestinian with them, the invitation was retracted.

'But my impression is that the majority of Israelis want peace,' she added. 'Very few people we met have said negative things. Maybe we met five people that were against it. But peace for them means freedom from bombing, from young people having to go into the army. They never talk about the suffering of the Palestinians.'

'People are so much in their own drama,' said Shai. 'They are not able to see the suffering of other people'

Dany talked about his experience of military service which he had done about fourteen years previously. 'It was exciting and it was scary. I was in Lebanon and in Gaza. I heard people shouting *Allahu akbar* and wanting to kill me. I considered myself humane. I wasn't thinking about the moral aspect, whether I thought it was OK.'

But since then he had been thinking. He recalled conversations with settler soldiers inside the tank he was driving while on reserve army service a few years ago. 'I can't recall the exact words but what I can't forget is the raw hatred my fellow fighters expressed towards the Palestinians who were in the focus of our sights. My mates clearly felt that these people were the enemy and that therefore even a minor reason would justify killing them. I don't agree with this view and will not take part in any killing.

'I'm well aware of my vulnerability. I remember an incident in Gaza. My platoon was cornered in a street full of locals who threw stones and came at us shouting *Allahu akbar*. I felt like the land itself was shouting and it was clear that we were in imminent danger of being lynched. I can't think of another incident at the moment but I think I've suppressed a lot of what I've seen. I know I may die at any minute, should a suicide bomber choose to explode near where I walk in the street, or should someone hit me with a brick when I am on reserve duty. Yet this knowledge doesn't encourage me to hate or to kill or to want Palestinians dead. It does encourage me to do something so that they will no longer want to be the enemy. Unlike some of my mates from the army, I don't want to kill or maim every Arab or Palestinian I see. I would much prefer to invite them to meet and talk.'

Dany had participated in listening circles with Palestinians.

'When I come to such meetings I bring with me an anticipation that they will hopefully lead to some kind of joint action. By bringing together people who have not had the chance to talk before we enable a platform in which information and opinions can be exchanged. Such personal encounters also bring us closer to understanding human needs on both sides, which is fundamental if we are ever to attain mutual recognition. I feel this is something very basic that we must strive towards. With all our differences, we're all human, and we're all destined to live on the same small piece of land.

'I don't see myself as a political person. My approach to the conflict is on a very personal level, and comes from a social-humanist perspective which is focussed on the here and now. I'll give you an example: I had a long chat with an eighty-year-old Palestinian some months ago in Bartaa, one of the Palestinian villages where Middle Way had organised an event. He brought up historical facts in an attempt to discuss the issue of 'right to the land' from a historical point of view. I told him that if that's all we do, then we have a very small chance of ever making any progress.

I was interested in talking about the present, as there is nothing I can do to change the past of this place we all call home. I do believe, however, that there is a lot I can do to change things for the better in the present. I know it requires an open heart and mind, and a lot of willingness to listen, but this is the centre of my world view today. By fighting over the past we avoid, or at least delay, solving urgent problems we face in the present and may also impede any attempt to deal with what awaits us in the future.'

Shai and Dany were going back to Tel Aviv that evening. One of Mohammed's friends offered to give us a lift into Jerusalem.

We had one more checkpoint to pass on the way there. A soldier stuck his head into the car and questioned Dany.

'Where are you from?'.

'Tel Aviv.'

'What have you been doing here?'

'Visiting friends'

'Arab friends?'

'Yes.'

He gave Dany a long, hard look and then nodded at us to drive on.

'He speaks like that because he can't believe we have Arab friends,' said Shai. 'He doesn't think they're human beings. Poor guy.'

[10] Quaker peace activist, pioneer of Compassionate Listening projects for conflict resolution

A PARABLE

As told to me by Shatha

A couple with a son and a daughter and some sheep were living in a two-roomed house. The couple were in one room, their children in the other and the sheep were outside. The husband went to talk with a holy man. 'We're not comfortable,' he said. 'We're not happy.'

The holy man said, 'That's easily fixed. Take your son into your room.'

The following week the man returned, complaining that they still weren't happy.

'Take your daughter into your room,' the holy man said.

The week after that the man was still complaining, so the holy man told him to take the sheep into their room.

The next week the man was back again, complaining even more bitterly. The holy man said to him, 'This is what you do. Put your sheep outside the house.'

The next week the man came to the holy man saying, 'OK, that's a bit better but we're still not really comfortable.'

'Well, put your daughter into the other room,' the holy man suggested.

The following week when the man came back saying things still weren't quite right, the holy man told him to put his son into the other room.

After that the man was very happy and didn't need to go to the holy man again.

GLOSSARY

ahlan	welcome
al quds	Jerusalem
aliya (Hebrew)	migration of Jewish person to Israel
Allahu akbar	God is great
dabka	traditional Palestinian dance
dishdasha	long white robe worn by Arab men
dunum	1,000 square metres
eid el fitr	holiday at the end of Ramadan
fatwa	Islamic legal ruling
fiqh	Islamic jurisprudence
hallas	enough, finished
halwiyat	sweet pastries
haram	forbidden
hijab	head covering for women
iftar	evening meal at which the fast is broken
intifada	uprising
jellabiya	long robe worn by Arab men
jilbab	full-length coat worn by women
kippa	round cap worn by Jewish men
maghrib	sunset (referring to time of prayer)
maqata'a	headquarters of the Palestinian National Authority in Ramallah
merkaz (Hebrew)	(town) centre
molokhia	green vegetable dish
muazzin	call to prayer
nakba	catastrophe (speaking of the events of 1948)
narguila	water pipe
ramadan	Muslim fasting month
sahur	meal eaten just before dawn during Ramadan
shabaab	young men

shabat (Hebrew)	sabbath
shabibi	Fatah youth movement
shahada	profession of faith recited when converting to Islam
shofar	Jewish battle trumpet
shukran	thank you
surah	verse of the Koran
tawjihi	final-year secondary school examinations
yanni	untranslatable (like, you know, well)

(Footnotes)

[1] Bad News From Israel: television news and public understanding of the Israeli-Palestinian conflict, by Greg Philo and the Glasgow University Media Group

[2] Military wing of the Fatah party

[3] Term generally used for foreign peace activists present in the OPT

[4] Democratic Front for the Liberation of Palestine

[5] Christian Zionists believe that the return of the Jews to Israel is in accordance with biblical prophecy and is necessary for the second coming of the Messiah

[6] Israeli Defence Force

[7] "Zion's Christian Soldiers", CBS-Sixty minutes, 5 October 2002

[8] Their beliefs are bonkers, but they are at the heart of power - US Christian fundamentalists are driving Bush's Middle East policy
George Monbiot - The Guardian - 20th April 2004

[9] Arab-Israelis, resident in Israel

[10] Quaker peace activist, pioneer of Compassionate Listening projects for conflict resolution

About Eye Books

Eye Books is a dynamic, young publishing company that likes to break the rules. Our independence allows us to publish books which challenge the way people see things. It also means that we can offer new authors a platform from which they can shine their light and encourage others to do the same.

To date we have published 60 books that cover a number of genres including Travel, Biography, Adventure, Reference and History. Many of our books are experience driven. All of them are inspirational and life affirming.

Frigid Women, for example, tells the story of the world-record-creating first all-female expedition to the North Pole. Sue Riches, a fifty-year-old mother of three who had recently recovered from a mastectomy, and her daughter Victoria are the authors – neither had ever written a book before. Sue Riches is now a writer and highly-sought-after motivational speaker.

We also publish thematic anthologies, such as The Tales from Heaven and Hell series, for those who prefer the short story format. Here everyone has the chance to get their stories published and win prizes such as flights to any destination in the world.

And here's what makes us really different: As well as publishing books, Eye Books has set up a club for like-minded people and is in the process of developing a number of initiatives and services for its community of members. After all, the more you put into life, the more you get out of it.

Please visit www.eye-books.com for further information.

Eye Club Membership

Each month, we receive hundreds of enquiries from people who have read our books, discovered our website or entered our competitions. All these people have certain things in common: a desire to achieve, to extend the boundaries of everyday life and to learn from others' experiences.

Eye Books has, therefore, set up a club to unite these like-minded people. It is a community where members can exchange ideas, contact authors, discuss travel, both future and past, as well as receive information and offers from Eye Books.

Membership is free.

Benefits of the Eye Club

As a member of the Eye Club:

• You are offered the invaluable opportunity to contact our authors directly.
• You will receive a regular newsletter, information on new book releases and company developments as well as discounts on new and past titles.
• You can attend special member events such as book launches, author talks and signings.
• Receive discounts on a variety of travel-related products and services from Eye Books' partners.
• You can enjoy entry into Eye Books competitions including the ever popular Heaven and Hell series and our monthly book competition.

To register your membership, simply visit our website and register on our club pages: www.eye-books.com.

2006 Titles

Fateful Beauty – the story of Frances Coke 1602-1642 – Natalie Hodgson

Fateful Beauty is the true story of a young woman who, at the age of fifteen, was forced to marry a mentally unstable man by her ambitious father, the Lord Chancellor, Sir Edward Coke, auther of the Petition of Rights. The book is well researched and gives a vivid picture of the late sixteenth and early seventeenth centuries - political intrigue, the Elizabethan and Stuart courts, civil war, domestic life and the place of women in society.

ISBN 1 903070 406. Price £12.99.

On the Wall with Hadrian – Bob Bibby

The newly opened Hadrian's Wall path, 84 miles (135km) long, stretching from coast to coast in the north of England, inspired travel writer Bob Bibby to don his boots and explore its Roman origins. The book describes Hadrian, his period and the life of his soldiers and provides an up-to-date guide on where to stay, eat and drink along the Path.

ISBN 978 1 903070 499. Price £9.99.

Siberian Dreams – Andy Home

Journalist, Andy Home realised that without the Siberian city of Norislk and its inhabitants, the lives of Westerners would have to change. He visits this former Prison Camp now mining city in the Artic Circle to find out what life is like for the 200,000 people living in sub-zero temperatures in Russia's most polluted city.

ISBN 978 1 903070 512. Price £9.99.

Changing the World. One Step at the time – Michael Meegan

Many people say they want to make a difference but don't know how. This book offers examples of real people making real differences. It reminds us to see joy and love in every moment of every day, and that making a difference is something everyone can do.

ISBN 978 1 903070 444. Price £9.99

The Good Life Gets Better– Dorian Amos

The sequel to the bestselling book about leaving the UK for a new life in the Yukon, Dorian and his growing family get gold fever, start to stake land and prospect for gold. Follow them along the learning curve about where to look for gold and how to live in this harsh climate. It shows that with good humour and resilience life can only get better.

ISBN 978 1 903070 482. Price£9.99

Also by Eye Books

Zohra's Ladder – Pamela Windo
A wondrous collection of stories of Moroccan life that offer
a privileged immersion into a world of deep sensuality.
ISBN 1 903070 406. Price £9.99.

Great Sects – Adam Hume Kelly
Essential insights into sects for the intellectually curious – from
Kabbalah to Dreamtime, Druidry to Opus Dei.
ISBN: 1903070 473. Price £9.99.

Blood Sweat & Charity – Nick Stanhope
The guide to charity challenges.
ISBN: 1 903070 414. Price £12.99.

Death – The Great Mystery of Life – Herbie Brennan
A compulsive study, its effect is strangely liberating and life
enhancing.
ISBN: 1 903070 422. Price £9.99.

Riding the Outlaw Trail – Simon Casson
An equine expedition retracing the footsteps of those legen-
dary real-life bandits, Butch Cassidy and the Sundance Kid.
ISBN: 1 903070 228. Price £9.99.

Green Oranges on Lion Mountain – Emily Joy
A VSO posting in Sierra Leone where adventure and romance
were on the agenda; rebel forces and threat of civil war were
not.
ISBN: 1 903070 295. Price £9.99.

Desert Governess – Phyllis Ellis
A former Benny Hill Show actress becomes a governess to the
Saudi Arabian Royal Family.
ISBN: 1 903070 015. Price £9.99.

Last of the Nomads – W. J. Peasley
The story of the last of the desert nomads to live permanently in the traditional way in Western Australia.
ISBN: 1 903070 325. Price £9.99.

All Will Be Well – Michael Meegan
A book about how love and compassion when given out to others can lead to contentment.
ISBN: 1 903070 279. Price £9.99.

First Contact – Mark Anstice
A 21st-century discovery of cannibals.
Comes with (free) DVD which won the Banff Film Festival.
ISBN: 1 903070 260. Price £9.99.

Further Travellers' Tales From Heaven and Hell – Various
This is the third book in the series of real travellers tales.
ISBN: 1 903070 112. Price £9.99.

Special Offa – Bob Bibby
A walk along Offa's Dyke.
ISBN: 1 903070 287. Price £9.99.

The Good Life – Dorian Amos
A move from the UK to start a new life in the wilderness of The Yukon.
ISBN: 1 903070 309. Price £9.99.

Baghdad Business School – Heyrick Bond Gunning
The realities of a business start-up in a war zone.
ISBN: 1 903070 333. Price £9.99.

The Accidental Optimist's Guide to Life – Emily Joy
Having just returned from Sierra Leone, a busy GP with a growing family ponders the meaning of life.
ISBN: 1 903070 430. Price £9.99.

The Con Artist Handbook – Joel Levy
Get wise as this blows the lid on the secrets of the successful con artist and his con games.
ISBN: 1 903070 341. Price £9.99.

The Forensics Handbook – Pete Moore
The most up-to-date log of forensic techniques available.
ISBN: 1 903070 35X. Price £9.99.

My Journey With A Remarkable Tree – Ken Finn
A journey following an illegally logged tree from a spirit forest to the furniture corner of a garden centre.
ISBN: 1 903070 384. Price £9.99.

Seeking Sanctuary – Hilda Reilly
Western Muslim converts living in Sudan.
ISBN: 1 903070 392. Price £9.99.

Lost Lands Forgotten Stories – Alexandra Pratt
The retracing of an astonishing 600 mile river journey in 1905 in 2005.
ISBN: 1 903070 368. Price £9.99.

Jasmine and Arnica – Nicola Naylor
A blind woman's journey around India.
ISBN: 1 903070 171. Price £9.99.

Touching Tibet – Niema Ash
A journey into the heart of this intriguing forbidden land.
ISBN: 1 903070 18X. Price £9.99.

Behind the Veil – Lydia Laube
A shocking account of a nurse's Arabian nightmare.
ISBN: 1 903070 198. Price £9.99.

Walking Away – Charlotte Metcalf
A well-known film maker's African journal.
ISBN: 1 903070 201. Price £9.99.

Travels in Outback Australia – Andrew Stevenson
In search of the original Australians – the Aboriginal People.
ISBN: 1 903070 147. Price £9.99.

The European Job – Jonathan Booth
10,000 miles around Europe in a 25-year-old classic car.
ISBN: 1 903070 252. Price £9.99.

Around the World with 1000 Birds – Russell Boyman
An extraordinary answer to a mid-life crisis.
ISBN: 1 903070 163. Price £9.99.

Cry from the Highest Mountain – Tess Burrows
A climb to the point furthest from the centre of the earth.
ISBN: 1 903070 120. Price £9.99.

Dancing with Sabrina – Bob Bibby
A journey along the River Severn from source to sea.
ISBN: 1 903070 244. Price £9.99.

Grey Paes and Bacon – Bob Bibby
A journey around the canals of the Black Country.
ISBN: 1 903070 066. Price £7.99.

Jungle Janes – Peter Burden
Twelve middle-aged women take on the Jungle. As seen on Channel 4.
ISBN: 1 903070 058. Price £7.99.

Travels with my Daughter – Niema Ash
Forget convention, follow your instincts.
ISBN: 1 903070 04X. Price £7.99.

Riding with Ghosts – Gwen Maka
One woman's solo cycle ride from Seattle to Mexico.
ISBN: 1 903070 007. Price £7.99.

Riding with Ghosts: South of the Border – Gwen Maka
The second part of Gwen's epic cycle trip through the
Americas.
ISBN: 1 903070 090. Price £7.99.

Triumph Round the World – Robbie Marshall
He gave up his world for the freedom of the road.
ISBN: 1 903070 082. Price £7.99.

Fever Trees of Borneo – Mark Eveleigh
A daring expedition through uncharted jungle.
ISBN: 0 953057 569. Price £7.99.

Discovery Road – Tim Garrett and Andy Brown
Their mission was to mountain bike around the world.
ISBN: 0 953057 534. Price £7.99.

Frigid Women – Sue and Victoria Riches
The first all-female expedition to the North Pole.
ISBN: 0 953057 52 6. Price £7.99.

Jungle Beat – Roy Follows
Fighting terrorists in Malaya.
ISBN: 0 953057 577. Price £7.99.

Slow Winter – Alex Hickman
A personal quest against the backdrop of the war-torn
Balkans.
ISBN: 0 953057 585. Price £7.99.

Tea for Two – Polly Benge
She cycled around India to test her love.
ISBN: 0 953057 593. Price £7.99.

Traveller's Tales from Heaven and Hell – Various
A collection of short stories drawn from a nationwide competition.
ISBN: 0 953057 518. Price £6.99.

More Traveller's Tales from Heaven and Hell – Various
A second collection of short stories.
ISBN: 1 903070 023. Price £6.99.

A Trail of Visions: Route 1 – Vicki Couchman
A stunning photographic essay.
ISBN: 1 871349 338. Price £14.99.

A Trail of Visions: Route 2 – Vicki Couchman
A second stunning photographic essay.
ISBN: 0 953057 50X. Price £16.99.